D1319543

4 YEARS
— and then some

by Mary Harrington Bryant

Mary Harrington Bryant
2007

ISBN 978-0-9733372-1-1

Printed in Canada
by
Pro Printers
1010 Belfast Road
Ottawa, ON. K1G 4A2
http://www.proprinters.ca

This book is printed on acid-free paper that contains
30% post-consumer paper and is FSC Certified

Published by
Mary and Joe Bryant
447 Thessaly Circle,
Ottawa, ON K1H 5W7.

ACKNOWLEDGEMENTS

Over the years many friends have urged me to write about my years in northern Canada. I resisted in the belief that it was much more important to live today's life than to reminisce about yesterday's. Perhaps age had something to do with it but at 88 I finally gave in and embarked on writing this story. I cheerfully acknowledge that my friends finally won out.

I very happily acknowledge the assistance of the Prince of Wales Northern Heritage Centre in Yellowknife, N.W.T. for granting permission to print photographs of some of the Mary Harrington oil paintings in their collection. The Centre also very kindly provided images of several artifacts that I had donated and permission to use them in the book.

I also thank Eric Gill and his staff at Pro Printers in Ottawa for their skill, patience and efforts in the production of the book.

I especially wish to thank my husband for his many hours of advice, his skilful editing and conversion of my handwriting to typescript in "4 YEARS" and for his contribution later in "and then some."

PREFACE

In putting together this story of my years in Aklavik, I have used references from my daily journals, letters to my supportive family and friends as well as a vivid memory.

Many persons urged me to write of those days in the '40s, now more than sixty years ago. It has been my desire to put forward a positive picture of residential schools as I have known them.

When I began my life in the schools and their communities at Lac la Ronge, Saskatchewan in 1942, there were in the Dominion seventy-six Indian Residential Schools. Of the 76, sixteen were administered by the Anglican Church, two by the Presbyterian Church, ten by the United Church and forty-five by the Roman Catholic Church. In many parts of Canada, mostly where the native peoples lived, the only "schools" available were in the missionaries' homes and because of the hunting, trapping lives of the people, attendance, if possible at all, was erratic. An alternative was to have residential schools. Elsewhere in Canada and in other countries, other peoples had used similar schools and still do, when needed. In the North, dedicated and caring workers went forward not only to spread their Christian faiths but also to facilitate the education needed for Canadians to face the changes taking place in Canada.

In the delta of the great MacKenzie River the native people, since the visits of explorers such as Alexander MacKenzie (1789), had felt that their ways were going to be affected. Before long they encountered new languages, new challenges, even new foods. The Eskimo and Loucheux were, and are, perceptive and adaptable people. Some of them had attended the early Anglican residential school at Hay River and were now leaders in the Delta. When the new school was built in Aklavik they and many others eagerly brought what children they could spare from their own domestic needs. The first member of a family to attend school often passed along some of his or her new knowledge to younger members at home, giving them a running start when they, too, were able to attend. The residential school was a part of the growing Aklavik Community, moving along with its demands. At the same time as much as possible the students were provided frequent contacts with their families, their languages and their customs.

CONTENTS

Part 2 – AND THEN SOME

APPENDICES

49. Arctic Mission Uniforms for Women Workers
50. Menu, S.S. Distributor, September 5, 1944
51. Hudson's Bay Company advertisement for travel,
    Waterways to Aklavik, 1933
52. Artwork by Children at the
    Anglican Mission School, Aklavik, 1944-48

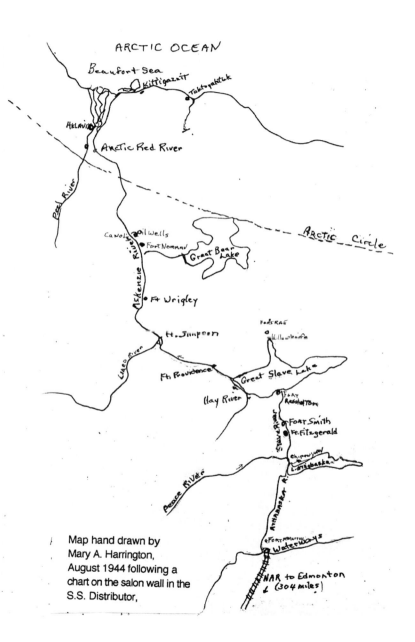

ARCTIC OCEAN

Beaufort Sea

Kittigazuit

Tuktoyaktuk

Aklavik

Arctic Red River

Peel River

Canol · Oil Wells

Fort Norman

Great Bear Lake

ARCTIC Circle

Mackenzie River

Ft Wrigley

Ft. Simpson

FORT RAE

Ft Providence

Great Slave Lake

Liard River

Hay River

FORT Resolution

Slave River

Fort Smith

Ft Fitzgerald

Chipewyan

Lartiebaskan

Peace River

Athabasca R.

Fort McMurray
Waterways

NAR to Edmonton
(304 miles)

Map hand drawn by
Mary A. Harrington,
August 1944 following a
chart on the salon wall in the
S.S. Distributor,

1

INTRODUCTION

It was mid-July when I flew out from Lac la Ronge, Saskatchewan after teaching for two years in the Anglican Residential School there. I looked forward to visiting with my family on the farm. My next venture was to begin on August 1, 1944.

La Ronge was quite isolated, without road connection unless the muskegs froze and allowed tractor trains to come in the winter. M & C Aviation from Prince Albert made charter flights using very small planes, mostly DeHaviland Moths. They operated on skis in the winter and pontoons in the summer. The school had no means of communication with Prince Albert in emergencies but a local trapper operated a Ham radio that could sometimes be used. Although that lack of emergency communication very nearly cost me my life when I had a burst appendix, I nevertheless felt confident and undaunted about my upcoming four-year venture in the delta of the MacKenzie River at Aklavik.

My parents, however, must have been concerned. One day I found my father studying a wall map of North America. I asked him, "What are you looking for, Dad?" and he pointed to the top of the map, then turned to me, "I wonder why you chose North and not South." I couldn't really tell him. I just wanted to go and I was sure I could help the Canadian children there. I'd be doing something useful like my brothers and friends while the war was on. Dad knew my fiancé was overseas, nearly all of the young folks my age were.

Both of my parents were very supportive of my decisions, and I usually had a feeling that they wished to come, too.

The Indian and Eskimo Residential School Commission had sent me a brochure with pictures of the Canadian Church of England schools and a long list of clothing requirements. [See Appendix] Filling those requirements in just two weeks proved very difficult. Eaton's was our only source from the farm. We shopped in the catalogue and wrote up the order, including measurements from which to have the required navy blue uniform made. With the order completed, we drove 10 miles to our nearest town, Ardath, bought a Money Order and mailed the order to Eaton's Winnipeg store.

The one tailored uniform had a pleasant princess fit and neat detachable white collar and cuffs. It was to be worn when travelling or representing the Arctic Mission. I also needed several additional navy blue uniforms made of less expensive cloth and half a dozen white ones that could be laundered with the school machines. As soon as the order was off to Eaton's, Mother and I set to work making the additional uniforms. As we sewed or gathered things on the list, we put them into the trunk. The biggest difficulty was obtaining warm underwear, especially size small, woman's. Eaton's replied, "Not Available."

Understandable, perhaps, as this was the middle of July. I was confident, regardless, that I could get along and anyway, I could send a letter when possible and they could send me a box on the 1945 boat.

As Mother pedalled the old Singer Sewing Machine and I stitched and sewed on buttons, etc, we visited. My sisters and other family members came. I had missed seeing them for two years. Now it would be four more. Members of several local churches heard about my experiences with the Cree which seemed very remarkable to them, and asked me to speak at their gatherings.

The time came. The trunk was filled, locked and labelled. Seeing the label made it final. Excitement, fear and sadness all at once. In 1944 in Aklavik we were not to expect the mail to come or go during the autumn freeze up or the spring break up, owing to the river conditions. There were no airports, no roads, no telephones and very, very little radio reception.

We loaded the trunk into the box of the farm truck and it was time to go.

THE ADVENTURE BEGINS
– Saskatoon to Edmonton

With my face as close as possible to the window, I waved and watched my parents fade into the distance as the CNR train pulled me slowly away from the Saskatoon platform. The silent, tearful couple had said good-bye to one of their eight children. It was 1944. War time had seen my brothers leave, my older sisters marry and leave, now it was my turn.

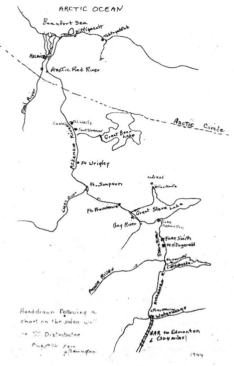

Uppermost in my thoughts was a contract of "four years in the far North" which loomed like a thick wall of time, at the moment opaque, huge and frightening. A silent, choking barrier between security and dreams. Meanwhile, an adventure to learn the unknown, to challenge the barrier brought excitement!

As the train gathered speed I daubed at my tears, then found the number of my place in the Sleeper car. Night had fallen over the prairies. I needed to be silently alone. To replace what was past and think – yes, think about what was ahead, the structure of the wall now moving toward me or I to it.

A jolly big porter helped place the ladder to the upper berth. This was a new experience for me and an interesting one. None of my former travels had provided the luxury. I slept little. I thought a great deal. What if the conductor failed to call me as we approached Edmonton?

August 6. I am here now in a fine room in the Macdonald Hotel, reputed to be a safe place for a young woman travelling alone. The charge is Three Dollars a night and I am to wait here until the freight designated for the Western Arctic is loaded on the Northern Alberta Railway (N.A.R.). Someone will call the hotel desk and I will be informed. Consequently, I don't go far from the telephone although in several short jaunts I have seen a little of the city. It appears to me to be poorly laid out, homes and businesses are intermingled and there are few names on the street corners

THE MACDONALD
EDMONTON, ALTA.

THE DREAM BEGINS.
–on to Waterways

After three long days the call came, "come to the Strathcona Station by early afternoon." I was prepared and knew the Strathcona Station was on the verge of Edmonton. I had been reading in the Hotel's library and learned its history. When, in 1891 the rail connection between Calgary, on the main CPR line, and Edmonton was completed, its terminus on the south bank of the North Saskatchewan River was named after Lord Strathcona. He had been Donald Smith, a one time HBC clerk in Labrador and subsequently a very wealthy Canadian entrepreneur. When the CPR line was completed sea to sea in 1885 he drove the last spike at Craigellachie, B.C. When the N.A.R. reached Waterways, Alberta in 1925, it used Strathcona as its southern base.

I took a cab to the Strathcona Station. There were many travellers and their friends milling about on the old station platform. I looked for young women who, like myself, would be wearing trim navy dresses with crisp white collars and cuffs. The Church of England required their workers to wear these uniforms for public appearances. It was easy to spot two others in the crowd.

Reka Elkink, a tall, shapely Dutch girl, a Saskatchewan teacher going north to Aklavik and Marjorie Sutton an attractive young lady from Gimli, Manitoba made three of us on our way to All Saints Residential School in Aklavik. From the beginning we were a compatible threesome.

Elkink and Sutton (it was the custom to use surnames) had arrived at Strathcona a few hours before and anxiously awaited me. "Oh, Harrington! Have you got our tickets?" I did have them. Evening departure was approaching so we picked up our hand luggage and boarded the sleeping car. (We had all previously checked our other luggage through to Waterways.) Numbers on our tickets indicated our places. The berths had been made up so in the dim light we sought the numbers on the curtains. As I pushed the drapes aside, I was surprised to see a fully uniformed soldier asleep in my place. Sutton had the same discovery. The porter saw our consternation and rushed up, "Vate, vate, I git 'im out dare." "No, no" I heard myself saying, "It's wartime, we'll go to the day coach." We learned later that military personnel superseded lay persons in wartime. The Station Master

6

had unilaterally cancelled our sleeper reservations but we hadn't been notified.

The coach was old, shabby and filthy. The travellers were a motley 'Canadian' lot: Nuns, trappers, Cree, French, Half Breeds, old, young. Nearly all seemed to be speaking French. I had never experienced the atmosphere before. It was like being alive in a novel. I wondered if it were typical of that part of Canada and I felt uncomfortable.

Sitting ever so sedately in my coach space, mulling over the challenges I might be going to face, I dozed off. A voice wakened me, "Are you Miss Harrington?" It was Frances Jukes, whose step parents were Reverend and Mrs. Morrison at Fort McMurray. She offered to share her upper berth with me. Elkink's berth had not been reassigned to a soldier so Sutton was going to share with her.

I went back with Frances to the Sleeper car. We went up the ladder through the smoky curtains. She said, "I never really undress as one never knows." She kicked off her shoes and lay down on the far side.

There was no way I could sleep in my new uniform so on the outer edge of the upper berth I somehow managed to change into the voluminous cotton night-gown my mother had supplied.

The train was starting to move. With quite a number of jerks, blasts on the steam whistle and clangs of the bells, we left the station. For some time the bells kept clanging as we crossed the streets and roads, slowly leaving Edmonton behind. Since we were in an upper berth we had no window from which to see it disappear. I had hoped to see the river as we crossed the High Level Bridge.

Frances was still awake and we, lying in the dark, had a giggly time as, separated from the other passengers only by swaying drapes, we heard every sound. Everyone seemed to be talking. It was hot, humid and foul with smoke but not without its drama.

I was hanging on for dear life to the edge of the berth as the bumping train threatened to throw me off until, slowly, the train stopped. What a relief! Then little voices from the next upper berth started crying, "Mummy! Mummy! I want a dink." Sometimes all three of them cried at once. Several female voices tried to help but the children screamed even louder. After what seemed about an hour the coach door banged, the babies got quiet and we were on our way again.

Frances, who had travelled this way many times, said a similar episode happens on most trips. It seems the NAR engineers accommodate one of the regular passengers who has a friend living a short distance from the railroad. She does his shopping in Edmonton and delivers whatever she has for him while the train crew eat their supper.

The talk in the coach diminished and we could hear snores in various "keys," the opening and closing of heavy coach doors, the clang of the wheels. Then I heard a door slam shut, something crashed to the floor with a loud bang, a torrent of blasphemous language and shouting. Soon a heavy odour rose throughout the area and I heard among other laments, "Mon rum! Mon rum!" Francis who had been nearly asleep woke. Finally I heard Elkink, who was more worldly than I, say, "It's strong enough to pickle us all!"

The coach door banged again and I heard the deep voice of the porter mumbling as he swept up the broken glass.

Frances was soon asleep again. I was afraid to relax as I clung to the edge of the mattress. Every lurch could have sent me off into the aisle. However, perhaps it was the alcoholic fumes that brought on quietness and rest until early morning. Then violent bumps and lurching brought the coach to a stop leaning slightly so that I was rolled against Frances and safely away from the edge.

A general commotion set up around us and people in lower berths pulled open their window blinds. As soon as we had dressed we looked out. Our coach seemed to be partly derailed in a wet, soggy muskeg. We followed others and got off to look about. It was already quite light. Most of the men seemed to be

prying, pushing and lifting the coach to get it back on the rails. We moved back on to a little drier footing where we weren't in the way.

I was very curious about the muskeg and had my first discovery of a pitcher plant. Before long mosquitoes found us. We heard shouts telling us "Hurry up! Get on again."

After we had returned to our places tin mugs of black tea and some big biscuits were passed around.

The second day on the N.A.R. was quieter until we came to a little settlement, Lac la Biche. The train stopped and when the porter called, "One 'our and one 'aff." Elkink, Sutton, Jukes and I got off in search of the Mission

—Pitcher Plant—

house. The town was muddy and dirty as we trudged to the Mission where we were greeted by Archdeacon Little. I was excited to see a familiar vehicle in the yard – the Sunday School by Post van – and the two van ladies, Misses Sawyer and Paris.

In the 1920s and later there were thousands of prairie families

who lived on farms and ranches far from towns and community services. Each summer it was a highlight to have the Sunday School by Post van ladies come. The driver was a well-trained auto mechanic, the other a friendly likeable teacher of versatile abilities. Both had training in First Aid which was often useful.

They drove the prairie roads and trails bringing cheer and Sunday lesson supplies to countless homes. The funds to buy and service the vans were raised in England. The ladies' personal needs were usually gladly supplied by their Canadian hosts.

As a child I was always very excited to see the big square vehicle driving slowly into our farm yard. So was our entire family as it brought such happy visitors. The ladies gladly accepted our invitation to join us at meals but always retired early to sleep in their van.

Usually I was their guide each day to go with them to find the homes of other children waiting for the annual visit. If we asked we would have a little service, learn to sing a hymn but as often they offered to enrol the children with the Sunday School by Post in Regina which would send regular lessons and even mark work sent in. Always the ladies left a supply of colourful Bible story leaflets.

These ladies brought a sense of universal Christian ethics and morality that often the busy parents couldn't define. Never was religion promoted but was always available if asked for. No place was too far nor inaccessible despite the roads or the distance. We heard many tales of their adventures which they told with much merriment. Archdeacon Little added, "Lac la Biche is a bit off the beaten track, you know."

Along with Misses Sawyer and Paris we went to visit the unfinished church.

Back in our places on the N.A.R. the old steam engine jerked the train away from the town. We got into more bush and muskeg. Our ride was less firm and more unpredictable. The porter came in, "Lunch, real fresh all the way from Edmonton," as he served paper bags of dry sandwiches and bottles, no straws, of Orange Crush. Later he made the rounds with a bottle opener.

Hours passed by while we watched from a window and talked, getting to know one another. As the train blew its whistle and slowed down, there were long line-ups in the aisle as the passengers sought one last visit to the only washroom.

Finally we were near our destination. We were glad to come to the end of the line for this railway at the dock on Clearwater Creek near its entrance to the Athabasca River. The area, "Waterways" was a vital point on our schedule.

I clutched my hand luggage and hurried off into the fresh air. Sutton and Elkink were ahead of me, marvelling at the view – there on the river we could see our crisp, white paddlewheeler, the Northland Echo. I turned to get one last look at the N.A.R. – it hadn't been luxurious, comfortable or restful BUT it had given us a 310 mile start on our trip to Aklavik.

END OF THE LINE
— Waterways, Alberta

Elkink, Sutton, Jukes and I followed the well worn pathway from the train down a stairway to a platform at the water's edge. A lady's voice called, "Is one of you Miss Harrington? Come on over the gangplank." It was the ship's housekeeper, Mrs. Rogers, who welcomed us aboard the S.S. Northland Echo. The purser had assigned our staterooms and directed us to them. None of us had previously travelled by ship and we were all eyes, marvelling at everything. We were asked if we'd like some breakfast.

After the pioneer conditions of the train, the formal table with white linen and silver was a welcome sight. We four young women chattered excitedly as we ate with hearty appetites, grapefruit, bacon, eggs and toast.

Probably because I was a veteran of the Anglican Mission Society, I seemed to have become 'head' of our group. When the Captain came to greet us he asked for "Miss Harrington" and introduced himself. I made the introductions and he told us about what amenities the Northland Echo could provide.

As we talked I watched a crane lifting huge cartons from the boxcars on the rails to a barge beside the steamer. I counted 63 dog toboggans, tied in threes or fours being placed on another barge.

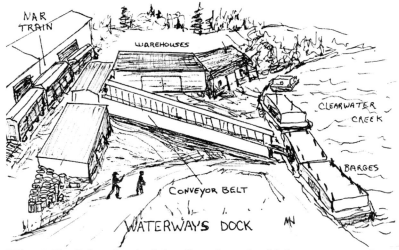

NAR TRAIN
WAREHOUSES
CLEARWATER CREEK
BARGES
CONVEYOR BELT
WATERWAY'S DOCK

When Miss Jukes thanked the Captain and said she must get going to her home at Fort McMurray, the Captain asked, "Why don't you all go? You're welcome here, but we'll be several days loading and it'll be a change. I'll send word when the loading is complete." Miss Jukes was delighted and suggested we stay with her at McMurray. So we gathered a few things and at 50¢ each for a taxi, travelled the muddy, rutted 3-mile trail to Fort McMurray.

Miss Jukes' step parents, Rev. and Mrs. Morrison were away with a barge load of 34 Scouts and Guides at summer camp so we shared the empty rectory. Most northern homes have basic supplies in their cupboards so by searching the shelves we chose things for dinner. I went with Jukes to the well for a pail of fresh water. Sutton was great at lighting up the wood-burning cook stove, Elkink opened cans and we had a good meal.

In the evening the four of us went to a show at the hotel. It was, "First Comes Courage," a tale of the invasion of Storvik, Norway. The walk after, back to the rectory, led through the bush and was as black as night can be. If Jukes hadn't been so much at home, we'd have been quite terrified by the strange noises from this unfamiliar place.

The Fort McMurray rectory of St. John the Baptist was a quiet restful place in its clearing near the village. I was up first and finally

13

WATERFRONT, WATERWAYS, ALTA., CANADA

WATERWAYS, ALTA., CANADA

FORT MCMURRAY, ALBERTA, CANADA. SUTHERLAND FOTO.

14

managed to find the ingredients I needed for some pancakes.

It was after 12 noon when again, at 50¢ each, we took a taxi back to Waterways. Waterways was the end of steel where the rail freight was unloaded from the train to be re-loaded onto barges to be pushed northward down the Athabasca River . A frontier Canadian outpost, the place held much diversity and interest. It was a good place to get some summer employment and that attracted a variety of people, mostly "Breeds," Cree and French, one British-Japanese family and a few Scandinavian men. The general impression to a visitor was that over indulgence in alcoholic drink was causing a social problem. During the time in 1943 that some 4,000 American and Canadian troops had been stationed here the soldiers had been allotted unlimited liquor rations and now in 1944 while most of the military had travelled on to Norman Wells, the quantity supplied remained high. Unlike most of Canada where the beer parlours were not open to women, here they were unrestricted. We were told that an accomplished woman could consume 40 glasses at one visit. The rows of baby carriages outside the parlours were a common sight and in 1944 venereal diseases and child neglect were a challenge to the workers in Roman Catholic, United and Anglican churches.

Waterways had a brine salt well where about 35 employees provided enough salt for all of Alberta. The old Hotel was getting a new coat of paint and a new Mission church was waiting to be  furnished. Other than those signs of prosperity the buildings were old and run down. However, the Hudson's Bay Company (HBC) store was very well supplied. I bought a sweet grass basket and for $2.00 a porcupine quill and birch bark box. The latter was round and designed especially to hold the stiff detached collars that gentlemen wore. How a native artisan got the dimensions – and the inspiration – to make such a box is hard to guess.

Fort McMurray was a contrast. The houses, stores and roads were all better despite the muddy streets. Fort McMurray, with only a few hundred residents, had a three-room public school. The "New

Franklin" hotel was undergoing a slow renovation. The Canadian Government had a well-run signal station. Further along the road was "Petrosands," a company intent on developing the extensive oil or tar sands, making them give up their petroleum. The gardens and flowers seemed especially lovely in this far-off lonely place. The Anglican Mission church was being furnished by an active group of people working together to enrich their lives and the community.
While we were at Waterways checking on the progress of loading our ship's cargo, the Rev. and Mrs. Morrison, their helpers, Charles and Mrs. Head and their 34 campers returned. Our barges were far from ready so we returned to Fort McMurray. We had a lunch of Crumpets and I jotted down the recipe:

2 eggs
2 1/2 tbsp. sugar
1 small c. milk
1 1/2 tsp. baking powder
1 c. or more flour

Right after lunch we went from the rectory next door to Mrs. Daniels' for the Women's Auxiliary (W.A.) meeting. Mrs. Ross was president, Mrs. Hill secretary and with the Mrs. Mitchell, Jewett, Cripps and Crowls, along with we 'travellers', the little house was full. Miss Jukes and I walked home with Mrs. Jewett. It was almost the same as being at my mother's prairie auxiliary.

The Morrisons had a good garden between the church and the rectory. The long summer days produced prolific plants. We picked and shelled peas. It was August 11, a rainy day so I stayed in to help where I could and also to glean more knowledge of the life in this outpost. Rev. Morrison was very amused by a story gathered at the Post Office. It appears that while the United States forces were at Waterways the previous year they had their own Post Office but now the American and Canadian officials worked side by side in the Canadian office. The U.S. officer, named Goodwin, was a huge, very talkative fellow. By the end of the day the village postman was nearly at the end of his endurance and as Goodwin closed his wicket and left for home, the village postman exploded, "If those hot-aired Americans don't soon get out of here we'll all be in the banana belt!"

While I helped Mrs. Morrison, the others went back to Waterways to check on the Northland Echo. Once assured it wouldn't leave until the next day, we spent another restful night at the rectory. Everyone slept late and Rev. Morrison had to scramble to get to a pre-Communion Class at 10. We went to Waterways again that afternoon and Mr. Petty, the Purser, advised us to stay on the boat.

We began days of sumptuous meals and leisure time to read, play cards, and enjoy life aboard ship.

MARY HARRINGTON

WE'RE OFF!
– on the Northland Echo

A letter home.

S.S. Northland Echo
Athabasca River
Outbound from Waterways, Alta.
Aug. 12, 1944

Dear Folks,

We are, at present, on the Clearwater River, a small river which flows into the Athabasca. Our steamer has been pushing the barges, one at a time, up [sic] as far as the Athabasca. We are on our way back for the third barge; then, we hope, we will be able to proceed with the three together. The river is narrow — flowing swiftly, though shallow, and churned to angry mud by our energetic paddlewheel. On either side steep banks of poplar, spruce and pine rise away, now and then broken by deep descents of rock and shale — uncolorful but scenic. Our paddlewheel goes, "swish, swish," in unbroken rhythm, two to a second, as if constantly daring a sandbar to interfere.

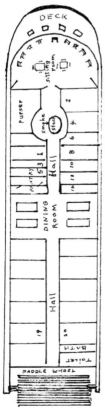

The steamer or "Northland Echo" is a fine boat — flat on bottom, like a raft, only dropping two feet into the water. The whole thing is painted white, trimmed blue and very clean. In the bottom is the huge boiler and the supply of spruce poles to keep up steam. The next floor is the passengers'. Perhaps a sketch will show you how it is laid out.

No. 10 stateroom is shared by Miss Sutton and myself. Across the hall in No. 5 is the other worker for Aklavik, Miss Elkink. We are comfortably placed. There are two 'bunks,' an upper and a lower. I am assigned to the upper. There is little room but we will spend all our spare time about deck.

Above our stateroom level is the upper deck. It is interesting to go up and look down on the churling paddle wheel, or on the barge tops. One small barge has a cattle rack — about 15 cattle, some pigs and sheep. Once in a while we hear the hogs.

We have just heard that there are 21 passengers besides a staff of probably 15. The meals are excellent. We had orange, bacon and eggs, toast, marmalade, coffee this morning. There is a choice of eggs any style, hotcakes, etc.

This trip is truly beautiful. We pass on and on, always passing through an unbelievable panorama of scenic beauty. Every window, every minute, shows a vivid portrait of nature in its summer garb. One of the young men just dashed in and out again with his camera. We jumped up to see what the object was. It turned out to be only a horse, grazing by the river side. I suppose he thought it was going to be a moose.

We passed a U. S. army plane turned over on its back and anchored on a sandbar. It reminded me of a dead beetle! Our purser said that it had flipped over taking off. No one was injured but the propeller was damaged.

At first rocky shale showed on the banks but now about 100 miles "down" river the trees and grass grow down to the water. The river is full of sandbars and it keeps our

19

steamer winding in and out to find a passage.
A deck hand is always ahead on the barge
sounding the depth — even three feet will clear
us. Yet it is surprising how many times the
forward barge has been stuck. In such a case
we stop, back up, turn, and manoeuvre until we
are free again. You can imagine that I enjoy
every minute of it. It even seems too risky to
go to sleep — in case I miss something! We
don't travel from about 10 p. m. to 5 a. m..

Clouds and light rain encouraged after dinner naps. I tried, then tried to write to a very special friend. I couldn't – every slap of the paddlewheel seemed to be creating a barrier – a big void between the past, the places, the feelings and emotions – and now and the future were dominating me. I gave in to now and went to the salon to watch.

At several places along the river billows of smoke rose from the dark areas of the shore. There the oily shale rocks had been smouldering as long as people remembered. Old accounts record that about 1715 a Cree Indian named Swan wintered on the Athabasca River somewhere near Fort McMurray. He collected a dark sticky lump
from the banks of the river and took it East when he returned. This was the first record of the Athabasca Oil Sands. Later, in the early 1900s one of the ships, the S.S. Grahame was recorded as carrying chunks of the tar collected from where it oozed at the Athabasca River Bank. When they got their furnace going they threw in chunks of the tar, the fire then quickly heated the water to provide steam more rapidly.

At pre-arranged riverside places wood cutters stacked cordwood for fuel. About five o'clock we stopped at a cabin to load aboard 15 cords of spruce logs. The Indian there cut and piled it by the shore, selling it

to the HBC for $3.50 a cord.
The ship burned cordwood
to produce steam to drive the
paddlewheel. We slowly
moved close to the river bank
and stopped. The crew
lowered a plank catwalk
which they used as a bridge
to wheel-barrow the wood
across to the hold. When I questioned an officer he replied, "Yes,
spruce cordwood, $3.50 a cord, about 15 cords a day."

Diary. August 13, Sunday.

The boat started to move again about 5 a.m. I believe. At least I was first aware then, of the crew – voices, steps, and the paddle wheel. When I finally arose at 10 to 7 and found that all this stirring about had accomplished only putting the barges into their positions – one afore, two beside – and the journey had begun again. I was resigned and really relieved to know there'd be no more delay.

The bathroom was conveniently vacant so at 7:15 I was dressed and out on deck. The Radium Queen went by, returning for her other barge. In the early morning sun it was lovely. The breakfast bell rang at 7:30. Miss Sutton and I went pronto. Bacon, eggs, toast, coffee, orange. The diamond drillers were there. Miss Elkink came later. [She had been up late making new friends with the diamond drillers.] Then we tidied our room. Miss Sutton and I took pictures of one another on the upper deck. A pyjama clad figure appeared at a window, "Hi, ladies, this is sleeping quarters. You shouldn't be up here . . ."

Now the morning has clouded over. Dinner [noon] – roast pork, blueberry pie. We all seemed to be trying to nap after dinner. The dull, cloudy, rainy day encouraged rest. I tried to sleep and almost did. Then I tried to write a letter to my fiancé. It is a hard task. . . . We passed an old mine – Poplar Point. Later we came to a point where we stopped and re-fueled, the men putting another 15 cords of wood into the boat. We were about 3 hours, until 8 o'clock there.

As soon as our supper was over we three, Elkink, Sutton and I went across the catwalk to land, first being assured that the Echo wouldn't leave 'til at least 8 p.m.. We followed a trail through the woods and arrived at a fine garden – potatoes, carrots, peas, cucumbers, etc. Beyond the garden the trail led on, presumably to the woodcutter's home but we didn't continue.

On the shore near the Echo we played with some little stones, trying to skip them on the water. Elkink was good at it. Meanwhile the crew loading the wood were also enjoying themselves. Their faces were blackened with charcoal from carrying the logs that had been scorched in a forest fire. Laughing and singing in bits of English about "O' Susanna" and "Old Black Joe," they lightened the evening in merriment, their voices breaking the stillness of the wilderness.

The barges were again attached to the ship and we were underway. In the evening there were flashes of low sunshine and we had two pretty rainbows. Memorable.

While not one of us was a sailor, we were beginning to feel at home on the Northland Echo. I found the translocation from firm prairie sod quite fascinating and determined to record details to enhance my memory. I clicked my little box camera to get  visual images such as Sutton on the upper deck, the "Echo" from the shore, the woodcutters' settlement.

I watched the fire boy feed each of the ships' three dogs a bone and a thick slice of bread. This fellow's real duties were to watch the steam gauges and hoist cordwood into the hungry fire pits.

August 14, Monday. Feeling quite happy and at home, I hummed "Home Sweet Home" and commandeered the bathtub to do a wash which I hung on a line on deck. The sun and breeze dried everything before lunch. Rejuvenated by the fresh air, I decided to get some handwork going. Mrs. Wiley, a passenger, held her arms out while I draped the red skeins of wool on them and wound it into balls. I cast on stitches to make socks.

Afternoon travel on the Athabasca river brought a variance in scenery – fewer sandbars, no evergreen trees, and finally only willows which were low and scrubby on the marshy shores.

We passed some scattered cabins and a fine, white painted farmstead where the sign said "Mr. & Mrs. A. Reid." One of the settlements had racks of fish drying in the sun. Here one of our deck hands changed places with one of the shore fishermen.

Two small boats passed us carrying a huge screen cage, probably 10' X12' X 8'. Later we saw a sign on shore reading: "Ducks Unlimited" and we surmised they were related and that the Ducks Unlimited men would use the screen cage when tagging captured birds.

Around noon many of the passengers spent several hours basking in the sun on the barge ahead. My freckled skin being easily sun-burned kept me indoors, knitting and thinking of my special friend away in the war.

Just after supper everyone rushed to the deck when they heard we were meeting a steamer. It turned out to be a Northern Transportation (N.T.) boat taking several barge loads of U.S. Army trucks and equipment back south. I became so occupied in trying to focus my little camera that I missed the details except the large letters U.S.A. on the freight.

By 6 p.m. we were nearing Lake Athabasca where, despite seeing the hills in the distance, the nearby land was low and marshy.

Mrs. Wiley, who had been out visiting her daughter in Ontario was now returning to Chipewyan, warned us that the lake could be rough. Immediately we wondered if, like in the stories we had read, we'd be hanging over the rails.

But on this evening the lake was calm, stretching out before us like a gigantic slough towards the horizon. This huge delta was strewn with countless dead trees lodged in the sand, their bleached limbs, like skeletal bones, reaching skyward. Gulls and ducks rose from the water, circled and landed on the shallow waters. The ship slowly stopped and I thought we would not be attempting a crossing that evening.

It had been an interesting day. For hour after hour the steamer chugged onward, ever onward. I happened to note the shadows, and yes, we were going north, north. A feeling came over me – every chug of the paddlewheel was taking me farther away from those I loved. It lasted for only a moment.

Earlier I had been speaking with Mrs. Rogers, the ship's matron. After supper she asked if we'd like to see the view from the wheelhouse. A senior passenger, Mr. Henderson and his secretary, Miss Abell, were there and as we thought they wanted privacy, we didn't go in.  But from the steps we had a distant view. Other vessels, the "Beaver Lake," "Pelly Lake," and "Radium Queen" were anchored near by waiting for morning light. We learned that we were not only anchored but stuck.

So from the wheelhouse we went down to the galley for coffee and got to see the engines, the boilers and learn about the inner "Echo" and how it worked.

Our night's rest on the sand bars stretched on. Around us in the delta of the lazy Athabasca were other craft, all immobile over

Another log on the furnace

night. During the early hours our short wave radio talked to theirs. We even heard them contact the S.S. Distributor now windbound at Wrigley Harbour for three days. I was interested in communications as the "Distributor" was to be our final ship.

We were only 15 miles from Chipewyan but it may take four days waiting for an east wind to blow across the lake gradually increasing the depth of the delta water and freeing us from the sand bars.

However, by afternoon the Radium Queen and Beaver Lake were free and came to our rescue. We watched them edge nearer and crewmen lowered small boats from which they attached heavy cables to the largest of our barges. After it was pulled clear and anchored, the refrigerator and cattle barges were towed away. The Echo was next.

We gathered up the barges and moved into the lake which was somewhat rough. By 4:30 we could see Chipewyan. The Radium Queen was ahead but it didn't stop at Chip.

When well advanced across the lake we met a craft, "Ste. Marie" being steered by a priest in cassock. The very rough water made his approach to our Echo quite precarious.

We were curious to watch as our crew assisted the French R.C. priest to come aboard with his luggage as well as a crated piano. He said he was going to Resolution to fix the school roof. The HBC had a custom of assisting all who approached needing help. Before the "Ste. Marie" pulled away, three Indian boys also boarded the Echo. They hoped to get to Fort Smith where the doctor could do appendectomies.

That mid-lake stop turned out to be our "dock" for Chipewyan. Only our refrigerator barge had goods for Chip so the Pelly Lake took it to the village, allowing us to continue towards the Slave River. The refrigerator barge would catch up with us later.

That left us with two barges, one of which had the cattle, sheep and hogs in their enclosures on top. I had interest in seeing how the animals were cared for. Fodder was baled and in bags, easily doled out. The deck hose was used with a hand pump to swab the manure over the side. The pens were small so the poor creatures could scarcely move about.

From my Diary, August 15, Tuesday.

Around Chipewyan I liked the rocky islands and shores

although their black hues were not nearly as pretty or striking as at Lac la Ronge. First came the old fort and the Hudson's Bay buildings, the Church of England mission church, the new Hudson's Bay store and lastly the Roman Catholic Church and hospital. It was a well-painted and pretty settlement. I took a snap from the deck after we had passed.

Chipewyan is credited to be the longest continuously settled community in the province. Roderick Mackenzie established the first trading post named "Fort Chipewyan" on the south shore of Lake Athabasca in 1788 but moved it to the present site in 1798.

A NEW RIVER, NEW ADVENTURES
– Chip to Fitz

Much of the load of silt carried by the Athabasca River is left behind in the marshes between Lake Athabasca and the Slave River. The water as we entered the Slave was much clearer but was joined almost immediately by the muddy and much larger Peace River entering from the west.

The Slave River is deeper than the Athabasca and is without obvious sandbars, allowing more rapid travel. To a question, "Is it free sailing now?" the Captain replied, "We've traded one hazard for another, sand for rocks." The steady "Chug, Chug" splashing of the paddlewheel took on a faster tempo. Expecting other changes, I spent much of the day on deck.

Just before noon the Radium Queen came alongside and some of us were invited over for a visit. Unlike the Northland Echo, the Radium Queen was not a HBC vessel. It was a Northern Transportation Company boat, diesel-powered, modern and compact. We had met the Captain's sister, Miss McKinley, when we were on the train and it was pleasant to see her again and also to meet the Radium's two passengers, Roman Catholic nurses from Montreal going to Fort Norman.

Back on the Echo, we travelled steadily until 10 p.m. when we arrived at a woodcutter's site. I drifted off to sleep listening to the rhythmic thuds of cordwood being loaded.

August 16 A new day. I rose early and joined the rest for the regular 7:30 breakfast. We were nearing the end of the Northland Echo's northward journey. Some of us knew that because of a 16-mile series of treacherous rapids in the Slave River, we'd have to make a portage from Fort Fitzgerald to Fort Smith. As many of the other passengers were busy packing up to leave, Sutton, Elkink and I took advantage of the unused bathtub to do some laundry.

Thanks to the muddy contribution of the Peace River, the bathtub filled with brown "soup" but we decided to do some of our things, hoping that the drying wind would whip out the silt. Actually we soon faced a worse problem: getting the soupy water out of the tub again!

Shortly after dinner we sighted Fort Fitzgerald. Some of the passengers were waiting to go ashore even before the barges were docked. They hurriedly loaded into a truck and left. In a couple of hours they returned, disappointed, having endured sixteen miles each way of rough and very dusty travel. Fort Smith had "no room at the inn." The town was still being affected by the building of the Canol Road and Pipeline from Norman Wells to Whitehorse, a U.S.-Canada project that brought many transients north. At the same time local administration was needing more staff and accommodation.

There was very little to do at Fitzgerald so I persuaded Mrs. Beatty, Mrs. MacDonald, Elkink and Sutton to go for a walk. I was especially anxious to get a glimpse of the notorious Rapids of the Drowned. The very name aroused questions. Who drowned? When? What were the circumstances? Did it happen more than once? etc.

First we went into the old Hudson's Bay Store. Home-made chocolate ice cream was selling for 10¢ a cone. Enjoying our cones, we wandered further along the trail until we came to a native graveyard. It was  different from any I had seen. Some plots had little houses over the graves and many had neat picket fences around the edges. All were painted white. Since there were no crucifixes, I surmised that they were the graves of Protestant Indians.

FORT FITZGERALD '44

We continued walking on the sandy road asking anyone we met if any of the trails leading off would take us to the Rapids. We finally got there. Our position up on the high rocky bank, looking through the trees, gave us a poor view but we could hear the roar down below. Not wanting to be left in the dark, or miss our dinners, we plodded back along the sandy road to the Echo. When we arrived, the staff had news that our next ship, the Distributor, had been delayed and wasn't yet back to Fort Smith. So, while the trucks hauled freight across the portage, we stayed aboard.

Thursday, August 17.   Elkink went to Fort Smith with Clara

McKinley, the sister of the Captain of the Radium Queen. Sutton and I were a bit restless and thinking of the days delaying us from reaching our journey's end, decided to explore a bit more. At Chagira's store and Post Office we each bought a whistle. What for? Well, if we got lost? or maybe to scare wild animals? after all wasn't it quite wild country?

I knew there was a school at Fitzgerald, the most northerly public school in Alberta and we found it. It was a desolate scene: door open, holes in the blackboard, whitewash peeling off the log walls, very few books – not at all a happy state to greet the new teacher who was on her way to Fitzgerald. We heard that she had 20 years experience. She would need it. I felt great sympathy for her with such a task ahead.

School - Ft. Fitzgerald '44

On the way back we stopped at the Hudson's Bay Company store for a few minutes. The manager's wife, Mrs. Milne, who had been a nurse at the Aklavik Hospital, invited us back at three for tea. After our noon dinner I knitted until it was time to join Mrs. Beatty, Mrs. MacDonald and Sutton at Mrs. Milne's house. I found her most pleasant, with an easy, friendly kindness and hospitality. I enjoyed doing some of her darning while she made tea. Sutton used her washer to do some laundry. On our way back to the Echo I took Mrs. MacDonald to see the school. She was a journalist gathering items for stories for the Edmonton Bulletin.

Meanwhile, adventurous Elkink had been to Fort Smith but returned in time for supper. She was not at all backward in approaching interesting ventures and always had lots to tell us.

Travelling with us on the Echo was Bill Apetagan, a quiet, shy, young Cree man. He had been working for the HBC in northern Manitoba and was being transferred to the Western Arctic. It was an apprentice promotion and I imagined well earned as he seemed both thoughtful and intelligent.

Bill, Sutton and I took our cameras to take pictures of the graveyard but stopped by the little store for ice cream cones, this time orange. We hurried back to Mrs. Milne's in time to hear the 8 o'clock news on the radio. Unfortunately the Milnes had left on a trip to Smith. Since we hadn't yet visited the renowned metropolis, we were disappointed as very likely we could have joined the passengers in the truck box.

It got dark as we played Rummy on the Echo. When tied up in dock without its engines running, the electricity was limited and as evening came no lights burned. Water pressure was off at 10 p.m. Just then our ship's matron, Mrs. Rogers, appeared with a tray of tea and a candle which she set up in our room. We were so well cared for by this gracious woman!

August 18. At Fitzgerald the sky was very cloudy and the air warm. There was still no word of our transfer to Fort Smith so I went to Milnes to see if I could help her.
She had a bright idea to plan a picnic and go up the Dog River, a small stream leading into the Slave River near Fitzgerald. It was Mrs. Beatty's birthday so Mrs. MacDonald made a cake. I cut a huge bouquet from Mrs. Milne's garden – sweet peas, mignonette and gypsophila (baby's breath). About 1:30 Mrs. Milne, her sons Douglas and Lindsay, Rae Shapira, Mrs. MacDonald, Mrs. Beatty, Sutton, Bill Apetagan and I went off in Milne's boat. All was

very restful and pretty. The water was low and we had trouble (and fun) getting over the stones until we got sticks from the shore and used them to pole. Then we broke a shear pin. That meant paddling and pushing, getting exercise we badly needed. We came to a landing place near a small, happy waterfall and went ashore.

Lunch was delicious – canned sausage, olives, pickles, and toast. Then marshmallows, well browned and the surprise birthday cake. Drinks of grape and cherry were soon mixed using the clear water of the little Dog River.

To top off our wilderness picnic we were planning on fishing. A quick shower that soaked us thoroughly helped us decide to put the tackle away. Meanwhile knowledgeable Bill had replaced the broken shear pin with a nail. Navigating the stones was less difficult with our fresh experience and we were soon on our way back to the ship.

Mrs. Beatty invited the Milnes to the Echo for supper. Then we all went back to Milnes to hear the 8 p.m. news. The war was still the 'news' and with all the wild noisy static coming from the radio we could have been involved in battle right there in Fitzgerald.

As there was light enough for a drive, Mrs. Beatty, Mr. and Mrs. Milne, Sutton and I drove in the HBC truck as far as "Halfway," so named to denote the halfway point between Fitzgerald and Smith. It was amusing yet interesting to see the marker at Halfway: it was a huge stuffed buffalo, now very flea (or moth!) eaten and weather beaten! It was indeed a pathetic, memorable sight, standing so dejectedly on a wooden platform.

Scruffy Old Buffalo at Halfway House
Ft. Fitzgerald ←...→ Ft. Smith '44

Just as we got back to our cabins on the Echo, the lights went off.

August 19. There had been rain in the night but we were up early and packed right after breakfast, expecting to go to Fort Smith but not knowing when.

We went over to say good-bye to Mrs. Milne. Elkink went to get her curlers from the Radium Queen and to say farewell to Clara McKinley. She brought back word that we were to go after dinner. That gave me more time to enjoy Mrs. Milne's company. I washed dishes, mopped and picked flowers.

After dinner we were excited to cross paths with Canon and Mrs.

Shepherd and their four children who were coming south from Aklavik. They were transferring from the Distributor to the Echo, the reverse of our travels. The Shepherds were so much of what I had previously heard of the North, I was sorry it was such a short meeting.

The big old car that took us to Fort Smith gave us an unpleasant ride and smelled strongly of petroleum. The sandy road had been widened and built up with more sand as it wound along through the trees. I saw some tin cans tied to trees and linked with wires along the right side of the road. Eventually I found out it was a telephone line! Incredible, I thought until I was assured it would relay a code of vibrations from one can to the next. Later we tried it and sure enough one could send an SOS, at least.

Telephone Line '44

I was glad to get out at "Halfway" for a walk and some fresh air. Most of our luggage was left in a truck and we were anxious to be sure it was following us. That portage, only 16 miles, seemed one of the longest portions of our journey.

N.W.T.
– the S.S. Distributor, Fort Smith

We realized that we had left Alberta and were now in the Northwest Territories (NWT). We were entering another exciting part of our Canadian Map.

Fort Smith was much larger than Fort Fitzgerald and built up on a hill where the homes were almost hidden amongst the trees. I had never seen so much sand! You seemed to wade through it. As soon as you stepped on the road it came over your boot-tops. Our first look over the edge down to the wide, wide Slave River was memorable – there on our side, close to the shore was a very large, white paddlewheeler. Slowly we drove down the curved approach, marvelling at our new ship, the "Distributor." It was sitting at the foot of the Rapids of the Drowned, 124 feet lower than the Echo at Fort Fitzgerald.

We were shown to Stateroom #6, a large room which in 1937 had been occupied by Lord Tweedsmuir on his trip to the Arctic. He was the first Governor General to take the tour to the Arctic and the accommodation was suitably modified. So it was a special room changed to accommodate the three of us. Along one wall were two single bunk beds, one above the other and along another wall a well appointed single bed.

What I see at night !

The latter had a special spring mattress, goose down comforter and fine percale sheets. Its unique luxury was a bed light on the head of the bed.

When we were first shown to our room I immediately suggested, "Let's rotate, take turns." Maybe each had her eyes on the real bed but that suggestion settled it. The night light was the chief attraction – if you had it you could read late and reach up to put the light out. If your turn was the top bunk you had to climb the ladder to get up and sleep with varied temperatures, sometimes hot and stuffy and you couldn't see to get up again after you turned off the ceiling light at its switch by the door. The lower bunk was dark – no light at all. We had our own hot and cold water with basin which meant we didn't have to wash in the public washroom.

At the evening meal we met some new passengers who had flown in from Edmonton. From my letter home: *Dr. and Mrs. Hayward are going to Aklavik to relieve Dr. Linvingstone. They have a boy about 10, a girl 6 and a baby girl 2. Dr. Hayward is also a Major in the Canadian Army and is dressed as such as the government is sending him to Aklavik. He was in China 5 1/2 years but still looks like a tall thin school boy. Mrs. Hayward used to be a teacher. We think we will like them.*

Mr. Henderson and his companion, Miss Abell, tourists who had been with us on the Northland Echo, also moved to the "Distributor."

<u>Sunday, August 20.</u> Sunny, cold, windy. I had breakfast at 7:30. Sutton was tired so I took her a cup of coffee. Elkink, like myself, was full of energy and eager to explore Fort Smith. We climbed the road up the bank and along to a small Anglican Church near the old Army Camp. (The U.S. Army had a camp for their men and equipment en route north to construct the Canol Road.) We knew there was temporarily no missionary at the church and no other protestant church in town. I wondered if we could have a service. I also knew that the Hayward family had recently returned from a mission in China so I approached Dr.

34

Hayward who agreed that we should hold a service.

We asked the Distributor's Captain Naylor whom we should see to get the keys to the church. He suggested that we go to the HBC Manager who referred us to another but eventually we obtained the keys from Sgt. Grey of the R.C.M.P.

It was a very nice little church. I swept, dusted and cleaned while Sutton played the little Thomas organ. Bill Apetagan and Mr. Davies also helped. Soon we had attractive wild flowers on the altar and fresh air and sunshine pouring in.

When we returned to the Distributor we found our luggage in our stateroom. Dr. Hayward and I, using my hymn and prayer book, planned a short service. Now to let the community know. A fellow in the dock office said we should find the Taylors as they would know everyone in the town (population about 250). He sketched a wee map to help us find them. After misinterpreting his directions and going much out of our way, we finally found the Taylors. They gave us some names of Protestants and said, "Why don't you put a notice in the Hotel?"

The notice I prepared said:

NOTICE
Prodesdant
Service
in
St. Johns Church
7 p.m.
All Welcome

We never knew how many saw the notice but at least one did: Dr. Hayward said, "I agree, we all need a little prodding!" Oh, my! And a teacher made the sign!

Sutton stayed at the church to practise on the organ and I hurried along the paths to find the people whose names the Taylors had given me. Naively I took it for granted that the local believers would really respond to a chance to attend a service. This gave me courage to approach the strangers in this new-to-me town.

Right after supper, dressed in our formal navy dresses with white collars, we hurried back to the church. It was warm and sunny so we sat on the church steps waiting. At 6:45 I pulled the old rope that hung just inside the church door. The heavy clang sounded loudly and compelling in the quiet town until it roused some dogs that began to howl.

About twenty people came, almost filling the plank seats. Dr. Hayward, a United Churchman, took a short but interesting service using some of the Anglican prayers, Deuteronomy 8 and hymns 350, 296, 102 and 27 which Sutton had practised. As we left the church I overheard one of Mrs. Milne's sons ask her, "What will we do with our money?" No one had taken a collection.

The Milnes returned to the boat with us for another little visit.

<u>Monday, August 21.</u> Woke up early but the boat was chilly. Sutton and Elkink stayed in bed 'til eleven. I put on an extra sweater when I saw the frost on everything on shore. Nearly everyone had a cold and there had been no heat or hot water since we came to the Distributor. By law, the crew had to clean out all the boilers in port so the steam was off. It had taken two days but the water was getting warm again. We were still using candles for light.

After breakfast some of us went uptown to visit the stores – HBC, Sutherland's Drugs and Brodie's. There was no mail for us. I had silently hoped for some. I bought a kerchief to keep my hair from flying about (89¢) and seven postcards (40¢). By the time we walked back over the sandy road to the Distributor, it was sunny and warm.

After noon dinner Elkink, Sutton and I walked up town as they hadn't seen the stores. I looked at a pair of woollen slacks. I needed them but $6.00 seemed more than I could pay. However, I did buy some wool at 25¢ and 35¢ a skein. I also bought some nice towels to take for gifts.

Supper was at five so we had the whole evening ahead. What should we do? We had heard that there was a film to be shown by the staff out at the airport. Should we try to hitch-hike the four miles out of town? I wasn't keen – what if the thumb didn't work? Instead we went to see Ernie's Reefer Barge. This barge was equipped with a generator to keep its cargo frozen. Ernie Shags, in charge of the reefer, was a small, friendly fellow with a head of curly brown hair. He'd been on the Smith to Mackenzie Delta run with the reefer and had some interesting Eskimo pictures to show us.

There still being plenty of evening to kill we, Bill Apetagan, Sutton, Elkink and I, walked up town and found a path from which we could see the <u>Rapids</u>

SLAVE RIVER RAPIDS AT FORT SMITH. N. W. T.

<u>of the Drowned</u>. It was an interesting walk and the notorious rapids really were impressive.

Elkink decided to lead us back to the boat by walking along the shore. At one point we were quite near the rambunctious water so she attempted to ascend the bank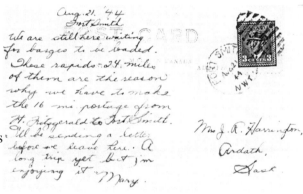

and got one foot very muddy. We found some very curious round and flat stones which we carried home.

<u>Tuesday, August 22.</u> A day of Emotions.

Up at 7:30 for breakfast. Lots of hot water so we all tried to do a little hand wash. Then the crash: I received a radiogram from Dr. Alderwood (Church of England Supervisor of Mission Schools, Toronto) "Take Plane to Aklavik." I had privately been concerned as we were getting quite delayed, had a long way to go and winter comes early in the Arctic. However, the journey was so wonder - full, so

2 VED LS BC   50 NL   CN WINNIPEG MAN AUGUST 21

MISS HARRINGTON
PASSENGER FOR DISTRIBUTOR
CARE H B CO, AGENT
FORT SMITH

ADVISED DISTRIBUTOR DELAYED AND NOW ONLY GOING GOOD HOPE STOP

UNDER CIRCUMSTANCES HAVE ASKED CANADIAN PACIFIC AIRLINES TO TAKE THREE

PASSENGERS TO AKLAVIK STOP REGULAR PLANE LEAVES SMITH NOON THURSDAY

STOP SEE AGENT MAKE NECESSARY ARRANGEMENTS STOP BAGGAGE MAY BE

DIFFICULT STOP ENQUIRE IF TRUNKS COULD GO OTHER BOAT AKLAVIK

ALFERWOOD

M. HARRINGTON,   WINNIPEG,
PASSENGER, S.S. "DISTRIBUTOR",   AUGUST 22/44
FORT SMITH

PLANE CANNOT ACCOMODATE SO BETTER CARRY ON HAPPILY
BY BOATS

ALDERWOOD

interesting, I had tried not to face the possibility until now – it hit. Right after lunch and much discussion with the ship's officers, Sutton, Elkink and I went to the telegraph station and sent a wire to Dr. Alderwood about the possibilities of boat travel.

I met Mr. Leslie at the HBC store. He used to be with the HBC at Lac la Ronge before my two years at the school there so we had an interesting discussion of mutual acquaintances and events.

Back on the Distributor we were still in a quandary; should we unpack or not? Elkink, who was quick and very efficient with clothing care wanted to iron so I stayed in the galley with her. Then I was summoned, "The purser has a message for Miss Harrington." It was a radiogram from Dr. Alderwood, "No plane accommodation available, better carry on happily with boats." Wonderful. Relief. Very happy!

After supper Elkink and I walked up to the Post Office (still hoping to get letters and also posting our cards) then through the R.C.M.P. compound, taking back the church keys. We met Mr. Milne and a constable Jansen. There was a nice trail down to the Rapids so we followed it. I took a photo of Elkink with the river behind her. We gathered some more of the flat round stones. (I had learned that the stones were concretions, formed by the eddying currents of the fast moving water on pieces of clay.) There was still hot water on board so I opted for a bath while the others worked on a huge jigsaw puzzle.

Wednesday, August 23.
Another fine day, actually very hot considering we are at 60° N. latitude. Rumour says we may leave today. Mr. Milne came from Fitzgerald with farewell letters.

Elkink and I went down town (or, from the boat "up" town) with Mrs. Hayward for one last bit of exercise. Mrs. Hayward and I each decided to buy a pair of the $6 woollen slacks. (So far on this trip most of the ladies wore dresses or skirts but we knew that in winter at Aklavik something much warmer would be necessary.)

When we got back to the boat for lunch we met some travel rumours and difficulties. Word came that Norman Wells is a WAR area – we could not proceed to that place without a guarantee that a plane would take us from there to Aklavik. We were much disconcerted. Of course, besides the three of us, there were other passengers including Dr. and Mrs. Hayward and their three children. The Doctor, being an army Major and an experienced traveller, went up town with us to the Canadian Pacific Airlines (CPA) office. It was closed. Sutton, Elkink and I waited on the steps while Dr. Hayward went to the government office and had a wire sent to Ottawa.

Right after supper, Mr. Hutchinson, Superintendent of Transportation and the one who was changing our travel plans, called us and the Haywards to meet with him. He explained that we could go to Norman Wells but from there on we must see to our own transportation arrangements.

Mrs. Beatty gave up on her northern plans and flew south on an afternoon plane. Mrs. Davies went over to the Radium King to proceed to Yellowknife.

After all the excitement and uncertainty of the day I found sleep impossible. Besides the boat was very hot from sitting like a huge bird in the sun all day. Our room had an outside window but no through air circulation.

AGAIN NORTHWARD
– Smith to Great Slave Lake

<u>August 24.</u> Very early I heard people moving about, saw the sky golden as it heralded the solar light, then the shrill whistle sounded. We were underway. By 6 a.m. we were well down the Slave River – northward bound again.

The S.S. Distributor was built at Fort Smith by the Hudson's Bay Company in 1920. It was the largest paddlewheeler in the Territories. At one hundred and fifty-one feet long with a thirty-five-foot beam and a draft of six feet it was registered at 876 tons – much larger than the Northland Echo. The ship provided service to passengers and freight from Fort Smith to the Arctic Ocean – a distance of about 1200 miles. It had accommodation for 96 passengers and 30 crew. Since we were only 14 passengers, we had ample space in the dining room and the comfortable, pleasant salon. I learned that to produce enough steam to push the paddlewheel, the engine burned at least a cord of wood every hour.

As in the case of the Northland Echo, the HBC arranged to have woodcutters cut and stack large piles of 4-foot long cordwood at intervals along the river. Daily the Captain manoeuvred the ship as close to the woodpile as he could. Then the crew appeared in full force to lay planks to bridge from ship to shore. By using a relay line, the logs were passed from one man to the next from the pile to the ship's hold.

At our first stop there was some excitement when a pig jumped from a pen on a barge into the river. It swam downstream and finally to shore. Perhaps the woodcutter would enjoy a welcome change of diet, if he could capture

it. The assortment of animals cared for on the deck of one of the barges constituted the fresh supply of meat for the voyage, outbound and return. When required by the chef, an animal was slaughtered in the night and all aboard had delicious meals. One milking cow was kept well fed for milk until the end of the journey.

There was always something to see from the ship as we chugged along. Going around Brulé Bend there was a raging forest fire making the atmosphere very smoky. Another diversion was supplied by Jack Coburn, the purser. He had made many trips north and other travels which he liked to recount to new passengers.

We travelled another few miles and stopped again, this time for six and a half cords. Elkink, Mrs. MacDonald and I went across the gangplank to the shore, then climbed the steep bank to the wood stacked above. We gathered autumn foliage to take to Mrs. Greber for the tables.

Down on the shore, among the flotsam of trees and driftwood we found the remains of a birch bark canoe. The painted canvas was mostly ripped from the "waskwi" (birch bark), a strip of leather was used for a keel and a sapling bent for a frame. A home-carved paddle lay broken on the sand beside it. The discovery stirred my imagination and I tried to salvage little bits of the canoe to carry with me. As I did so I envisioned the circumstances by which it had come to this place and how it had been made. I saw the face, the hands, the birch tree without its pink-white bark, then the first trip before the tragic end.

The crew was ready to pull in the gang plank and called, breaking my reverie. We went aboard and watched from the deck.

Friday, August 25. Morning came, smoky and cloudy with a strong cool wind. I didn't see the Hearne Lake when we met it near McConnell Island.

We chugged on and on, slowly diminishing the long waterway before us. We went around bends, past burning spots and past golden poplars in autumn foliage until we left the morning clouds behind and emerged into brilliant sunshine and clear skies. Glorious, but not enough at times to keep my thoughts from hearing the paddlewheel with every slap of the river, saying "farther away!, farther away!"

During the afternoon I finished my knee-high socks and read well into another John Buchan book. When this prolific author got home from his Governor General's tour north he donated a complete set of his already published books (37), fitted into a fine wooden library cupboard for use on the Distributor.

Meanwhile Elkink played cards with the Haywards, so completely free of responsibilities we each found our activities. At one point we passed a big saw mill which seemed to be vacant. So many hours  passed and it felt that our steamboat was all that moved. Any wildlife would have heard the sounds of the paddle and retreated into the vegetation.

When we finally reached the delta it was exciting to get a glimpse of Great Slave Lake. It had always been on the maps and now it was real for us. There were numerous gluttonous gulls that sailed like little boats upon the ripples, each making its own wake: or they hovered in perfection in the blue sky, watching for a tidbit from the boat.

The steamer and barges were tied in the delta just beside a log cabin. A romantic tale about this old cabin was passed on to us. It caused me much wonderment. An old man had lived there. He kept the delta navigation lights by each evening lighting the lamps. Summer after summer he kept his lonely vigil, probably happy in his own way. People said he was "quite daft." Then last fall, 1943, taking a small boat, he set out alone for Yellowknife and no one has heard of him since. What happened? Who saw him set out? And now no one knows and no one seems to care. Maybe some day some bones will be found and someone will say, "Oh that must be the old light-keeper."

While we listened to the story, I noted young Robert Hayward's concerned face and when it came to the end, he turned to his Dad, the doctor, and said, "But God knows, 'cause God knows and cares, doesn't he?" I didn't hear his father's answer as the deck hands were moving a large pile of lumber from the shore and noisily stacking it on one of our barges.

Elkink and I, being careful not to meet crew balancing lumber on

wheel barrows, crossed the gangplank.
We gathered bits of plants. Elkink was
attracted to the cone-like growths
(galls) on the willows. I found Rumex
(wild rhubarb) which had turned subtle
shades of red, some wild parsnip – the
seedy umbels like miniature parasols,
and some silver willow twigs. There
were some faded Indian Paint Brush
plants, too weathered to collect.

Gall on
Willow

From our vantage point up on the bank
we could see, not far ahead, an old broken
scow which seemed to be tied to the bank.
Mr. Coburn, the purser, Dr. Hayward, Robert,
Jean, Elkink and I walked along the shore with
the Captain to look at it. Everything had been
removed from the old scow except a barrel
which was unnamed. The Captain supposed
it was full of paint since it was too heavy to
carry away.

Saturday, August 26. Each time I wrote
in my diary I tried to be certain to note the
date and day. My thoughts were that this
journey was a unique experience, so many
days, no commitments – at least not
physically. "Is this what holidays are like?"
I was trying to make the best of such a rare
change but it was hard to mentally blank out

Silver
Willow
Silverberry
Elaeagnus

starting a new class in the next week or so and even more I wondered
if I were going too far to ever be able to reattach to other precious
things.

The boats started to move about 5 a.m., leaving the Delta of the Slave
River. I quietly moved the curtain but from the window I could see
nothing except a white wall of fog turning pink at the top in the
morning light. Then the paddlewheel reversed and we were back in
the place we had been and got anchored again. "There is a big lake
ahead, it is very windy. We'll probably be here all day – and then
some," I was told.

I finally arose at 7:20 and had grapefruit, bacon, eggs and coffee. I felt grateful to be on the thin side and could happily enjoy the good foods. Mrs. Greber planned on waxing the dining room floor so I helped a bit by sweeping it for her. I set Sutton's hair and started Elkink knitting some socks with green wool – Elkink has a sense of humour, "They'll match my eyes!"

Our clean linen came so we had time to change our beds before noon dinner. I always had to make the big single bed since it was the one where I pressed plants between magazine pages under the mattress!

After dinner I felt tired, went to bed, knit more on my blue sockees, then finished reading "Witch Wood" by John Buchan – an enjoyable read.

Sunday, August 27. The morning air was gray with smoke although the sun was still high (nearly another month to the equinox) and the day was bright. The Distributor still held us comfortably, though restless, in the Slave River delta. The gentle breeze we felt at our sheltered anchorage was probably a stiff wind out on the open lake. Being Sunday I read a book I found in the library. Called "Atonement," it had some good thoughts though I couldn't venture a guess as to what society the writer belonged to or even what he really meant.

Sunday dinner was always special. We began with canned fruit cocktail, then boiled chicken with sauce, green peas, asparagus and mince pie. I had gone often to the large deck to watch the chickens crowded in their wire crates. Each Sunday would make more room in the crates.

Once, in the afternoon the ship moved out about a mile into the lake so that we practically lost sight of land. The water was too rough so we swung back and left our barges at our old mooring while we returned a short distance up river to a site of a recent U.S. Army camp.

The crew started to take on slab wood from a sawmill when the bell rang for provender (maybe I got that term from John Buchan?).

We really weren't as isolated as we felt for, although we couldn't see their home, a family of five watched us from the shore and nearby six dogs bayed on their leashes.

An advantage of the Distributor's new anchorage was that we could go ashore. Right after dinner Mrs. MacDonald, Elkink and I went for a walk inland, bringing back some osier dogwood with white berries. I got my camera again and Elkink took a snap with me in the foreground, the Distributor behind.

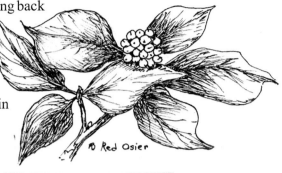

Red Osier

Captain Naylor picked up the barges and took a look at the lake again. As before, we had to return to anchor. The "Dease Lake" came to moor beside us. I slept about two hours in the afternoon but still didn't feel very rested. Maybe it was because I was used to being very busy and now had too much time on my hands. Was I tired of doing nothing?

After supper we went up to the wheelhouse with Captain Naylor. Despite the calmness at our anchorage the lake, as seen through the glasses, appeared a spread of whitecaps. The Captain showed us pictures of his baby, "Nancy." He must have missed his family back in Victoria while he worked on the Mackenzie River.

Elkink went to sleep early but I stayed up to write to brother Bob, as this was his birthday. I felt a bit selfish about not doing more to initiate a church service today. I hesitated, not having been asked.

Monday, August 28. There was a strong north wind so we remained at our moorings. The "Smith" and the "Radium King" came and anchored on either side of us. Constables Osborne and Jansen and the two nurses came aboard to visit until the dinner bell rang. The "King" left her barges and tried the lake but soon returned. Early in the day Mrs. MacDonald, Elkink, Mrs. Hayward, Jean, Robert and I started out to cross the island. The grass was wet knee-high with dew and frost so Mrs. Hayward and Jean turned back. Robert persisted in grumbling but we went until a stream barred our way. Actually I quite liked and admired Robert. For a ten-year-old boy to be trapped on a paddlewheeler so many days without complaints seemed remarkable. The whole Hayward family seemed patient and calm. But one can enjoy sitting, playing cards, doing puzzles or reading for only so long.

Some of The Passengers.

L to R. Marjorie Sutton, Mrs. Hayward,
Doris Ibister, Mrs. MacDonald, Bill Apetagan,
Robert Hayward, Dr. Hayward, Dave Miller (Purser),
Reka Elkink.

Photo by Mary Harrington using a box camera.

I finished knitting one blue socklet. Elkink and Sutton and the pursers who have nothing to do while we are between forts, sunbathed on top of one of the barges. After supper we visited on the "Smith" then the "King" before they departed, towing their barges. By towing, each vessel can ride independently in the rough water. Normally they are all lashed to the boat, one barge in front and one on each side.

Tuesday, August 29. At 4 a.m. the paddlewheel began to rotate and churn as we left our sheltering bank. At 4:20 a.m. we passed the brilliant delta lights. The world was lovely. The night sunlight was enshrined into an arch, and up above, each star shone like a diamond. I watched until the chilling breeze came through the screen and I covered up in bed. Then at intervals I couldn't resist jumping up again to see our progress. At breakfast it was a surprise to find that on account of a smoke wall, we had turned around and were headed back "home."

I went out on deck and stayed there until we left our barges and continued on to the woodpile.

Elkink and I were working on our birch bark souvenirs from the old canoe.

We started out again but it got too rough. The "Hearne Lake" came and anchored near us for the night. Jack, our former Assistant Purser was aboard.

After supper we went ashore and had a wiener roast instead of night lunch. The fire was very pretty in that far off lonely bit of Canada. The cook (Paul) gave us four cans of wieners (very salty), a loaf of bread, coffee, cookies etc. A deck hand was persuaded by some to come and sing cowboy songs. I came back early with Haywards, about 10:30 p.m.

Wednesday, August 30. After six days we left at 5 a.m. and were able to continue. The sun came up hazy and warm. I stayed out on deck until we came to Burnt Island after we had passed Loutit Island. (There was a large framed map on the inner wall of the ship so we could follow our progress.) Burnt Island appeared in striking autumnal hues, predominantly  crimson. The Captain charitably said we'd dock and he'd take the passengers ashore to see the York Boat.

York Boats were used by the early traders to travel from Fort to Fort. Dr. Hayward said the last one travelled in 1876. The old boat we saw was sitting on the stony shore, quite badly weathered but still holding its proud stern and bow aloft. I estimated its length to be about 40 feet and its beam about 12 feet. I acquired two of the hand-smithed nails for relics.

Many of us took pictures and I had many mental images of what it used to be.

When we had first started out following Captain Naylor, Mrs. MacDonald had gone back to the ship to change her shoes and got left behind. Later, Captain Naylor and I retraced our steps looking for her. When we met her he continued back to the Distributor while I went with her to show her the York boat.

We decided to return to the ship via the south shore of the island. We came upon a large, almost square rock which appeared to be full of fossils – clams, snails, sea larvae, corals and other. I saved some specimens. The ship's whistle blew! We made great haste but soon had to sit to rest.

The whistle blew again!

We scrambled all out of breath across the gangplank as the crew waited to pull it aboard. It was good-bye to Burnt Island, we thought.

Shortly after twelve o'clock we left the shelter of Burnt Island but on reaching the main lake the water was so choppy we had to seek refuge back there again.

At noon the dining room was attractively rearranged so that we all sat together for a birthday party to honour Miss Abell's birthday. Beside our usual fare we had a jelly cocktail, sardine and hard-egg salad, and a tasty fruit cake for desert.

The conversation turned to the weather, "getting colder, days shorter, less light – when will we get another chance for a good swim?" On a dare, Elkink, Sutton and I hurried ashore. We had just got into the clear, cool water when the ship's whistle blew. Pulling our coats over our wet suits, slipping on our shoes, we gathered our other things and hurried back to the gangplank as the whistle blew again! We were soon leaving Burnt Island.

We spent the rest of the afternoon in our stateroom. I slept a little.

I don't think I have written earlier about any of our other fellow travellers. I just mentioned Miss Abell's birthday. Of course we weren't given any personal information but somehow we seemed to learn, or maybe just speculate, about them. Miss Abell was with an older man, tall, thin, very rich and we didn't know if she was just his secretary! Their rooms were side by side on the other side of the ship from ours. Sometimes she took a tray in to him and she seemed to serve his lunches in his room.

Since supper, the sky had been beautiful with dark storm clouds, rain and sunshine, then rainbows and gulls flashing white against the darkness. Always we had gulls following our travels. Refuse from the galley and from the livestock on the barge was thrown or swept overboard but didn't have time to pollute the waterways – the gulls scavenged it clean. I watched a gull try to swoop and carry off a cardboard box when it was attacked by several other gulls. Finally the box fell and bobbed up and down on the wake. At times the cry of the gulls is forlorn and tended to bring lonely, homesick feelings. At other times their beauty and grace were a joy to study.

GREAT SLAVE LAKE
– on to Hay River and Fort Simpson

After dusk fell we came to the harbour lights at Hay River. I stood on deck watching the skipper on the front of the first barge as he called out soundings to the pilot.

The "Smith" and "Hearne Lake" were lighted in port. We could see the Roman Catholic residence and church, the Hudson's Bay Company buildings, the Church of England residence, church and the old Indian Residential School.

We passed farther up the Hay River to tie the outer barges before we docked.

The crew immediately began to unload the forty tons of freight. Two cows went very awkwardly off to the Roman Catholic Mission. Flossy, one of our ship's kitchen help, went to see her father, Mr. Dodman, the Manager of the Hudson's Bay Company's store in Hay River. We watched the activities until midnight then went to bed.

Thursday, August 31. We had very little sleep as the crew worked noisily until 4:15 a.m. then the steamer moved farther down river to the woodpile. Very tired, the men ate breakfast and went to bed until dinnertime (noon).

Mr. Henderson and Miss Abell decided to walk back to town. Mrs. MacDonald, Bill Apetagan and we three followed at 10:45. Our trail, a two to three mile hike, was built by a caterpillar tractor and was known as the "Grimshaw Highway" that the U.S. Army used to bring in winter freight. [The "Grimshaw Highway" was at that time just a winter road from the town of Grimshaw, near Peace River, Alberta, to Hay River. Many years later it became an all-weather highway.]

We went first to Miss Neville's hospital. She was the sole nurse, the only Protestant teacher and leader of the Protestants among the 150 residents of Hay River. Truly a wonder! She wore a white uniform with a square veil over her head. Her cottage had seven hospital beds. We all felt awed by her fortitude and efforts and wondered at her ability to do so many tasks. As she talked we were aware of a strong antagonism to the aggressive R.C. domination. We heard her depth of faith in her literal interpretation of the prophesies contained in the Bible. My mind found neither consolation nor justification in this emphasis so I kept silent.

Nurse Neville took us to see Charlie Norn, a Scotish-Slavey métis who had long been the mission interpreter. His wife was crying, much grieved by the loss of her son by drowning at Fort Smith. Mrs. MacDonald helped to comfort her.

We visited five other homes, among them Sibbeston's and Isaacs'. All were roomy and well furnished (Mantle clocks, etc.). Maybe they weren't as clean as one would hope but I remembered and old saying, "Circumstances alter cases." All of the people talked fairly good English and without reluctance. I enjoyed the visits but I had been used to natives from my two years at Lac la Ronge. It must have been novel to the others – Sutton and especially Elkink as this was her first employment among native people.

I have one vivid memory of going to one very tidy log house. The door was open but no one came. I stepped in to the doorway in case it was an old person's home and they hadn't heard. Still I saw no one. But I did see a single room, neat and clean, several wooden chairs, a little iron stove and a table. There was one article on the table – a large metal hospital tray and on it was a complete fish skeleton. From head to tail it was completely picked clean. The white bones stood like a model for a biology class. I left wondering not only how it remained so intact but who was so hungry to do such an impeccable job? And are they still hungry?

One of our conversations with an Indian man told us about a quarrel with the priest over unfair distribution of the rations between R.C.s and Protestants. "So," he said, "we all chipped in 5¢ each to send a wire of complaint to the doctor." [In most settlements if there were a government appointed person, e.g. a doctor, that person was also the Indian Agent.]

We visited the Hudson's Bay store where I purchased two postcards (20¢) and twenty bobby pins for 10¢. [I mentioned costs in my diary as money was scarce. For two years I had worked at $30 per month less deductions for War Bonds. I had many expenditures for preparing required uniforms, etc.]

St. Peter's, Hay River, N.W.T.

In 1875 an Anglican Mission was established at Hay River. The Anglican church building (St. Peter's) was especially interesting as it was covered with tin inside and out. In 1920 Canon A.J. Vale founded St. Peter's Residential School and was its Principal until 1927. The old school now stood empty – a huge shell in a place of small structures. Previously it had housed and taught hundreds of northern young people from as far away as the Delta of the Mackenzie River, the Arctic Coast, Old Crow in the northern Yukon and from many points along the Mackenzie valley. They spoke many different languages but at the school, learned English, "reading, writing and arithmetic" and some of the white man's domestic ways. [For many years thereafter in nearly every settlement, the person or persons able to interpret and assist in the changes of the area had been at the Hay River school. They shared and passed on their well-taught skills. Their enthusiasm and gratitude for Canon Vale was often noted by other workers helping in the North.]

Several years later the old school was declared a fire hazard. Modernizing it was deemed too expensive and so it was closed. Fortunately, by then other schools had been established closer to the homes of the northern children. Rev. Ralph Gibson, who would be our Principal at the Aklavik Anglican Residential School was the stepson of Canon Vale.

We returned to Miss Neville's and had a cup of tea. I felt famished but the cupboard seemed bare. I wondered how she survived and often had patients to feed, too.

We visited the graveyard on our way back to the Distributor. We could hear the ship on the river so Mrs. MacDonald returned to it while we three went on to the Camsells. This family intended to send three children to the Aklavik school next year so we were anxious to meet them. We enjoyed the meeting. (This home even had a wind charger to produce electricity!)

We had time to prepare for supper and were pleased to see that Miss Neville had been invited. Three U.S.Signals men were also guests.

At 7:30 p.m. several of us went with Mr. Camsell and the Signals men on the "Pilot" up the river through picturesque scenery to the U.S. Army barracks. The mess hall and kitchen were also the recreation rooms, the centre of activity.

We played at the pool table until the windows were covered and the movie began. There was a short on birds then a film "Impostor," a story of the fall of the French Army and of the Free French under General de Gaulle. At nine o'clock it stopped and we all went out to see the Signal Corps send up a balloon for weather and wind observations. We went to the chart room to see the balloon flight charted and the information radioed to Edmonton and Norman Wells. We returned to watch the film again and after a few more breaks in the film, it was finished.

It was interesting to see the audience – only seven Service men and us. They played the Victrola. Elkink, Flossie, another girl and I danced. The floor was very rough but these men appreciated having partners with whom to dance. Elkink and I came "home" in the Pilot with some of the others. It was a conclusion to Elkink's birthday.

By 1:30 a.m. we had our lights out. It seemed but an instant before the ship's whistle blew at 5:20 a.m. as we left Hay River.

Friday, September 1. Elkink and I did our wash then dashed out to see Wrigley Harbour in sight by 10:15 a.m. There we met up again with Ernie Shags: the Distributor took him and his reefer barge in tow. Another

55

barge with about 300 empty 45-gallon oil drums was also attached. Trying to rest didn't work so at 2 p.m. I went with Elkink to iron in the galley. We had delicious lunches there, e.g. pineapple pudding with canned plums on top, coffee and cheese. Captain Naylor and Ernie came in and talked while we worked.

Several times we passengers had wondered why the native passengers were not seated with the rest of us. It seemed very unkind to leave Bill Apetagan and Doris Ibetson alone while all the "whites" were at the other table. Finally I was delegated to ask the Stewardess if we three girls could move to Doris Ibetson's table. She didn't like my asking. "We don't do that," she said and wouldn't allow it.

As I had eaten well in the galley, I stayed in bed through supper until 8 o'clock. The boat had stopped when I woke up. There had been a tragedy: the co-pilot received a message that one of his sons had accidentally shot the other so Jack Cockburn and a deck hand took the co-pilot by speedboat to Providence and probably on to Simpson.

I played cards with Sutton, Bill, Doris and Jean – "Old Maid" and "Fish." We all enjoyed tomato sandwiches, fruit cake, tarts and cocoa for night lunch.

Saturday, September 2. We pulled anchor early and took two barges (the Aklavik and the Reefer) up to the shore past Fort Providence. This took over two hours, manoeuvring the rapids. Once through, the crew tied the barges and we started back to where we had left the other three. A wind storm moved in and many of us felt quite sick until we were anchored again close to shore. The river paddlewheelers like the Distributor have flat bottoms and  when the water is rough they get tossed about like corks.

Fort Providence sits up on a shelf-like shore about 20 feet up from the water. It surprised us to see such a large settlement, mainly Roman Catholic, a convent, stately church, a new Hudson's Bay Company store, very much like the one at Lac la Ronge but not yet finished.

There were some communication towers and many native dwellings. We didn't land and as we travelled along, an island cut off our views.

Fort Providence

Today I finished knitting my blue sockees and wrote two letters. In the afternoon nearly all of the passengers became quiet, probably succumbing to the steady chug of the big paddlewheel. I had a sleep, too. By evening the wind dropped. Some of us played a word game called "Guggenheim."

Sunday, September 3. The day's activity started about 6 a.m. but a fog rolled in and we had to wait for it to clear off. We finally got the big barge up over the rapids and started back for the last two. The wind became so strong that we had to give that up and remain wind bound with the barges all the rest of the day. Elkink had a cold so spent the morning cozy and warm in bed. I spent the time reading, "Great Britain Feels Her Oats" from the ship's library. Then I started reading "Russian and Christianity" – a Student Christian Movement book that Dr. Hayward lent to me.

After noon dinner we all rested 'til nearly six.

In the evening I held a service, selecting mostly the evening prayers, Psalm 121 and St. Mark 13, "Holy, Holy, Holy, " "Near the Cross," What a Friend" and "Abide with Me." The congregation comprised Misses Elkink, Sutton, Abell, Flossie Dodman (staff), Jean Hayward, Mesdames Hayward, MacDonald, Greber (staff), Messrs Henderson, Dr. and Robert Hayward, Shags (staff) and David Miller (staff). I was pleased to hear the hearty and well-timed singing despite the lack of a musical instrument. Responses were good and feelings warm.

Later we played Guggenheim for a short time before night lunch. Lights out at 11:30 because of fuel (wood) shortage. Still a strong wind and cold.

Monday, September 4. We left the down (north) side of the rapids just before 7 a.m. and arrived at the barges at Fort Providence by 7:40 a.m. There we left the oil drum barge, and the reefer barge and Ernie Shags to be brought by the Hearne Lake. Now we are proceeding down river with our three original barges.

Shortly before dinner we stopped at the woodpile where we were scheduled to pick up the woodcutter, his donkey cat [a small caterpillar tractor] and equipment as well as 40 cords of wood. Consequently we were able to go ashore. Elkink and I walked along the road, through the woods and along the shore. We saw a red squirrel, a downy woodpecker, a flock of sparrows and a few cranberries. Sutton walked about with "Shorty," the little red fireman.

Elkink heard the short wave radio: "We are at the woodpile and are taking aboard forty cords and the woodcutter's cat!"

Cranberry
Vaccinium

After we returned, we slipped into the galley for coffee and cream pie. I went up and bathed. We rested until 5:30. by then the work on the woodpile was done. The Distributor gathered up its barges and continued across Mills Lake.

At the far end of Mills Lake we came to the old U.S. airport. It was deserted but there were huge piles of barrels and equipment. A girl, Rhoda Fields, and her brother came aboard. A large caterpillar tractor was also loaded.

Tuesday, September 5. From a letter home: *There is a full moon so for the first time we've travelled all night. We stopped at 3 a.m. at Brownings, a white settler's homestead. We took on board 5 tons of vegetables for the Aklavik Mission. They say Browning makes $1000's of dollars every year. Potatoes are $6 for 98 lbs. I'm sure he earns it. Every fall he sells not only potatoes but huge cabbages and bags of carrots to the School. Otherwise they have only dehydrated vegetables of which only onions and cabbage even slightly resemble the real things.*

Browning came north from the USA to trap. He married a Dene wife and settled along the river where they cultivated several acres of fertile land. The growth during the days of perpetual sunlight was tremendous. Some cabbages reached twenty pounds. Browning was a resourceful settler. For many years he also ran a small lumber mill. From the local woodlands, in a mill he himself constructed, he supplied a much needed supply of lumber.

A fellow from one of the Northern Transportation Company's boats that had a radio came aboard and told of the gladsome news — "Allies march across Belgium." We hunger for news. There is a shortwave but no reception for radio on the Distributor.

When we stopped at Brownings, Mrs. MacDonald and I got up. I called Elkink. It was a lovely sight by the light of a full moon to see the deck hands work so cheerfully, putting out the gangplanks, then wheeling out the freight for Head of the Line and Brownings. [Some freight destined for small communities not serviced by the large ships was stored at the "Head of the Line" for pick-up and delivery by smaller vessels.]

We brought a bull and two cows for Brownings. When the crew tried to lead the cows from the barge down the gangplank, they found the animals had become very stiff from being penned so long. The sloping planks were a problem. One cow slipped and fell with a mighty splash into the water. We watched but she stood up in the shallow water, dripping with mud and made her way with difficulty to the shore.

The three of us walked up the path to the red-roofed, white log cottage. A horse running and blowing in the corral, an up-turned kiddies wagon, the sight of the Distributor's barges, and workers with the lights – all gleaming in the moonlight. Lovely! But the night was chill so after over an hour we crept back to bed.

I was up when we started to leave at 7 a.m. We were forty miles from Fort Simpson. We stopped and waited while the "Fitzgerald" came through the rapids. The "Hearne Lake" came too. We tied for the night above the rapids (Green Island) with our last barge.

We set our clocks back an hour to Pacific Standard Time.

NEVER A DULL MOMENT
– Fort Simpson to Fort Wrigley

Having taken two of our barges, one at a time, through the angry water of the rapids we now had one left. We spent the night anchored at Green Island, above the rapids, about twelve miles from Fort Simpson.

About 7 a.m. the paddlewheel began its push, chug, chug, slapping the water and slowly leaving to face the challenge. Suddenly we struck a rock! There was a bang and a strong vibration shook the whole vessel. Almost at once the loaded barge began to sink. The Captain quickly manoeuvred nearer the shore. The water was nearly to the barge's deck level when it grounded. Since the valuable cargo was carried on top, not inside, it was, at least for the time being, unharmed.

We stayed on deck as we went safely through the rapids to the other two barges which we proceeded to take to the docks at Fort Simpson. The crew worked feverishly to unload one of the barges so that it could be taken back to salvage the approximately $90,000 cargo of the stranded barge.

It was a big occasion for the white populations of those isolated northern places when the supply ship and passengers came – maybe only once each summer. Always quite a few came on board for a meal – some invited, some paying. At dinner time Elkink's friend Fred Vitsinge was among them. Later Sutton, Mrs. MacDonald and I, anxious to see the settlement, went ashore.

Fort Simpson was located on fertile soil deposited as silt through many centuries by the muddy Liard River as its current slowed upon meeting the Mackenzie. The Nor'West Company recognized this

The Liard River joins the mighty Mackenzie River at Fort Simpson

advantageous location and set up a trading post there in 1804. From then, York Boats and later steamboats, loaded with furs, came to trade for provisions. With fish and game plentiful in the surrounding area, it was an ideal spot to stay and trade and some stayed to settle. The Klondike Gold rush also brought new settlers. Fort Simpson became the home of prominent persons such as Charles Camsell and Albert Faille.

After our climb up a steep incline from the water, we followed a good road about a mile to reach Dr. Truesdell's home. Mrs. Truesdell welcomed us. Her son, Donald, aged 14, was home preparing to leave for Calgary to take Grade Ten. The doctor returned and we had a visit with him before returning to the Distributor.

We had heard much about Dr. Truesdell. He was a new graduate of Queen's University in Kingston, Ontario, when he came to Fort Simpson. As medical doctor and Indian Agent, he found great satisfaction in service to the people. He was gentle and kind, especially appreciated by all. He enlarged the garden area, grew crops for fodder for cows, vegetables for local diets. His agricultural activities took much time but when needed to perform surgery he took time to review his textbooks and follow them precisely.

In the evening we went to Dr. Truesdell's again – Dr. and Mrs. Hayward, Mrs. MacDonald, Sutton and I. Everyone visited, we heard the news on the radio and had lunch of salad (from the garden), rolls and chocolate cake. The doctor brought us home to the Distributor in his car (an old Model A Ford) about 12:30. (This car and the one mile road constituted a unique feature of the entire N.W.T.)

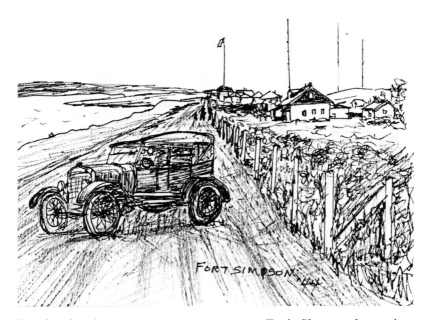

Previously when we were up town we met Ernie Shags and went into a Free Trader's store while he did some shopping. There were some interesting things to buy but we did not have access to money! Next stop was the HBC store. There I did buy a film and a copy book in which to continue my daily journal. Ernie bought a lovely blanket for Mrs MacDonald's birthday.

<u>Thursday, September 7.</u> Up for the usual breakfast time at 7:30, to a very fine day. I wrote to Dr. Alderwood on behalf of the three of us, since I am the "senior" member. I had received two letters when we arrived yesterday and was so happy to get them that I answered them, too. Small pontoon planes came in occasionally from the south and always they brought and took out our letters.

Mrs. Hayward was very good company for me and we went uptown together to the HBC store for nylon hose (the brand, ORIENT, were $1.25). Then we went to the Post Office where we found Elkink. We met Mrs. Wilderspin, a tall, blond lady, the wife of the HBC Manager. We had time to see St. David's church, too.

After dinner I took Sutton to see the church. It was truly lovely, all freshly painted, waiting for the pews to be put in again. Since Rev. Cooke left in June 1943 there had been no missionary. A Signals man

and his wife lived in the rectory.
She was out digging potatoes so
we had an interesting talk with
her. She told us that the two
steers that had come on the
Distributor for the R.C.s were
jumping over the fences here and
there. In a small place like

Simpson such things can be provocative.

After we returned, we went to the galley with Captain Naylor, Ernie
and Mrs. Hayward for coffee, apple pie and red plums. I was sick
after that and stayed in bed the rest of the day. Maybe I was trying too
hard not to waste one single moment of that once-in-a-lifetime
journey, to see and do all, and my physical system was not quite able
to cope.

Before supper the Distributor
left Fort Simpson and went
back to the Green Island
Rapids to the submerged
barge. The "Hearne Lake"
also went. Dr. Hayward
missed the boat so Dr.
Truesdell brought him after

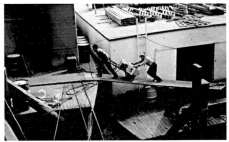

supper. A priest and three Sisters also came.

Friday, September 8. Not a cheerful day – cloudy, dull and raining.
The crew was busy loading wood out of the Hearne Lake's barge and
cargo from the stranded barge. Bill Apetagan and all the available
men were helping with the work.

Dr. Hayward received a telegram to fly from Simpson to Aklavik as
Dr. Livingstone was on his way out. So they took him, Jack
Cockburn and Elkink to Fort Simpson on the "Hearne Lake" before
dinner. Elkink stayed there so that she could see more of Fred. I
wrote, knitted and rested – and day dreamed.

After supper, Dave, Sutton and I started to play Rummy until Mrs.
MacDonald came with pencils and papers ready, desiring to play
"Guggenheim" So Ernie came too and we played until lunch time. I
didn't eat lunch but retired and wrote a letter.

Saturday, September 9. We were awakened by Ernie and others from the Hearne Lake calling to our kitchen men that they had finished breakfast, having had hot cakes and tomatoes. When we got up about 7 a.m., the atmosphere was so smoky that even the opposite shore was blue. The loading except for a few oil drums was finished,  even the D8 Cat. was loaded. The Hearne Lake pulled off and gradually so did we.

I went down to the front of the 500 barge and took a picture of the abandonned barge. I then finished my letter and changed from my slacks to a skirt by the time we got back to Fort Simpson again. Fred was escorting Elkink down the hill as the whistle blew. Mr. and Mrs. Wilderspin came aboard.

The Hearne Lake returned from Green Island for the barge load of oil drums so our Captain said we had time to go up to the store. Sutton and I did. Mrs. Greber asked me to get her some wool but there wasn't any. I bought a #120 film for 40¢ and half a pound of peppermints for 25¢.

We were on our way again before 11 a.m. with three barges – the Aklavik barge, the big 500 (loaded high on top with oil drums) and the barge of oil drums. All together we must have had  about 2,000 empty drums for Norman Wells.

After dinner we all crawled into bed for a rest. Shortly after 3 p.m.

Jack and Mrs. MacDonald woke us to say that the scenery was beautiful.

I did not expect that the scenery would hold such a pleasant change. There on the horizon over the river stretched the hazy blue ghosts of the Nahanni Mountains. At first they appeared like pyramid points over the tree tops. We got closer and closer. The huge mountains with trees of every autumnal hue climbing up their sides, doing homage, stirred our souls. I, at least, felt the deep joy, a pang, for the beauty and awe of life which I hadn't felt before on this trip. I was loathe to leave the barge top even for a moment. Mount Nahanni and Lone Mountain stood out singularly and massive as we passed. Again, I felt inspired. If only they could but talk and unravel the threads of traffic from the Mackenzie history, like cotton from a spool! Other mountains were in a continuous range with similar forms. In some places the golden poplars crept like flames up from the foot, and as the calm water mirrored reality, everything was warm and glowing.

At supper time Mrs. Hayward was not well so I took care of her younger daughter, Helen, until her bed time at 7:30. Then I set Sutton's hair and washed my own.

I sat alone on the deck with my pen and journal on my lap, watching the beauty turn to solemn gray, the mountains like clouds hugging the tree tops

We were preparing to tie up for the night by an island. Jack Cockburn came and broke the spell of my thoughts, my dream. The wake of the steamer in turning has broken the water surface and the voices of the men and the bell have broken the rhythmic "push, push" of the paddlewheel's sound.

From a letter home: *Every night, as darkness fell and sleep in her grey cloak approached, we went in to shore, fastened the cables to trees, and heard the rhythmic "chug — chug" of the paddles slow to rest. The days of perfect leisure were like a dream – time for reading, time for handwork, time for talking, and, best of all, time for thinking. There was no radio on board, except the wireless, so we were oblivious to all else – just the white river steamer churning its way around the bends of a mighty river through the beauty of God's creation.*

<u>Sunday, September 10.</u>   The day began with wind and rain. My companions remained in their warm beds. I watched as occasionally the wind blew the clouds so that we could get a vision of the mountain tops. And lo! they were snow-covered! Even the afternoon sunshine couldn't cut the icy air. What could we expect – we were travelling NORTH!

Around noon we stopped for five and a half cords of wood. The woodcutter, E. Beauchamp, got off with his Cat. and pulled the wood down to the shore. He stayed there, supplied with provisions, to cut more wood. I took a snap.

Anxious to get some exercise, some of us walked up the wooded hillside which was deeply carpeted with rich wet moss. We found a babbling brook and followed it to the river. There I picked a bouquet of Indian Paint Brush.

At super time we stopped about ten miles above Fort Wrigley, below the airport. The U.S. Army men were waiting with a D7 Cat and built up an approach to the barge so that they could unload another Cat. By 8:30 p.m. we were on our way again.

Jean rang the "church" bell and with a congregation of thirteen in the saloon, we held a short service: Hymns 18, 724, 485, 520 and Lessons Proverbs 15 and Matthew 5. Hymn 520, "Unto the hills . . . ." seemed especially appropriate to match our feelings with this beautiful section of our journey.

Just as we finished, the whistle blew for Fort Wrigley. It was 9:20

p.m. but very dark. We met the new HBC post manager and his wife and daughter (Mr. & Mrs. Scoles and Veryl). Flossie, Kay, Mrs. Greber, Elkink, Jack and I went to the store but got back again for night lunch.

Earlier in the day I spent the morning making novelties from prunes, raisins and jelly candy that I had bought in Fort Simpson, to decorate Mrs. MacDonald's birthday table. She had a cake from Mrs. Beatty and a card and gift from Ernie. We all had a delicious chicken dinner.

S.S. DISTRIBUTOR
Fort Wrigley

Monday, September 11. We left Fort Wrigley very early and travelled rapidly through the morning gloom, past Blackwater River and shortly after dinner stopped across from where the Saline River empties into the Mackenzie. The crew had to throw the wood down to the shore then load it into wheel barrows. It surprised me how long they took, there must have been many cords. When they finished, darkness was falling so we remained over night.

The evening was lovely but cold. I remained up for night lunch – cocoa, salmon sandwiches, cookies and tarts. As it seems on all cruises, the meals and food take on much importance and are an effective time to meet and socialize with other passengers.

Tuesday, September 12. A fine day, but smokey. We travelled right along until mid-morning when we left our barges and went to pull a barge from the shore into the river. During the next three hours cables snapped, pegs broke, etc. but we got it into the river where the Hearne Lake took it onward.

The river banks were very high all along, the mighty river having cut its way through silt and centuries of deposits. We saw the red stones at the place where the coal vein has been burning for hundreds of years. Bear Hill was veiled with smoke but even that didn't hide it's size and strength.

WARTIME SECURITY
– farewell to the S.S. Distributor

<u>Tuesday, September 12.</u> About 5:20 p.m. we arrived at Fort Norman. It looked trim and well painted, sitting up on a hill. Sutton and I took Doris Ibister ashore to meet Mrs. Craig for whom she is going to work. Then I went on up and took a snap of the old log mission church, a truly historic and interesting building. A Signals man, Patricks, and his wife lived in the mission house. She was out tending a flourishing garden and took time to talk. I had hoped to learn some local history and in a way I did: the floor in the house had a one-foot slope! (I was later to learn that northern buildings sitting on the ground often became unlevel as frost in winter and heaving in summer moved the base.)

The Patricks, Mrs. Harvey (the Doctor's wife) and her little Judy, Mr. Craig (HBC Manager) and his wife, son Eric and daughters Ruth and Joyce, and Mr. Bartleman (HBC Transport) came to the Distributor for supper. After supper we went to the Craig's, then to the Harvey's. The Harveys had two boys, Micky and Peter as well as little Judy.

Next we went to see the hospital. It used to be an Anglican mission but the church lacked resources because of war demands and the government took it over. Pat and Barbara, the nurses whom we met earlier travelling on the Radium

Hospital, Fort Norman, N.W.T.

Queen, were already deep into work, with thirteen patients. The hospital is fine and is being renewed with additional staff.

Wednesday, September 13.
Bright sunshine at nine when we got up for breakfast. I persuaded the girls, Mrs. MacDonald, Mrs. Hayward and Helen to go to see the Bear River which flows into the MacKenzie river at this point. Instead of following the Mackenzie shore, they decided to take a trail up over the hills, through the woods. The berries, rose hips, cranberries, coloured leaves along a brook and little path were truly beautiful and the vegetation quite fragrant.

We couldn't seem to find a way down to the shore of the Bear River but kept going on and on. I was nearly forced to stop when shortness of breath and pains racking my body were nearly all I could bear. Finally we found a path leading back through the damp moss to the village. I went into the little church for a while before Elkink and I went to the small store where I bought some licorice pipes, cigars and whistles, 3/5¢. I bought 25¢ worth. Mrs. Craig asked me to take some mauve wool for Mrs. Greber, our ship's hostess.

We were home (on the Distributor!) by 11:45 a.m. in time to prepare for dinner. Although quite exhausted, I enjoyed the meal of braised beef, soup and apricot pie. I stayed in the cabin until 2 p.m. when the whistle blew. Outside I saw the Signals men unloading a steer from our barge. It was a big black animal with a white head. I estimated it would weigh about 800 pounds. After being in a pen on the barge for weeks, it showed its joy of freedom by jumping and throwing itself, making the people scatter for dear life.

About 2:30 p.m. we left Fort Norman.

I tried to rest while Elkink and Sutton, knowing we might be at the end of our time on the Distributor, packed until suppertime.

Thursday, September 14. The morning sunshine was soon hidden by smoke and fog. A strong wind kept the water stirred. We were anchored at Bear Island but we could see Norman Wells about a mile to the east. The shiny oil tanks were visible through the smoke.  Some lively little red flames danced on the shore. And above all this the mountains towered bleak and foreboding.

Because of wartime security, the HBC was not allowed to carry us farther. Flying was the only option.

Captain Naylor and Jack Cockburn had gone to Norman Wells and all morning we waited for their message to tell us when a plane would be ready to take us to Aklavik. I passed the time playing with Helen Hayward and knitting. The message didn't come. Then after dinner the Hearne Lake arrived, bringing the Captain and Jack. They reported that the plane was out of commission but would be ready between now and three days. Disappointing!

Mrs. MacDonald wanted to go to Canol so Elkink and I went with her on a ferry. "Shorty," the little red fireman from our ship was all dressed up and went, too. The ferry passed Goose Island, a low sort of sand bar formation where some drilling was going on.

Letter home: *Dear Dad, I was over to Canol yesterday and while it appeared little but machines, buildings and disorder to me, I thought of how you would like to have been able to see it.*

The Distributor, with its barges, is tied to Bear Island out in the middle of the Mackenzie River. It is an island about seven miles long. To the east we see Norman Wells — and countless oil tanks gleaming. In every direction you can see them. The project must be scattered over miles and miles.

A boat with a roof and with room for about twenty-five people runs hourly between Norman Wells and Canol. If you beckon from the Distributor it will pull in. We did so yesterday afternoon. It took about 30 minutes to arrive at the first of Canol. We waited on the shore in a little shack where an old barrel heater is made into an oil burner until we learned that the Bus (a station wagon) had been stopped the day before. So, although we knew it was four miles, we started to walk over the dusty sand hills. The highways were perfect but a multitude of trucks kept meeting us and leaving us blinded in brown dust.

The Imperial Oil Exploration Camp came first. It was a series of buildings, laboratories and machinery. There a "kind Canadian" picked us up in his truck so we rode the rest of the way. The scenery was certainly ruined — either burned or bulldozed up, for sheer love of destruction (or so it seemed).

The administration buildings were our destination as Mrs. MacDonald had to conduct an interview for the Edmonton Bulletin. While she was there we went to the Canol dentist as Miss Elkink had a bothersome toothache. We found him reclining in his bunk but he consented to investigate so we went to his office. He found the tooth dead, removed a filling and fixed it so that it could drain. The igloo sleeping quarters seemed the regulation kind but all the other buildings were just tacked up of big slabs of veneer, or ten test, etc.

We got a ride back to the ferry on a light delivery [truck]. It was windy and dusty but a quick ride. A "wine-sopped" fellow nearly sat on top of me all the way. I didn't appreciate him or his language either.

We had to wait a long time for the ferry but found some Canadian men to talk to. There is such a difference between them and the Americans. The Americans are to leave soon and are gradually being replaced by our men. They are certainly leaving their marks here — and it is not all good, either, especially at the smaller ports where they have contacted the native people. For example, they get liquor rations and bootleg them. The Indian Agent told of having tried to catch some who were giving drinks to the Indians then selling small bottles for $100 each — and drinking half of it themselves. There are so many evil things they've done. I suppose there are good points, too, but I haven't heard much *about those.*

    Well, Canol is behind now. Miss Elkink and I may take the ferry to Norman Wells and I will mail this. The ferry is free.

We were to fly yesterday but got word that the plane was out of commission and it would take up to three days to fix. So we are still here. The Distributor will be here for a week or more so we have accommodation. However, we hope to leave at least before the boilers are cleaned and the boat gets cold.

    As for myself, I am getting over anxious to go. I never mention to the people here, but I am frightfully tired of the boat. The people who come on from the Wells in the evening aren't very good characters and seem to get worse. Furthermore I know we are needed in Aklavik and school should be started.

    I suppose I'll get a letter hearing how your harvesting is progressing by the time I get to Aklavik. It will be six weeks tomorrow since I left.

                        With love,
                        Mary

After arriving back at the dock shack we had a long wait for a ride to the Distributor. After several false starts, we, with eleven others, got going. We were dropped off at the Distributor, unfortunately too late for supper except for some tomatoes and pumpkin pie.

After supper the girls played cards while I knitted and listened to Mrs. Hayward read from the "Jungle Book."

Friday, September 15. A dull, dreary day with low clouds obscuring the mountains. Elkink and I wanted to take the ferry to Norman Wells but kept putting it off. The Distributor went over to the Canol side just before dinner. From the roof of the 500 barge I took a picture of the crane working.

All day long a stream of men poured into the ship's canteen. There were all sorts, some had beards, some had jackets with huge checks, some had hats that looked like a bulldozer had trampled over them.

They all departed with ginger ale (30¢) sticking out of their pockets and arms loaded with matches, tobacco and candy bars.

Letter Home. *Saturday, September 16, 1944.*

We are still at Norman Wells. A terrible storm of wind and rain has been continuing since yesterday. However, just now the sun has burst out and shines on the tanks, making them gleam silver across the river. The water is tossing in white caps. We have seen thousands of wild geese flying overhead all morning. Isn't it strange how they take advantage of the strong wind to help them southward?

We are on the Canol side now and two huge cranes are on the bank unloading the barrels from our barge. The crane swings over dangling 4 steel loops. The men slip the loops over the drums — up they go, then swing over and are dropped on a very strange-looking truck. The back is like a floor only two feet off the ground. There are eight wheels side by side across the back. Really, I never imagined there were machines like those we see here.

The lounge is the only warm place today so everyone is here. There are four card tables and about thirty modern wicker or leather chairs. Some folks are reading, others are knitting and still others are playing rummy. I have just written a little note to Mollie Alexander. I meet quite a few R.C.M.P. that know Sgt. Alexander.

Our plane is ready and only awaits better weather conditions to take off. I hope it is tomorrow, at least. The men on the radio hear that there is over a foot of snow at Aklavik.

You should see the men who work here. "All sorts and conditions of men," seems indeed true when you see this assortment. A very few are spruced up, some have loud checkered shirts, some are fully bearded with wild eyes, some look like cowboys, some like Eskimos in parka, a few wear uniforms, and so on — big and fat, long and lean, etc.

<u>Sunday, September 17.</u> The weather was clearing from the northwest and blowing the clouds south but where we were tied up there was no wind, not even a ripple.

We had our usual breakfast at 7:25 a.m. The Hearne Lake took our 500 barge, Captain Naylor and our men over to Norman Wells.

I prepared a Thanksgiving Service as we heard that <u>the lights are on again in England</u> for the first time in five years. How happy they must be! Decided to hold the service at 4 p.m. so that the boys from the Canadian Signals Corps could come.

After noon dinner Sutton and I went for a walk along the beach and up onto the top of Bear Island. Shorty was in the separating house and called us in. Eleven hundred to twelve hundred barrels of crude oil go through there hourly. We took the inland route and had fairly started when we heard the Distributor's whistle. When we got to the ship we found that the Hearne Lake had come over to take us to a waiting plane at 3 p.m.

How we hurried and packed! Mrs. MacDonald took our pictures. We shook good-byes all around and were gone. It was a lovely ride on the Hearne Lake. Jack Cockburn finished our bill and I signed it: $520.00 but with a 25% discount, just $390.70 for the three of us, from Fort Smith to Norman Wells.

A big red truck took us from the dock to the Hotel when we learned that the plane wouldn't go until the next day. We girls were taken to a very comfortable 2-room, 4-bed tent, Mrs. Hayward and the three children to a cabin. All were lighted electrically and heated with gas. We walked about with Mrs. MacDonald until she left on the 5:35 ferry. Then we killed time until 7:30 supper.

Meals were served in the mess hall amid such a conglomeration of men and women eating carrots, boiled beef, meat salad, potatoes, tomato sauce, pineapple, molasses cake and tea. There was such noise and such haste that I was breathless in amazement. The novelty, however, was exciting. Everyone looked at little Helen. Seeing a little girl at Canol was a novelty. Also our uniforms attracted attention. Friendliness. Met Mr. and Mrs. Bartleman on the street. We went to our "home" tent then to the "tin house" to wash. Mrs. Hayward came over then Robert followed in his pyjamas to take her "home."

I was designated to sleep in a top bunk. Just before I put my head down, I removed my glasses and reached over and put them on the sill of a little window. Then we decided that the gassy smell from the heater might not be good for us so we should open the window a bit. Somehow, I don't know how, but the window slammed back down on my glasses! I had only one pair, my second pair was packed in my big trunk somewhere on a freight barge.

<u>Monday, September 18.</u> We were late for the second breakfast and had to wait for the last one at 9:30 a.m. our time (8:30 theirs). There was a great assortment of food on the table. Mr. Bartleman ate with us. Then Mr. MacDougal of the CPA came, saying that the plane awaited us. I mailed my glasses with an enclosed cheque.

The station wagon took us down to the river. Mr. MacDougal went back to get some seasick bags. A good precaution.

We were packed into the silver Fairchild, ATZ, seven of us, sitting on our luggage and Robert lying down on some at the back. It was a first flight for both Elkink and Sutton. I sat next to the pilot so  relayed his shoutings about the earth below: the Ramparts, Good Hope, beaver lodges, etc. Without my glasses I couldn't see the details he described, a disappointment. However, it was smooth so no one was sick except Helen Hayward.

This flying episode was a quick pass over several places that we had on our list of stops when we left Edmonton:

1. The Ramparts – where the mighty two-miles-wide Mackenzie River is squeezed to a few hundred yards by high cliffs. Consequently the water rushes at great speed and constitutes a high point of the river traveller's experience.

2. Fort Good Hope where the Roman Catholic Church established a mission in 1862 and still dominates the area. Particularly notable are the murals and pictures inside the church. All of us had much looked forward to seeing them. The well staffed mission had also developed excellent gardens.

3. Fort McPherson, an old established Anglican mission but we knew that we would see it later as it was part of our school's itinerary.

We flew into a rainstorm and landed at Arctic Red River. A clerk came to the plane with some snacks: biscuits, bars, cheese, crackers. We each paid $2.00. There were no white ladies at Arctic Red River. Peering through the wet windows of the plane, I could see that the river banks were sheer and high and I also saw my first long parkas on some women walking along the shore.

The pilot put on some more gas and we were off!

As we flew low over the Delta, I tried to shout above the engine's roar that in July 1929 Punch Dickens had landed his plane at Aklavik – the very first. Only Robert heard me.

After 45 days travel we were in Aklavik in 45 minutes.

The river was too shallow for us to land in the usual place so we circled again and from the ground signals the pilot, Cameron, brought his Fairchild, ATZ, down gently, taxied a short distance and shut off his motor. I could see the crowd on the muddy shore moving along to our new spot, some were running. Starting at the passenger nearest the door we were helped one by one down onto the pontoon, across the planks and over to the wet earth. We recognized Dr. Hayward who was overjoyed to see his family.

We met Archdeacon Marsh and Miss Niven from the school and let them lead us through the mud, up a bank and along a muddy road to the school. It was almost like a dream. We were tired and had travelled so long, so far, then the little plane almost stupefied us with its fumes and now at last, here we are. I thought, "The first day of four years. It's great, it's finally beginning."

Thoughtfully we three, Sutton, Elkink and I were at once led up the front stairs to the second floor to our rooms and the Lady Staff Bathroom. Then back down to meet more of the staff and have a cup of tea.

There was a staff meeting in the evening but I for one was too tired to record it, maybe I didn't even hear. All my diary said was,

"COLD."

"Tomorrow school begins."

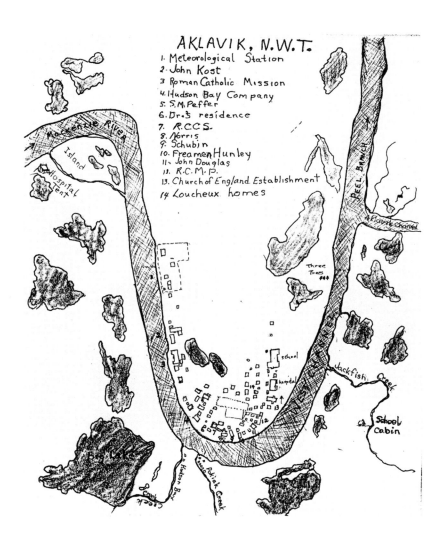

AKLAVIK, N.W.T.

1. Meteorological Station
2. John Kost
3. Roman Catholic Mission
4. Hudson Bay Company
5. S.M. Peffer
6. Dr.'s residence
7. R.C.C.S.
8. Norris
9. Schubin
10. Freamen Hunley
11. John Douglas
12. R.C.M.P.
13. Church of England Establishment
14. Loucheux homes

FULLY EMPLOYED
– at All Saints Residential School

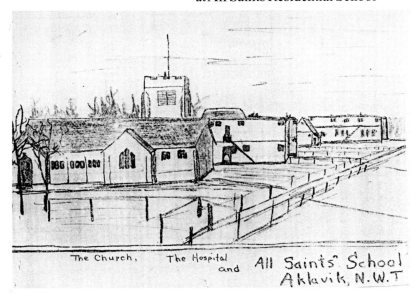

The Church, The Hospital and All Saints' School Aklavik, N.W.T

<u>Day 1. Tuesday, September 19.</u>   It was good after so many weeks of travelling to have finally reached that little dot on the map – up at the top of mainland Canada. It was good to be so earnestly welcomed by the staff who had been working so short-handed. It was good to start the next day with a classroom full of happy children – happy because they were going to "make school." The regular classroom day began: 9:30 - 11:45; 2:30 - 5 p.m. Maybe it was none too soon. The children weren't the least bit shy – they were excited, talkative and very happy. Some whistled, some sang and some even stood on the desks – all in fun! It snowed that night. The ground was white.

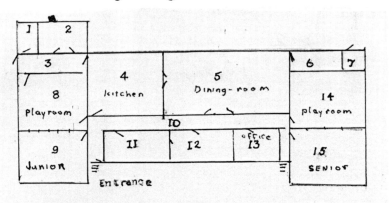

This may be a good place to refer to the building diagrams. My room was #2 on the second floor. My classroom was on the first floor and labelled "Junior." All of the children unable to read at the Grade IV level were in my care. So since children entered the school at any age, I had from age 6 to 15 or 16. Learning English and basic math was the routine in the Junior Room. I determined that this challenge would be fun and arrived at in creative ways.

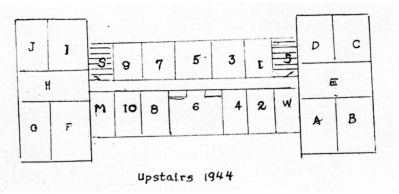

Upstairs 1944

The two Hayward children who travelled with us came to day classes after lunch and in the following days others also enrolled. Fortunately I was able to find primary supplies on the shelves – pencils, scribblers, etc.

Day 2. Wednesday, September 20. We only arrived on Monday yet the school already seems to be in full swing. I hadn't contemplated the social aspect of the community. My previous two years working at Lac la Ronge, Saskatchewan, had been involved totally with school and church. Here in Aklavik there appears to be involvement in everything. This day all the free moments were filled with preparations for a bridal shower. "Pauline," they said, "is marrying Doug." I didn't question that. No doubt I'd learn all about it. All of the white women in the village seemed to be at the school preparing for the evening's shower.

The matron, Miss Fulton, told me that Wednesday evening was my turn to do dormitory duty after 8:30. She told me I was to walk about to keep quietness and order in the dormitories. At the girls' end there were three dormitories and four at the boys' end. The hundred or so children would hopefully soon fall to sleep. Their lights were out and I carried a flashlight. I had been told by a supervisor of an incident that occurred on her first night supervising. Feeling quite happy that

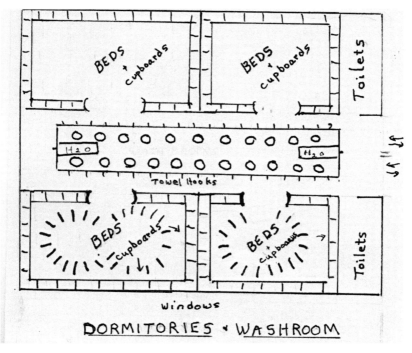

DORMITORIES & WASHROOM

the girls were settled down and very quiet, she nevertheless tiptoed into the junior room. Much to her bewilderment all of the first little beds were empty. Using her flashlight she slowly checked further – every bed was empty. Then at the far end of the dark room she found them all, sound asleep on the floor in close little humps under their blankets, together. When I asked what she did about it, she said, "Left them to feel at home."

Being on duty after 8:30 upstairs meant that I was not involved with the bridal shower downstairs. For this I was thankful. Meeting many new people at once was not something I enjoyed – a frightening experience I was happy to avoid.

Day 3. Thursday, September 21. The routine was becoming easier. Besides being a teacher many other 'school' activities had to be shared with other staff. We had breakfast at 7:30 then after prayers, I supervised dish washing and cleaning in the children's dining room. The classroom opened at 9:30. Teachers had from 12 to 2:30 free from classes as supervisors took the children walking after lunch during the lightest part of the day. We dismissed again at 5 p.m. and it was a rush to get the classroom clean by supper bell at 5:30.

I had an excellent classroom with fine windows facing south and east and many blackboards. It was, however, a little too crowded with over 60 pupils and their desks.

Thursdays both Elkink and I had a free hour after lunch without house duties before the afternoon classes. It gave us a chance to walk about town and size up our new environment. The Radium King was in port and Constable Jansen, whom we had met on our way in, had arrived. After supper was choir practice – it seemed that I was expected to be "useful" there!

Day 4. Friday, September 22. I was slated to be Brown Owl of the Brownie Pack but since I broke my glasses in Norman Wells and still awaited new ones, my eyes were too strained to cope with the added activity. A native girl who was on the school staff was selected to be my Gray Owl. However, she didn't seem to be in the school. So the little girls had a playtime in the playroom.

Day 5. Saturday, September 23. Teachers had one full day off every two weeks. Today was Elkink's, not mine. I spent the a.m. supervising the cleaning of the children's large dining room. This meant I had some girls, all eager to help, scrub benches, wash tables and scrub the entire floor. We had to be finished by lunch time. Any children who had family in town were allowed to leave the school to visit if their kin came for them. That happened on Saturdays. They had to be back in the school by 7:00 p.m.

That afternoon Elkink and I went to the stores, three of them, Hudson's Bay Co., Kost's and Robert's. We walked on farther to where the previous doctor had an experimental farm. Dr. Leslie Livingstone, possibly a descendent of the same

Kost's

Scottish family as Dr. David Livingstone, missionary in Africa, began to establish medical services in the Eastern Arctic in 1922. He came from a farming family in Ontario, studied at Queen's University in Kingston, did his internship at St. Luke's Hospital (now the Civic in Ottawa) and had many interests. After several years of service in the Eastern Arctic he moved to Aklavik in the Western Arctic in 1938. Besides his official duties he began to dabble in farming.

Before my journey to Aklavik I had read with considerable curiosity about his experiment – a barn built for cows, goats, pigs, chickens – and field crops growing fodder? on the permafrost? It seemed incredible.

Elkink and I saw with amazement the barn, fence and six cows eating amongst old tree stumps. Peeking into the barn, a long-bearded billy goat stared through at us. Previously I had noted a very lush patch of oats growing on the mud flat by the river. The plants were either frozen or trampled. As Dr. Livingstone had only just left Aklavik, the unharvested oats were an indication of the coming demise by neglect of the experimental farm.

BUTTER CUP

Harrington

Oat Crop - frozen

Day 6. Sunday, September 24. Our school, "All Saints Residential," was part of the Church of England Mission at Aklavik. The Mission also included the church and its ministerial staff, the hospital and its staff.

All Saints School, Aklavik

Each Sunday the church held Holy Communion at 9 a.m., a service for the Loucheux [Kutchin or Gwich'in] Indians at 11 a.m. and Sunday School and a service for the Eskimo [Inuit] at 3 p.m. Then in the evening at 7:30 there was a service in English attended by anyone wishing to come. It was a very full day. If we were free, we could go to Holy Communion at 9:00 a.m. and breakfast afterwards in the school kitchen. While the Loucheux children were taken to the 11 a.m. service in their own language, the Eskimo children at the school often sang hymns with Miss Robinson around the little organ in the dining room. I went to that activity as I wanted to hear and begin to learn the language.

I went to the choir loft early before the 7:30 evening service. This being my first time as "choir mother," I was impressed by the girls with red cassocks, white surplices and white crimped collars. The four women (Sutton, Robinson, Nurse Beach and I) had white surplices and black mortars. Many village folk came to the Sunday evening service. All were welcome to meet afterwards for late lunch either at the school or in the Hospital staff room. I enjoyed meeting many and we visited and sang requests. There always seemed to be one who could play the old piano and nearly any old favourite song requested.

Day 7. Monday, September 25. A week had already flown by. Very foggy but to our surprise, the mail plane came and on it, Mrs. Boxer (née Perrins) with her first baby, 4 1/2 month old Donald. She used to be a staff member and would stay with us until her husband returned. The school mail bags were dumped onto the floor of our staff living room. From there we gathered letters bearing our names. Since the Post Office would close at 8 p.m. I quickly looked over mine in case a quick reply was needed.

Mrs. Dewdney, the missionary's wife from Fort McPherson, had been staying here and she hoped to leave on the mail plane in the morning.

After 8 p.m. Mrs. Gibson and I went downtown to deliver the new issue of the "Living Message," the Anglican church magazine that had just arrived.

It had been a full day and ended a full week in All Saints School in Aklavik.

Tuesday, September 26. School, or more precisely, the classroom, was settling into a routine, already showing slow but noticeable change and progress. The children all knew their desks and seemed pretty proud to have their very own table with attached seat, in its own place in the classroom. At home most of the children dwelt with the whole family, maybe  others, too, in one small space so school became very special, indeed. And fun, too. I aimed for each to be in the ideal learning position whether it was age, previous time at school, grade level, if any, and influence. Some new students felt better near a sibling or friend who already knew the ropes. I liked the newest ones near me so they could catch the nuances of English words and I could hear them better. I found that if they taught me their words and I exchanged our English ones, it was a game. I also employed the chalk on blackboard and physical action where possible. For instance, saying the word "jump" writing the word on the blackboard accompanied by a sketch of a stick man jumping and having the children jump helped them to understand. They jumped and jumped and then sat down and made the action and word in a crayon picture. Bit by bit, rather "word by word," the vocabulary got built like snow blocks making an igloo. I anticipated that soon English would dominate as, with three languages, Loucheux , Eskimo and English, the class would lead into one in order to progress.

With about sixty children of varied ages, we had to have order coming and going. Joining the classrooms which were at each end of the building was a long hallway. The boys' playroom and senior classroom were at the other end from our junior classroom and the girls' playroom. The supervisors lined up the boys and girls in their separate locations and they came to classes in single files, each going to his or her own desk. At recess or dismissal times, I did likewise, alternating boys or girls leaving first.

We had to have quietness during the lesson times. All faculties, eyes, ears, touch, etc. needed to be able to take in the process. It worked well – improvements showed even in students who had been several years in the junior classroom. They listened intently to the other levels' classes.

On this day, the start of our second week, our last hour was spent on names. The new students were helped by the experienced students and myself to print their own names. We decided that my name could be "Miss Mary" as "Harrington" was too complicated. It seemed easy even for the young ones as "Mary" was already a common sound, putting the "Miss" in front was simple although it often came out as "sssmay" or "mmayee." By dismissal time at 5 p.m. each child had a paper with his or her name printed on it to leave on their desks for me to see.

This being Tuesday, it should have been Women's Auxiliary (W.A.) night but several leaders couldn't come so I spent time with Miss

Elkink, doing her hair. Then she did mine.

Wednesday, September 27. Today I obtained safety pins from a supervisor and the children pinned their names on their chests. New words, "pin," "on," "shirt," "dress." Older students – a sentence.
It was cold and the ground remained frozen all day. I had time at noon to do Miss Niven's hair. An exciting event for Aklavik – a wedding at 7:30 p.m., Pauline and Doug. Since I was a new arrival, I didn't mind being on duty, putting the girls to bed, helping Jessie with the boys, then taking night duties. Mr. Campbell came from the church and told me about the wedding. (Mr. Campbell was a retired accountant and a very good friend of the school.) I was also baby-sitting Mrs. Boxer's baby but little Donald slept all night.

Thursday, September 28. Two "new" day pupils arrived – Jim Sittichinli's two sons, George and Ephriam who came at noon. Jim, a Loucheux, was a deacon and Rev. Marsh's assistant. The class seemed noisy, perhaps anticipating the Doctor's coming to give diphtheria inoculations. My class was first. Dr. Hayward was gentle and only Rosie Jane ("Peanut") cried. After first recess the senior class was inoculated, including the children of the Marshes, Gibsons and Douglases. Choir practice was at 7:30, then at 9 p.m. the mission staff meeting where all Anglican workers met. Rev. Marsh led discussions on: visiting homes, Loucheux W.A., organ fund, church cleaning. So it was an 11:15 bedtime.

On Friday evening we held our first Brownie meeting. There were four "sixes." I was Brown Owl, and Jessie Bonnetplume, a Loucheux native on staff, was Gray Owl. Delightful.

<u>Saturday, September 30.</u> My first full day off. (and it was full !).

I spent the early morning preparing the prescribed classroom register which requires end of month daily records, and washing the black boards. There was a lot of tidying to do.

In the afternoon Elkink and I went with the two R.C.M.P. Jansens to see if the ice on the little lakes between here and the R.C. Mission was ready for skating. I was reluctant to go as I felt a bit unwell but the sunshine felt good. "Fair" Jansen and Elkink skated only a few strokes and declared the thin ice wasn't quite ready.

In the evening Elkink and I went to Haywards and the doctor said I must go tomorrow to the hospital. When we got home we found everyone eating corn-on-the-cob, a gift from a new meteorologist, Mr. Labelle, who had just come in from "outside."

<u>Sunday, October 1 to Wednesday, October 11.</u> I had a short stay in hospital to clear up some lung congestion and during that time I was enriched by learning more of the people there, the staff and the patients.

Meanwhile a barge had got through to Aklavik bringing our trunks and boxes that we'd had to leave at Norman Wells.

The Mission boat returned from the Reindeer Station with our yearly meat supply.

In an effort to stabilize the food supply for native people and others living in the Delta the Government of Canada had imported a herd of reindeer from Alaska. Originally from Lapland, the animals thrived in Alaska. The  epic multi-year trek across the arctic to the Mackenzie Delta was completed in 1935. Some local natives learned from the supervising Lapps to become herders. Now, in 1944 each year's surplus was made available for local needs and the residential schools and hospitals received their shares. All Saints School in 1944 received 49 carcasses.

The school had its own freezer – an underground "room" in the permafrost. A small building covered the entry. A door in the floor and a ladder provided access. Year after year the temperature remained constant. Often the carcasses were gutted but the skin was left on to keep the meat from drying out. Other than canned products or very salty cured pork, the deer were our only source of fresh meat.

<u>Thursday, October 12.</u> While I was hospitalized my classroom had been well attended to by other staff sharing their care, especially Miss Sutton. I soon noted that the children's English had improved as practice, songs and games, often repeated, had established the vocabulary. I realized how interdependent our staff and the community are in such an isolated place. Each one of us was important.

Staff, 1944
Front Row L to R : Mike Koziak, Mary Harrington,
Dorothy Robinson, Marge Sutton, Bizz Niven, Mr. Campbell
Back Row L to R : Bobby and Rev. Gibson, Eleanor Woodcock,
Edna Gibson, Beth Fulton, Mr.Elwell (missing – Reka Elkink)

Jessie Bonnetplume
Marjorie Greenland

I felt really excited to be back to routine. The children all tried to talk at once – to tell me things. Little Rosie Jane seemed to have lost control again and when Miss Niven came in to take pictures I had to take action – a couple of little pats with my short ruler – she was very surprised, and her noise changed to screams! Everyone but me laughed.

We were attempting to help the children maintain their own languages as we promoted English. Rev. Marsh, who was fluent in Eskimo, came in regularly to talk with the Eskimo students. Rev. Sittichinli did likewise with the Loucheux students. The English speaking students could go home early or, if they liked, join one of the other two groups.

We made paper snowflakes and snowbirds which we hung with threads from the heat pipes which crossed our ceiling. [There were two furnaces, one at either end of the building, fuelled by cordwood barged from farther up the river. Fans drove the hot air through the pipes which were attached to the ceiling. Outlets both down and up distributed the warmth.] When the forced air came on, the little paper birds and snowflakes seem to come to life.

Friday, October 13 and Saturday, October 14. After Friday's busy classes, a Brownie meeting and Rev. Marsh's "Camera Enthusiast" meeting, I was ready for Saturday, my day off. It was fairly warm and sunny so I went to the HBC to buy an alarm clock ($2.50) and to the hospital to pay my bill (all of $7.00 – subsidized, of course).

Mrs. Marsh and I kept our plan to go painting. She had her watercolour things ready and I my oils when it was time for the boys' walk. They pulled a sleigh with our things until we saw our chosen site by Dr. Livingstone's farm then they and Miss Robinson continued further for a picnic. The first loose ice floes coming down the river, the far-off mountains, the close-up berries on snow-covered bushes – my picture was only started when the boys returned. Mrs. Marsh had some delicate water washes on her paper.

I stayed at Marsh's for supper. We had roast reindeer. There were two community meetings going on at the school.

Sunday, October 15.   There were about 20 at Holy Communion. Sunday School was at 3 and I held a class of 8 boys in the kitchen. I was very interested to learn how very literally they fully accepted the old bible stories. My walk in the afternoon took us as far as Kost's and was pleasant. On Sunday there were some children away visiting with family so the smaller number made our walks a more informal time. The choir service in the evening finished my day as I didn't go with the others for a singsong at the hospital.

"We three who traveled to Aklavik in 1944"
L to R. Reka Elkink, Mary Harrington, Marjorie Sutton

FREEZE-UP

—a respite on the Peel Channel

On October 16 the river had a shiny ice covering which soon gave way to ripples when the wind came up. Summer activities gave way to others. Aklavik became an isolated little unit of the world with no invasions of outside events. We were wrapped up in Aklavik and that was all that mattered.

Being so isolated made the rest of the world remote except for our local Red Cross Society. It was made up of anyone who paid $1.00 for membership and was usually the recipient of funds raised by community events. Such events often meant a dance with a "pass the hat" collection, a card party, a race or contest, Peffer's restaurant getting a new movie would charge a small fee for the Red Cross, betting on when the ice would leave the river in spring, when the first plane would land and even when the first safe crossings occurred in the fall. Most events were entertainment, open to the entire community. Small prizes went to the winners and the rest of the proceeds to the Red Cross. The war was still on. At the meeting at the school today it was decided to send $1500 to the Red Cross headquarters.

School went merrily on. It was such fun and I was very happy. In the evening I made a hectograph. I had brought from home a pan – a jelly roll pan – about 12" X 16" with a half-inch rim and three tins of refills. I heated a pot of water and slowly melted the tins of "jelled refill" in the hot water. It was difficult finding a level place to put the pan where I could leave it undisturbed over night. Using water for trial, I finally levelled a place on my desk. Then, while quite fluid, I poured the clear, amber liquid into the tray and left it to set.

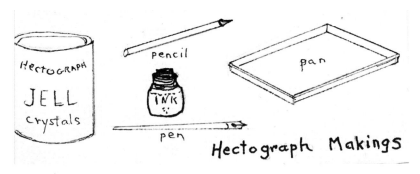

Hectograph Makings

Tuesday, October 17. Tonight was the G.A. (Girls' Auxiliary) meeting. Being my responsibility, I prepared the agenda at noon, using my newly made hectograph and the special pencil with an intense purple lead to write the script. The original was carefully placed, ink side down on the jelly. I waited a few minutes for the ink impression to transfer to the jelly and peeled it off. Then, by applying clean paper I got as many copies as I wished or at least until the impression became too faint. Overnight the ink sank to the bottom and the pan was ready for reuse.

Wednesday, October 18. I have now been at Aklavik for one month. It was a beautiful day, made special by an invitation from Mrs. Hayward to go there for supper – a Chinese supper – her husband, Dr. Hayward, demonstrated how to eat with chopsticks. I had to be home by 8:30 as it was my duty night. Everyone else was away to the newly weds' (Pauline and Doug McNiece) house warming.

Saturday, October 21 and Sunday, October 22. The exciting event of the week happened on Saturday. People crossed the river on the ice. The next day some cleared a space and had a vigourous game of broomball. Now Aklavik seemed to be re-awakening with the "freeze-up" agenda.

Tuesday, October 24. After the river ice formed, sewage and garbage that couldn't be burned were dumped on the ice. In spring as the ice breaks up and travels northward, the piles of garbage go, too. The school was the farthest north establishment so as break-up proceeded we led that disposal.

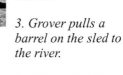

1. Burning the combustible garbage.

2. Tractor "John Deere" waits to be loaded.

3. Grover pulls a barrel on the sled to the river.

3. Mike and "John Deere" drive off to the dump.

In summer the unburned garbage was taken to a marshy site away from the buildings. The sewage was dumped into the river.

At the school and at many homes, chemical toilets were used indoors. Daily emptying and cleaning were carefully done. The contents were dumped into a large barrel, transported on a sled in winter, a wagon in summer and emptied into the river.

The Mackenzie River water was much too polluted for human use. However, as it froze the particles tended to descend and the ice was relatively pure. Hence the urgency to put up a good supply of ice in autumn to last through the next summer. Last year's supply was nearly used up. The men anxiously laid pipelines to the river. They pushed the line up close under the ice where the water was cleaner. Then a pump was used to move the water to our indoor cisterns to be used for laundry and washing.

Men daily brought huge blocks of ice from the ice house to be melted for table use. Every kitchen had tanks on or near the stove where the ice melted. Most folks seemed to drink their water in tea or coffee so it appeared to be safe.

<u>Wednesday, October 25.</u> Early sunshine was soon covered by storm clouds. Inspector Forest came for supper. It was my duty night.

As schools go, discipline other than talks, was seldom needed in All Saints. However, although rarely used, we did have a system which I learned to use on one of my first duty nights. If necessary a child is removed from the general gathering and made to stand in a hall, quiet, alone, hands at back. That evening I had four senior Loucheux girls who thought as I was "new" they could talk and laugh well past curfew when other girls were trying to sleep. Consequently I had four girls spaced at intervals in the hall!

<u>Thursday, October 26.</u> Rev. Marsh conducted lessons in Eskimo [Inuktitut] in my classroom so I had time to make butter tarts.

As the end of October drew near we had our staff meeting as

scheduled. We saw for the first time photos in colour taken by Robinson. Discussions covered fire precautions, pressing of choir collars (I volunteered to learn to use the crimper), using a suggestion box and the date of the Christmas Concert.

But first there would be Hallowe'en

Monday, October 30. There was a party for the children today. Halloween. A natural as, it seems, all aboriginal people have confidence in the supernatural, even if for amusement. We, on the staff, got into the act, too. We had boxes of old clothes sent in by church auxiliaries and by making a black paper "pointy" hat, wearing a size 20 black crêpe dress, carrying a broom, I was a witch; our matron, Miss Fulton was a clown; girls' supervisor, Miss Niven was a peasant; Miss Elkink was a perky Miss Muffet; Jessie, our general help, dressed up in potato sacks, was a peanut; Marjorie Boxer was a Chinese lady; Miss Robinson made a winsome baby in a long nighty, bonnet and bottle; Miss Sutton was a very fancy flirt. We all made a trip to the hospital to see the patients, or really, to show ourselves. Even the sickest laughed and tried to guess, saying "devil, devil."

At the school, in the dining room, Jessie and I with Mrs. Reiach (the wife of the HBC Manager) played games with the younger children. Other groups had fun activities, then all had a big supper, reindeer stew, pumpkin pie and molasses cake with orange icing.

Tuesday, October 31. The adults in town had their parties and played pranks. All disguised and aided by a full moon, they had a "witchy" fun party.

Wednesday, November 1. Since I was the one on duty last night, I seemed to be the only staff member not tired out. Being All Saints Day the school had special hymns and those who wished went to church. Our class watched eight of the Grade Ones jump (fly) over a pile of Grade One books to the Grade Two "shelf." I wanted their success to be understood and it really was. It worked well as a great incentive to get ahead, to remember

Graduation I to II

the lessons. They all wanted their turn to "fly ahead."

Friday, November 3. Lovely weather – just right to go to the river to watch the yearly event, "Ice Cutting." Besides our school team (men), the R.C.M.P. and Peffer's were also working. The thickness of the ice had been carefully watched. First the snow was cleaned from the surface. Then, in this case, a portable motor and saw cut the ice into blocks. They were pulled with a pick on the end of a long pole and were lifted from the water and either piled near shore or onto sleighs to be hauled up the bank to the residences. Timing of the cutting is important as each cold day thickens the ice and it soon becomes too thick for the saws and too heavy to lift.

The school's ice house is built with double walls, the space between the walls is filled with sawdust brought in the summer from mills up river. Since the floorless building sits on permafrost, and the winter is constantly frigid, the supply of ice is kept solid.

Many of the private citizens in the village chopped holes in the river ice and carried pails of water to their homes. When the ice became too thick they chopped pieces of ice to fill their pails, then melted the ice on the heaters or stoves in their houses.

In the school we did the same thing in the summer and winter, getting ice from the ice house for drinking and cooking. Occasionally in winter, if the pump broke down or the pipe froze, we had to use some of our stored ice for all purposes.

*Mrs. Greenland goes to chop
river ice for drinking water.*

That same evening, the ice being safe to walk on and not too thick to make holes in, the jigging for loche (burbot) began. We went across the river to the place where Pokiak River joined the main channel as it seemed to be the best place where the fish could be caught. There was nothing professional about the equipment, just a stick with a sturdy fish hook suspended on a string or cord from one end. Bait? Well, some people seemed to have chunks of fish but a young Eskimo I watched took his chewing gum, wrapped the silver paper around the gum, then put it on the hook. In only a few minutes after lowering it into the water he gave a yell. I looked to see what he had caught. I had never seen such an ugly fish before as he eased it head first up out of the hole. "You eat that? Good?" I questioned. "Hungry, boil, eat. No hungry, dog." and he laughed merrily. By then our feet were very cold so we hobbled back to the school.

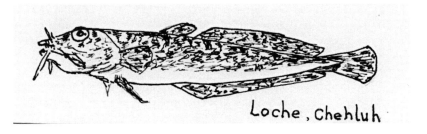

Loche, Chehluh

99

Saturday, November 4. There were no classroom classes today so I was free to clean the classroom – not an easy job with more than sixty desks on wooden runners to be moved when we swept the floor. We tried to wash the blackboards and desks, also. There were quite a number of younger girls not fluent enough to help in the kitchen or sewing room who pleaded to help me. They loved to scrub and clean and have something to do. My problem was to choose a few from the group, then as most adults know, it is hard to have "learning help" do the job as you'd like it done. This was brought home to me one Saturday when I saw the young helpers sharing the gum they had scraped from beneath a table!

I had some time and energy left after the cleaning so I went to help in the kitchen. Our regular cook could always accept a volunteer. Just helping her senior girls prepare meals for over 100 children was a full-time job. Something to enhance the staff meals was a welcome addition. That week I made four lemon pies and many pans of cheese straws with the pastry scraps. [After our fresh lemons had all been used, we relied on powdered lemon filling.]

After lunch I took the duffle cloth and Grenfell cloth I had purchased at the Bay store to Mrs. Jim Sittichinli, as she had agreed to make my "native" parka. She looked me over, and with a string in which she tied knots, measured my height, arm lengths, and shoulders (3 knots). She had use of basic English but being shy we talked little.

On my way home I noted that the village men had cleared enough ice to provide a skating rink.

Sunday, November 5 to Thursday, November 9. It seemed as though the "flu" was spreading through the Delta. By November 7 we had more than 30 children ill. And not only that but it was the season of a surge in head lice. Miss Fulton was tackling that problem with a fine comb and a small pail of coal oil. The flu is especially hard on some of the local people and our children. Dr. Hayward took time to come to the school daily to check on our most severe cases. I kept well and able to help in any place needed. One evening those of us still well (Mrs. Gibson, Misses Massey, Sutton, Fulton, Robinson and I) made 524 doughnuts to freeze for Christmas.

On Friday, activities, other than my regular teaching responsibilities included:
To Mrs. Sittichinli's to try on the parka as the first part was finished (the duffle under part).
To Robert Martin's to ask the price of Caribou shoes ($6.00).
Called to see Mary Jones, then went to hospital. Robert's leg is nearly better.
Called to check on the Marshes.
Planned a contest – draw a gingerbread boy! (a game but also English practice for my students in names of body parts). I drew a two-foot tall gingerbread man, then cut it into many parts. Each player received a part and subsequently a number. If, for example, the person who received a nose had also received #1, he or she would go first and pin the nose to a board. The player who received #2 would go next, perhaps with a toe or an ear, etc. Depending upon where the first parts were pinned, many hilarious combinations could result. It became an effective teaching tool.
Evening – Brownies. Mended and pressed uniforms.
Radio – Northern Messenger, but no messages for us.
Community Club Meeting at the school.
Camera Club at Marsh's. Fun.
And "outside," people think we've nothing to do in our spare time!

PRE-CHRISTMAS

Saturday, November 11. -14°F. I began writing a Christmas letter. Mr. Gibson mixed some diesel and gas to blacken my blackboards. They were much darker as a result.

Elkink and I went out to price moose hides – they were poor, full of holes and at $22, we didn't buy.

As a form of 'flu is spreading through the village, we went to check on the Haywards. Mrs. Hayward was better but Jean was ill.

I got my new parka from Mrs. Sittichinli and all she would take for making it was $5.00. It had a long tubular shape with sleeves and a hood. A wolf tail made a warm edging around the hood. Fur was also sewn around the edges of the bottom and on the ends of the sleeves. Over that another similarly shaped garment was worn. Mine was white and made of windproof Grenfell cloth. Both duffle and Grenfell were from Scotland. The outer cloth had fine geometrically-designed tape edgings instead of fur. Parkas like this were hung from the hood on a wall hook. One got into the  parka by diving into the bottom and arriving upwards through it to the hood. The last touch was a tapsy – a woollen sash, either woven or crocheted. The tapsy drew the duffle closer to your body for added warmth. In the Delta, the design when it had a frilled portion at the hem was called a "Mother Hubbard". That style had a printed cotton cover, not Grenfell like mine.

I got back to school in time to share in Miss Oldenburg's "left behinds." Margaret Oldenburg was a single lady from Minnesota who travelled in the Arctic for parts of 15 years. Financially independent, she was able to charter flights with the best pilots, such as Ernie Boffa. Her interests were diverse. She made collections of thousands of plants from many remote sites and took copious notes on her visits, showing her deep sociological interest in people. She was equally interested in geology and generally in all aspects of her surroundings. Many of her journeys included boat travel as well as flight. It seems that with her background of good schooling, three university degrees and librarian's status, she was always seeking new knowledge. She donated her plant collections to herbaria in both Minnesota and Canada. Northern people were very glad to see her come to visit and when in Aklavik she could always find a warm welcome with us. On this occasion she cooked the staff a sumptuous meal with recipes and contributions from her travels. I have a mimeographed copy of a unique collection of northern recipes that she kindly gave to her friends.

About nine in the evening Miss Elkink and I dressed very warmly and crossed the river to jig. It was -30°F but we had an exciting and satisfactory time – caught 6 fish, 4 of which we lugged home. The staff were amazed! One fish, a loche or burbot, was so large that when we put it in the large kitchen sink its grotesque head appeared at one end and the tail protruded at the other.

Loche - One of six caught Nov. 11, 1944.

On Sunday we had the loche for dinner. The local girls in the kitchen knew how to cook it, although they were reluctant. To them it was 'bad spirit – for dogs.' Man ate it only if starving. First the 'offending' head was brutally severed and taken out of sight. Now the creature was a 'fish.' They served it cut into big pieces, cooked first in a little water with a lid on, then salted and moved to brown in lard in the heavy frying pan.

I had never had a chance to use a typewriter but this year I knew I'd have a long Christmas letter to send, and many copies to make. Could I use carbons? At first, with sheer determination and concentration I proceeded reasonably well, until I noted that every error I erased and corrected made a very objectionable mess on the carbon copies. But I worked at it!

The evening service at the Cathedral (our Mission church) saw us going early and for the first time we wore the freshly laundered and pressed white cassocks for choir. Some of the congregation after the service went to the hospital but both Jansen and Storey (R.C.M.P.) came back to the school. There was an unwritten rule that our lights must be out by 11 p.m. This was not only judicious saving of the fuel oil for our lighting plant but for the staff who rose early and worked long hours. We were at a loss as to how we could politely convey this 'lights out' rule to our visitors, who stayed on and on, until 10 to 1!

The following evening there was a community-school meeting. Christmas entertainment was the main theme and it was left to the teachers. Fire Drills and electricity economy brought up a reminder of the 11 o'clock lights out rule. Timely, too, after last evening's event. During the week early Christmas preparations began.

After choir practice on Thursday we made 650 doughnuts to be frozen.

Many children were ill, some hospitalized. The promised plane still hadn't come but I continued writing letters.

<u>Friday, November 17.</u> A plane finally came at 10:30 this morning. It was an Army plane and it returned to Fort McPherson to bring in 3 patients and take out some of the men from the Signals Corps who were going on furlough.

The evening party on the river rink was a moccasin dance and fun. With a tent and some lights it was lively until the gramophone froze up. Carrying it back, it was dropped and the lid broken. Nearly everyone danced –  how does a real rabbit dance? We did it! And the most comical one was a jig tune in which each woman pushed a man, his feet sliding, a race in time to the music. At 11 p.m. we went to the Bay house, danced indoors and had a hearty lunch of canned wieners. We got home by 1:30. I was soon asleep.

From a letter to my sister Reata and her daughter, Jacqueline:

Dec. 13, 1944. . . . Everyone (except the 100 children) is out so I am on duty. There is a lot of social life up here — compared to most places. Every night something is planned. There must be about sixty grown-ups here — all still young. Some haven't had much to do except entertain or be entertained. At least six of the women in the village used to be on our mission staff. They are so friendly and hospitable. Every day off you are sure to be invited out. I usually do up my own chores, sketch a bit, then go in time for supper and the evening. Usually lights have to be out by eleven but on our day off we don't have to be in until twelve. Rising bell is at 6:45, on Sundays at 7:45.

We have breakfast at 7:30, then after prayers I supervise dish washing and cleaning in the children's dining room. Then school opens at 9:30. We have from 12 — 2:30 at noon as they take the children walking during the lightest part of the day. I usually wash, iron, or do class preparation. We dismiss again at 5. It is a rush to get the classroom cleaned by supper bell at 5:30

I have an excellent classroom with fine windows and blackboards. It is a little too crowded with over sixty pupils. We do not have as difficult work as I had at Lac la Ronge, but the social obligations are greater.

Last night our School Girls' W.A. held their party. We were invited to the hospital. There are thirty girls. I took them over at 7 o'clock. We played games, sang carols, had lunch and got home at 8:30.

Parkas hang and are easily put on.

The Loucheaux W.A. were having their W.A. here. We played "Nuts in May" and other similarly simple games. It was very gay and amusing to see the fun they had — some in their long parkas to their ankles, some old, some serious, some laughing. I came upstairs before lunch hoping to get this letter done — but I was too tired to write.

Our Christmas concert is on Dec. 23, Saturday evening. The senior teacher, Miss Elkink, and I share it. I am training my children to act "The Three Bears," do a sailor song and drill, fairies, stars, lullaby, etc. They love it. However, I do not expect a good performance as so many have been ill and I have had to do a great deal of substituting. It is funny when Father Bear gets excited and shouts,. "Who has been tasting my bed?" Miss Fulton, the Matron plays the music for us.

I have heard from home once since leaving last summer. Then last month I had a message over the "Northern Messenger." — C.B.C. It was quite exciting to hear it. We listen every week and generally someone gets a message. They are two weeks old but we don't mind at all.

Sometimes our radio is very poor and we only hear an odd word. And sometimes the signal station comes on the air and we hear nothing at all but their code.

After the plane comes we will be busier than ever so I will only have time to dd a note then. I am certainly waiting for it to arrive.

<u>Saturday, December 16.</u>   In the morning I made 4 lemon pies and 2 dozen tarts and thoroughly cleaned my room by noon.   In the afternoon I did some work on the Christmas costumes and went shopping with Elkink, searching for little gifts to keep for Christmas (staff). As Christmas got closer every spare minute was filled with preparations: sewing, practices, parties. Exciting!

The committee of the

Club of the
MIDNIGHT SUN. AKLAVIK

invites

Miss. Mary. Harrington.
to accept this membership card and to become a club member.

date. DEC., 20/44

Sec. Treas. R. Elkink

<u>Thursday, December 21.</u> The shortest day of the year — my first in the Arctic. You never saw such a glorious sky. The lovely hues lasted all the mid-day hours.

<u>Saturday, December 23.</u>   The concert began at 7 and went well.

Elkink and I shared the program.

Santa Claus came with gifts for the village children. We served coffee and doughnuts with pails of tea to the approximately 100 people who came, despite the quarantine for mumps at Fort McPherson and sick dogs to the north of Aklavik.

<u>Sunday, December 24.</u> We had invited two bachelors, George Chapman and Sid Scott, for supper on Christmas Eve.

CHRISTMAS 1944

After the midnight church service, we hung up the children's stockings replacing the limp ones they had hung on their towel hooks with well-filled ones. The next morning one little girl said, "I woke up and heard someone whispering. Santa Claus must have had his wife to help him." There was the usual delight that prevails the world over as the little ones explored to the toes of their stockings.

I took the Loucheux children to church at 9. Each little girl was preoccupied adjusting and readjusting a pretty new bow in her hair.

At dinner time the children sat in families or relation groups. They brought their gifts to show others. Their dinner was roast reindeer, split peas, potatoes, gravy and pudding.

After the dishes were washed a bell ringing announced that the

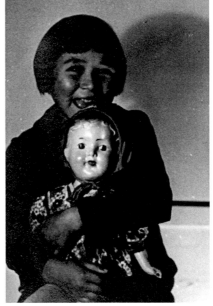

Christmas tree in the hall had its lights on and Santa Claus was coming. Mrs. Claus had done very well to leave a present for every child. When only the tinsel and lights were left, the children all went to their playrooms while we exchanged our gifts. My gifts contained a towel, a sweater, belt, a bubble bath, bed socks, 4 handkerchiefs and 2 spools of thread.

Elkink and I took the children for walks, calling and singing "Merry Christmas" at the homes in the village.

That evening our dinner was different.   In early December our Principal, Rev. Gibson, offered the senior boys 25¢ for each ptarmigan they could catch before the 24th. The birds were easy to catch. You could see only the black beaks as they sat in the snow. They were tame. The boys could toss a piece of ice or use the favoured catapult and soon return to exchange a fluffy white bird for the coveted coin. In the kitchen the little birds were skinned, cleaned, stuffed and baked until golden brown, then served, one each. What a pleasant change from rabbit and reindeer and our dried foods of wartime! No one mentioned the turkey dinner at home!

Some of us left after dinner to attend the concert at the Roman Catholic Mission. With fewer students it was an enjoyable carol program. We got home at midnight.

BETWEEN CHRISTMAS AND NEW YEARS, 1944

During the post-Christmas holiday we had fewer children during the afternoons because any who had family members visiting Aklavik could spend the afternoons with them. We tried to give each other more time off by doubling our care times.

I had 30 boys out for a walk one midday when we heard a strange sounding aircraft, then saw it land on the river by Pokiak Channel. It hit a very hard ridge of wind-blown snow and tipped over on its nose, breaking the propeller and the tip from one

The pilot patched up the plane and flew away after the light was better.

ski. Because of the darkness we could see only where there were flashlights and torches.

One afternoon Fulton and I visited the Pokiak families where I taught Sunday School – Jamesons, Lelands, Noel Firths, Kenneth Stewart, Albert Ross, Hvatums, Garlands, Lusiacks and others. It was -45°F and as we went from house to house we were breathing out frosty clouds.

In an effort to keep us all warm in the school, a little too much fuel was fed into one of the furnaces resulting in an alarming yet colourful chimney fire. For a short time flames and sparks shot up into the dark sky. Our fireman wasn't too concerned.

Our Principal advised us, "put on more sweaters while the furnace cools down."

During the week I had time to paint a portrait of student Eric Lester who kept me entertained with humorous stories while I recorded his happy expressions.

Painting of Eric Lester by Mary Harrington

All branches of the Women's Auxiliary had handicraft sales. The Girl's made $7.75 and the Seniors $135.00.

When late on December 31 I heard the bells ringing and guns firing I put away the 1945 requisition forms and, with excited anticipation, hurried to begin the New Year.

FROM DARKNESS TO LIGHT 1945

Mail Plane - New Year's Day, 1945
Flying over Mission buildings.
Two weeks before sun returned.

From a letter home

January 1, 1945   On New Year's Day the Loucheux people carry on an old Scotch tradition in preparing an elaborate feast. In the early trading days the scotch employees of the Hudson's Bay Company used to give this feast to Natives. In Aklavik it was held in Jim Coe's house and very well organized.

Many of the Loucheux hosts had attended the big Residential School in Hay River and were skilful cooks. One long table and one smaller one were laid ready. Meat soup, Platters of lean roast caribou, potatoes, gravy, corn, peas, tomatoes, cranberries,

pickles, catsup, peaches, plums, cherries, cake, cookies, cigarettes and candy were the luxuries provided in unlimited quantities. The young men wore aprons and waited on guests. As soon as you emptied a dish it was wisked away to be washed for someone else, who sat down as soon as you stood up. They welcomed everyone and in four hours royally fed around 300 people – Eskimo, Loucheau, white, and mixtures of all.

From the beginning of December less sunshine found us each day – until none came at all. At this season the day seems like dawn – a long prolonged dawn. It gradually lightens 'til noon, when you see beautiful colors in the southern sky for about an hour, then darkness falls again – slowly and unwillingly but certainly just as it had gone as noon approached. The Stars swim out into the sky, the Northern Lights wave shyly, and alluring. Night is here.

Very often the temperature is below forty degrees and, unlike the prairie where the cold days are usually calm and still with frost, the wind does not always drop. Those are the days when the fireman is the busiest and no one is really warm despite his effort. Then, too, we think of the log houses not properly mudded up or the nomad in his white duck tent which looks so pretty with the light inside. There is the usual clean covering of snow about a foot deep. In the bush it is soft and light, but on the river it is as hard as cement – so that even the sleigh runners do not mark it.

A lovely part of Aklavik is the smoke, it rises in silvery, billowy funnels from each chimney (and many little log houses have three stove pipes). On a cold, clear, moonlit night, I have often thought it was like a forest of silvery trees. Others think of factory towns in England, but industry could not be so serenely beautiful.

Thinking of Aklavik we remember its canine world – the dogs, white, brown, black, spotted and marked – the little motors of the north. Think of them running nose to tail in fives, sixes or sevens, conveying the toboggan and master to his destination. Perhaps the cargo is five sticks of cordwood, or a carcass of caribou with frozen legs stretching *stiffly up, or fish, or even a wife and the little ones. Think of the dogs beside the overturned toboggan at the journey's end, biting at the snow on their feet as they await their ration of frozen fish. This winter they have had great sickness with distemper and many have died. Hearing of these losses we realize the value and utility of an ordinary dog in the North.*

There is another method of transportation entering this area and that is the tractor – there are three here now and their owners seem to be able to earn a good livelihood hauling cordwood. One truck is also here. These vehicles were brought up on barges in the summer.

After the Christmas activities, the village moves into a slower tempo. Business, what we have of it, is as usual. Elkink and I, not having classroom duties, chose to give our ladies' washroom a thorough cleaning – and whether owing to her Dutch background or not, Elkink was indeed a thorough and expert cleaner – a veritable Miss "Bon Ami." That finished, I went to the Post Office to claim two parcels – one was just a card, $0.32 owing; the other was a small cake in a pound-sized coffee can from my sister Gladys. I had to return to the school for $2.50 in order to claim it. Never was a cake so rich!

Gradually the children who had gone home for Christmas returned and simultaneously "flu" took over the Delta. The cold weather intensified. Our school water supply became critical when the pipe to the river froze.

One by one the school staff had to give in and go to the hospital. Our dormitories were busy, too. Fortunately, I was able to resist and able to help with the extra care. I filled in on the medical care by opening our dispensary, checking temperatures, serving soup and keeping the doctor informed. To keep the well children occupied, Elkink and I held as much school as we could. The outside temperatures (low -30s and -40s) and strong winds made the classrooms too cold so we tried to have activities in the playrooms. You can imagine: trying to keep around sixty bouncing children in one room in reasonable contentment. Even with their outdoor parkas on it was cold. Some of the older students delighted in "teaching" the little ones to do adding and writing or sewing dolls' clothes. They play games like "Here we go round the willow bush." They could spend hours sitting on the floor with pieces of string making "Cat's Cradles" and telling stories. The boys liked most to whittle and carve pieces of wood. I delighted in the extra responsibility until I developed a very stiff neck, chest pain and fever. It was my turn to share the 'flu. The hospital heat lamp helped my neck. Mustard poultices were less successful and I was unable to assist anyone, or even write in my diary, for a week or so. Being confined to bed was not only inconvenient and annoying but also lonely.

Temperatures outside were -50°F or lower and the 'flu hung on to its victims. By the end of the month some were recovering, some had been flown out to Edmonton, and a few like myself were striving to get back to normal. The sun returned and its noon day brilliance was surely "good medicine." The winter moonlight, unusually brilliant for nearly 24 hours daily and the spectacular aurora borealis seem to provide the energy to cheer everyone.

We had an unusual visitor, George Schreiber, an artist from New York. He got a ride on a flight from Norman Wells where he had had an assignment. I was venturing out with some of our 'well' boys for a short walk when we met him carrying a large camera. When he asked one of my younger native boys his name, he answered "John Edmund MacPherson" which caused much merriment.

A letter from my parents surprised me as we hadn't expected a plane so soon. It seemed to open a crack through from Aklavik to "outside" and my preoccupation with the present. Up here the radio reception comes and goes in waves until finally we haven't desire to spend time trying to follow the world events. But their letter mended the link. They asked what I'd like for my birthday. And what about the summer box they could send for $4.60 a cwt. from Waterways? A quote from my reply read,

"I really don't want anything except some seeds, especially those little tree-like balsam and some curly petunias. I'd be very happy to try to make them grow [in the classroom]. Oh yes, some copies of the Free Press and MacLeans . . . I made a personal note not to tell you anything negative but now that it's over, I've been a little sick. With the classroom so cold I got pleurisy — left lung — and then pneumonia . . . mostly I was disappointed because I so much wanted to make a good showing and help a great deal here. But once I get going I'll make up for it.

"There are a few things I don't really need but I could use if I found them in my summer box: a couple of pretty feminine blouses and a dark dressy skirt. The other staff all have nice clothes to wear when invited out for dinner or to parties. I don't know what to say about size? I absolutely have to gain weight! The fruit juices I brought in have been a life saver. . . . I will have an art order coming to you and Sunday School supplies so that they can be packed together. . . . a box on the summer boat. Staff send orders to Eaton's and have it mailed to "outside" relatives who pack everything to get to Waterways by May 1. I may be late sending orders as I haven't had ambition to shop for next Christmas . . . Thank you for the photo. Some of the comments from people here: 'My your mother looks sweet.' 'Your father has a keen sense of humour.' 'You look just like them both.' 'You smile on one side like your Dad.' Then Fulton came in and said, "You're not a bit like either of them!" Did you adopt me!! . . . . "

The school routine has changed since March 1. March 1 to June 15 is "ratting" season. The "rat" here is a muskrat, similar to those that live "outside" in wet places, too. To begin with, our native assistants left to take the opportunity to "rat," not only to add money to their incomes but because it seems to be the major activity that makes the Mackenzie Delta so much a part of life.

Gradually about 35 of our children have been called for and taken home. So now I have around 30 pupils. We hate to see them go as they have just started to grow physically and mentally and the "ratting" to a teacher is like a frost is to a budding plant.

Yet the children are needed to trap, or, if too little for that, they can cut wood and mind the even younger ones while the parents trap. After open water two weeks of shooting is permitted. Rats [muskrats] are so plentiful here in these multiple lakes and streams that one of my pupils who was nine years old last season shot 300 during the two weeks. At $2.00 each, money is quickly made but it has to last all year, maybe pay the previous year's debts and at any rate affect the style of survival.

With so many children and the native staff away, we miss the help some of them gave in our school activities.

A quote from my March 17 letter:

The favourite child I have ever met in my profession is dying. He has just been sick since Christmas. His x-ray plate said, "Active T.B." which could have been curable until this week. Spinal meningitis has set in. You can't imagine the agonizing screams and pain of this affliction. I was the last he recognized and it is a new, hard experience for me to see one so young and loveable so ill. Aklavik reeks with tuberculosis. However our doctor is good in every sense of the word. In case you worry, he has ordered me to have another x-ray, which has been done. I actually feel better than I have for a long time.

"I brought in a collection of branches last week and already have a handsome bouquet of pussy-willows. The plants in my classroom are a verdant joy: ivy, jew, calla lily and amaryllis.

"I had a very happy birthday, my day off. We had fried muskrat for supper. It tastes like duck – good. Thank you for the seeds which I will plant soon as the sun's rays are getting stronger. The soil I saved last fall is just silt (what the Delta is) – a gift from the river.

"Oh, by the way, I need more envelopes. I've already used my 4-years supply and it's not a year yet!"

<u>April, 1945.</u> I've just had my first Easter in Aklavik and was able to adorn the church with pussy willows I had 'forced' indoors. There are buds on my calla lilies – a joy yet to come.

Since we had reduced classes with the children away, I endeavoured to clean the classroom by washing the ceiling and walls. Because we're on permafrost, a basement is impossible and our furnaces and classrooms are on the first level. Huge hot air pipes enter and hang close to the ceilings. They are a tin metal colour but the ceiling above them is painted. Imagine the job of standing on a ladder with a pail of soapy water and a big soft brush trying to reach in and over the pipes to clean the ceiling. I actually managed half of the room each day of the two-day holiday. Now the pipes look even worse!

On day Three, I had the eager help of Taddit Frances, and some other senior boys to scrub the floor. It is wonderful to see how they enjoy the exercise it requires. Meanwhile I washed desks. In the afternoon Jimmy Husky oiled the floor and the boys "o'cedared" the desks

1. *Boys bring frozen reindeer meat from the ice cellar.*
2. *Boys get rabbits ready to cook.*
3. *Time to make the dough into loaves.*
4. *Kneading dough for rolls.*

carefully counting and dividing the sixty into 12s so that each did the same number.

We all tried to get some rest and recreation during the week. I enjoyed time in the kitchen to bake and visit. Our girls' supervisor confided in me that she'd be leaving and marrying George Chapman, local meteorologist. No surprise!

The sun gets warmer every day. Kitchen staff supply me with tins, every time a butter or coffee can is emptied so I can plant more seeds. One day the cat took advantage of the unclosed classroom door and dug up my nasturtiums. Fortunately those seeds are large so we retrieved them and replanted them. The entire staff are becoming interested in my "greenhouse."

While it was still very cold despite wearing layer upon layer of clothing, we took advantage of the noon time warmth to clean the Cathedral. The men had long handled brushes and did the ceilings. The women did what they could reach and especially the pews. I had a very interesting time washing the stained glass windows. One of the village children noted that, "Miss Mayee washed Jesus' face." A few  people kept busy emptying the pails of dirty water and bringing clean water from the hospital kitchen.

Right after Easter Rev. Dewdney came from Fort McPherson to stay for a while to write his Doctor of Divinity exams, with our local clergy invigilating. Next May they will do that for me as I write a University of Saskatchewan course in History, which I am studying.

School with the reduced student load is so much easier and the students seem to learn so much more readily this term. I felt well and full of energy until one day while out walking with Sutton we looked in at Dr. Livingstone's farm to photograph the cows. Then we looked to see the goats. It was a sad sight. Buttercup had jumped over the rail stall and hung herself on her rope. We could see that no one had been into the barn to care for the animals for several days. This was disturbing.

When we got back to the school the mail had arrived. There was an Overseas letter for me postmarked March 28. Instinctively I felt a shock, hid the letter in my pile of mail. Later, upstairs I concealed it in my cupboard. The letter stayed unopened for several days as the busy school activities postponed my facing the inevitable.

The warm sun caused the heavy load of frost above our ceilings to melt. We had drips everywhere and everywhere pans, basin, pails and sodden quilts. The west rooms were especially bad. Woodcock, our kitchen matron, even had a big bread pan on her bed. The constant dripping, its sound in the various pans caused me to jot down a little rhyme.

DRIPS

A drip applies to the Commission	drip! drip! drop!
Sent to this Aklavik Mission	drip! drip! drop!
So there are drips overhead	drip! drip! drop!
Willing to fall upon your bed	drip! drip! drop!
Basins, pans to catch a drip	drip! drip! drop!
Patchwork quilts to make a sop,	drip! drip! drop!
Am aroused from a dream	drip! drip! drop !
By a semi-smothered scream	drip! drip! drop !
A certain Fulton's daughter	drip! drip! drop !
Stepped in a pan of water,	drip ! drip ! drop !
Every room is very wet	drip! drip! drop !
But Mike's is the winner yet	drip! drip! drop!
Sutton with no place to walk	drip! drip! drop !
Merely giggles at Woodcock	drip! drip! drop!
Who sleeping midst a scene of woe	drip! drip! drop!
Has a basin balanced on her toe	drip! drip! drop!
Elkink's only real complaint	drip! drip! drop!
Is that drips mar new paint	drip! drip! drop!
Robin's room, it's quite a crime	drip! drip! drop!
After quilts all the time	drip! drip! drop!

Niven hardly seems to mind	drip! drip! drop!
But we know that love is blind	drip! drip! drop!
There's no time to sit and mull	drip! drip! drop!
For Dripping Time is never dull	drip! drip! drop !
Harrington's rhyme is true to fact	drip! drip! drop !
Of drip and drop there is no lack	drip! drip! drop!

Our life became even more complicated as the weather warmed even more. The ceilings upstairs were of donna conna, pressed fibre that absorbed moisture and swelled until each 4' X 8' panel sagged down in the middle. Rev. Gibson, foreseeing that the extra weight could pull the panels from their nailed edges got a very sharp poker and with a strong man holding a large bucket beneath, pierced the bulge to drain the water. Then we felt safer and could put our pans in more strategic places. None of us could have dreamed of this diversion from our school routine.

On the 11th of April some of the tomato seeds germinated. The days lengthened rapidly. The differences of climate and yearly changes were a novelty. It seemed the seeds grew and in "no" time had second leaves – almost miraculous. Mr. Gibson came to help transplant the crowded tins into flats.

My first calla lily unfurled into white loveliness and delicate fragrance. Everyone enjoyed the phenomenon, came to see and breathed the fragrance. Rosie Jane (the little girl who used to be so naughty) wrote in her book, "I like saints and smells." She meant, of course, "I like school and the flower's smell."

Mrs Hayward brought Helen and Jean to see the plant and to say "goodbye" as they are flying outside because Helen hasn't recovered from the 'flu symptoms.

Colder weather stopped the drips but it took a long time to dry the consequences. A quick requisition went out to the School Commission for ceiling repairs to come in on the very first boat. For many days the furnace room racks were shrouds of soggy quilts. After I did what I could to put my room in order, I went outside with my sketch book. A dog viciously attacking a frozen piece of caribou made a good model.

I think, almost unconsciously, I was seeking to conceal to myself what I must do, what I must know for sure, what was in that letter I had hidden. Mrs. Marsh called, "Come in. We're having soup." A delay which I really wanted. Elkink was there and we enjoyed a jolly evening.

I knew I was trying to avoid bad news by finding any excuse not to read that final message. I excused myself a dozen ways and kept inhumanly busy, dreaming and guilty, too. When Freeman Hunley, representing the HBC river shipping concerns, came to ask if we would help clean the SS Hearne Lake during the next few weeks, I never hesitated and replied, "Oh, yes" before I had even consulted any of the other staff. "We'll do it on our days off." Another delay.

One evening we had a very different and enjoyable Musicale, put on at the hospital, with Nurse Beach, an accomplished violinist and Rev. Dewdney, a trained organist, playing together for us. I could have listened forever!

There was a special power in that concert. I felt calm and relaxed, went home, closed my door, calmly took the letter from its hiding place and sat on the side of my bed. I didn't hesitate. I opened the letter. Maybe I read it. I knew what it said. I folded it, put it carefully into my diary and got ready for bed. Yes, the wall had tightly closed around that part of my life.

And just as tightly I pulled another wall around my personal past life, I thought, and dived forcefully into the present – my students, my present friends and associates and even my studies. I told no one.

Spring galloped ahead but still winter grasped and grabbed a bit of the weather. It echoed "me," I thought, then rushed off to tend the children, the plants, the wonderful side of life. T.B. was still rearing its ugly disease. My dear pupil, Marion had to be segregated in hospital. I had lost 4 before Christmas, now several more.

There were wonders to enjoy in the area around us. A plane brought fresh food for Peffer's restaurant so I took the children to see 3 bananas, 1 cucumber, 1 pineapple, and 1 tomato. I filled every moment of the days with activities, then, exhausted, I went to bed early and often slept.

When Mr. Gibson preached for Sunday's evening service he pointed out that thoughts make acts, acts make character – and as experiences build our thoughts, therefore we should guard our experiences. It was thoughtful and maybe just the path I was choosing.

*The first nine paintings photographed here are in the collection of
the Prince of Wales Northern Heritage Centre, Yellowknife, N.W.T.
All were painted by Mary Harrington using oil paints and a spatula.*

High Noon, Aklavik, Jan. 26, 1946

"10 to 11 a.m. Sunday" Aklavik, 1947

Idling Motors II, 1947

All Saints Anglican Cathedral, Aklavik, N.W.T. 1945

School Cabin, July 1946

Tuktoyaktuk, 1947

Last Trip to the Arctic for S.S. McKenzie River, Tuktoyaktuk, 1947

Bringing in a Beluga, Tuktoyaktuk, 1947

Susie Umoach Hangs Muktuk, Tuktoyaktuk, 1947

Winter Noons, Aklavit

1955   *Jan. 10, 1956*

SPRING INTO ACTION
– but a reluctant winter

I have moved across the hall to a warmer room. The other will be used for storage. The new location is above the staff sitting room. When visitors came after church I could usually hear the conversations even when up in my room as the grate in the floor was my source of warmth from below. On Sunday, the 23rd of April I heard Constable Storey reporting that the Russians had taken some suburbs of Berlin. At the school we seldom heard of events beyond Aklavik.

Another sign of spring: a dogteam pulling a toboggan with a canoe in the toboggan and the driver in the canoe. He'll have his canoe here in town when he needs it. That was what I saw from the window during a rare lull in a very cold blizzard. A forward-looking optimistic outlook!

Now that Mrs. Hayward is away, we take turns in cleaning the doctor's house. He and son, Robert, often eat with us and sometimes Robert stays over night. I was curious and learned how to manipulate some of the dental tools in the doctor's office. Actually he had little to work with. The drill was run by a foot pedal like the treadle on an old Singer sewing machine. Several times when the doctor was away I was able to help in emergencies. Once, with the help of his brother, I extracted a tooth for an injured Eskimo. I made sure he had some aspirin for pain killers before and that his brother would be there to help either to hold him down or pull. He was so grateful to lose that tooth. The same chap sent another patient, a woman to find me at the school. She had several huge cavities. I made an effort to fill an easy small one, but didn't attempt more. Using oil of cloves I daubed the large cavities and gave her some oil of cloves and cotton, hoping it would help.

On Friday evening near the end of April, Elkink and I began the work to clean the SS Hearne Lake as I had promised. We loaded a toboggan with 2 bed rolls, a towel, canvas running shoes, my camera, and dressed in ski pants and parka, we set out after supper. At 7:15 we

stopped at Hunley's and got some bread, cake, caribou steak and strapped them onto the toboggan (See map) We followed the trail past Pokiak, over the two little lakes and at 7:45 we came to the S.S. Hearne Lake.

First we went to the galley – a cold sight – thickly coated in ice and hoarfrost over two inches thick. Mr. Hunley started the range and we used butcher knives to cut the ice from the walls. He shovelled it out the hatch. There soon were many drips as the galley warmed. We really worked. By 10 p.m. we thawed and heated two cans of soup (Scotch broth and chicken noodle) ate a can of frosty cherries and had coffee. The crew must have had short notice that the last plane out was ready to go, as everything was as they left – things in the icebox, dishes in the sink, etc.

There was no frost in the Purser's Office so before he left, Hunley lit the fire in the heater and we used it for our bedroom – I in the lower berth, Elkink above. The wheel house was above us and all night as we twisted and turned we could hear the clock strike its bells.

We had agreed to rise at 8 so at 8 bells, I threw my pillow on the floor so Elkink could land on it. She soon had the fire crackling. The galley fire was out but Elkink soon lit it. By 8:45 we were trying to drink some half-thawed tomato juice but it tasted horrid so we threw it out. Then we ate a can of peaches and some bread and butter.

*Cleaning S.S. HearneLake
on our days off.*

Sutton, Elkink, Harrington

We began work by moving quantities of pans, spices, food in cans, boxes, etc. from the panty to the galley table. There was still some ice and frost in the galley so while we waited for the galley to warm up, we started on the pantry. It turned out to be much more difficult than we had anticipated. The ceiling and walls were coated in an oily grime which required careful scrubbing with Old Dutch Cleanser – every square inch. Being V-joint and bolted well onto 2 X4 beams it was complicated for sure.

Freeman Hunley came about 10. While we worked at the pantry he turned out the cook's room. The upper bunk was stacked sky-high with cereals, beans, chocolate, Lux soap, etc. And the squirrels, intruding, had played havoc!

At 1:30 we dined on caribou steaks, pork and beans, and canned pineapple. Then Sutton arrived. Elkink and I did the cook's room which wasn't very dirty. Sutton borrowed Hunley's extra overalls and began to work. When Fulton and the school boys came over we stopped and had a lunch.

By 8 that evening we called it a day and cooked supper – steak and onions, steak and kidneys, corn, cherries, blueberries – all from cans. We washed up and the four of us went home by 10 o'clock. We all helped Sutton get in the school washing from the outdoor lines and I went over to tell Gibsons we were home. And so began a busy but pleasant experience.

The whole community began to talk and speculate, "How can the ice be out in a month?"

May Only slightly warmer. We combine as many school activities as we can so that other things can be done. While I had all of the pupils for classes, the free staff housecleaned the living room. Community activities continued unabated. R.C.M.P. Inspector delivered the first lecture on St. John's First Aid on May 1.

May 2: Very bad news. Elkink heard that her X-ray wasn't very clear. A blow to us all. She and I did a big laundry and she was sent to bed early. Of all of us she had always seemed most well. A blizzard raged on the 3rd when I went with Elkink to see Dr. Hayward. He looked at me and without further comment, said, "You need sleep. Take these." Elkink was admitted to hospital after supper. I helped her get ready and went with her. To show we still could have fun, I timed her first jump into a hospital bed – 3 minutes to 7. The children said, "T.B. too bad." Now we say, "T.B. to bed."

I had to hurry to choir practice, then do our ironing but I had a heavy heart.

Now I definitely had all the students but they were also so fine, happy and helpful. I took time to mend Robert Hayward's pants and mark some books at noon. Our First Aid lesson was on bandages. I enjoyed these lectures.

V for Victory
– over war, not over winter or old emotions

May 7. A memorable day as we learned of the Victory in Europe. World War II is over. The armistice has been signed. I feel disbelief. I feel numb. Flags are flying, people talking eagerly and excited. But I, I am not feeling a thing.

The next day Fulton and Niven got up at 4 a.m. to go to Pauline's to hear her good short wave radio – Churchill speaking. King George spoke at 11. The R.C.M.P., Wireless, RCASC, Scouts, Cubs, Guides and Brownies followed by the civilians all paraded to church at 3 p.m. It was a very impressive, spectacular service. Mr. Gibson took the Scouts, Miss Niven the Cubs, Messes Sutton and Robinson the Guides, and I, Brown Owl, was so ridiculously proud of my bouncing Brownies, even though I felt that I wasn't really a part of it.

The Brownies, Scouts and other groups get ready at the school for the parade to the church.

We celebrate the end of the War.

We had a scheduled W.A. meeting in the evening in my classroom. Then at 9 p.m. the First Aid lecture was on Fractures.

The hospital has been on quarantine but Elkink has been sending me notes. She, for the first time, is not feeling well. I am fine again and so happy to be able to visit her in the evening before my 8:30 duty.

On May 10 I saw a sea gull and on the 13th an eider duck flew overhead.

eider

As the days went by, the sun shone sometimes, snow and wind interrupted and still we were hopeful. Rev. Gibson worked, when he had time, to fix the greenhouse. I visited Elkink every day. Various staff members worked in pairs on the S.S. Hearne Lake. It seemed as if nothing had happened here in Aklavik.

When I took the girls out for a walk we could only walk up and down on the high river bank where the boats are dry-docked for the winter because there is so much mud and water down town.

Elkink had many visitors and she tried to "clown" her misfortune in humour. I wished I could but I was secretive, my misfortune locked up.

The days were very long and the plants never stopped growing. I put the sweet peas out into the greenhouse and immediately the searching little tendrils twined around the wires. Down town when the sun shone we saw mud but also people – the R.C.M.P. painting a roof, Eric shirtless, Doug McNiece also painting, Inspector supervising the renovation of the S.S. Immaculata.

The hollow before the school was a veritable lake as water on both sides of the river ice rose higher and higher. Thinking a plane may come soon, I rushed to hospital to shampoo and set Elkink's hair. This was my sister's birthday so I took Elkink my chocolates as she was my nearest sister here. On May 17 we had blackbirds and robins. Nine ducks swam on the water

before the school. All day countless blatant gulls stormed the Aklavik winter's garbage collections. While watching white geese I saw a plover.

I have Elkink's clothes all washed up and ironed to be sure all is ready before she has to leave on the first plane out.

Last night a mouse ate some of my sweat pea plants. Mr. Gibson is seeding cabbage and cucumber.

Woodcock and I were cleaning the doctor's house when he arrived and wanted to hear about Aklavik news. I almost missed the 2:15 school bell. On Saturday, after morning duties I did some baking, worked in the greenhouse helping Mr. Gibson set out tomatoes, pansies, phlox, nasturtiums, marigolds. Spent the afternoon with Elkink.

On May 20 there were thousands of ducks and gulls stopped in transit on the ice before the school. Spring was a rapid, vibrant movie. The winter ice still lay unmoved while the water on both shores widened. Some travellers left their toboggans on the ice and paddled over to town to shop or even to bring the children to see the doctor. However, on the 22nd we heard that the ice had moved at Fort McPherson. Our break-up is imminent. I went to the Bay to finalize Elkink's business there.

On the 24th of May, a holiday, we took the children on a longed-for outing. We tramped through water, snow and mud northward and then on a higher river bank. It was a very "sticky" place but with the joy of freedom the children soon salvaged something to sit on, pieces of drift wood, some old cans and boards. Soon tea was made and we enjoyed the food that we had brought with us, cold spare ribs, bread with marmalade and cake. Then the trek back home where I had the Senior Womens' Auxiliary and a visit with Elkink. The First Aid lecture was on hydrophobia, snake bite and such emergencies. The entire Delta was electric with growing energy, it is hard to cut the 24 hours into the work/rest lots. Work and excitement, "spring" takes over from sleep. Anticipation and excitement lengthens with the sunlight.

<u>May 29.</u> When I slipped over to see Elkink at noon, Nurse Brooks said, "Stay only a minute," Elkink had had her left lung tapped. For

First Spring Picnic

her sake we hope the ice soon clears away and she can get out to begin her cure.

The First Aid lecture was on Artificial Respiration.

The Community was having a lottery on the ice moving out. Markers on the ice and markers on the shore were carefully watched. At 5:30 p.m. today, May 29, the ice moved.

The 30th was the most beautiful. Too nice to be in the classroom so after last recess I took my class outside to see a white-crowned sparrow's nest in a willow clump behind the school. It had four grey eggs. We observed other birds on the river bank and played "cat and mouse" on the road.

The last day of May saw Rev. Gibson helping me make a border around the children's dining room walls of paper bird silhouettes which I had prepared. Then a big event: Elkink was brought back to the school on a stone boat pulled by the little John Deere tractor. Now I can visit her often and she can at least hear the school activities.

<u>June 1.</u> A big snow storm. Cleaning floors at the doctor's house as many visits to the doctor's office had left muddy tracks in the hallway. Big news: Tommy Ross and Caroline Moses won the ice sweepstakes!. After our First Aid class we could

see that objects on the ice in front of the school had really moved. By morning the main ice had gone with only ice floe pieces and bits of debris floating by. By propping her up in bed, Elkink could watch the exciting event. Before the day had passed, George Roberts, with his bulldozer and the R.C. Brothers with their "Cat" had pushed the "Immaculata" into the water. At supper time, while we ate our supper in her room, I gave Elkink a "Charmette" permanent. We must be

Elkinks going-to-the-San party.

*Friends carried Elkink to the boat
and to a picnic across the river. On
the way back to Aklavik she was
allowed to see the prime activity of
the Delta - a rat being harrested.*

ready when the plane comes. After the main ice has gone, the Mackenzie carries an assortment of ice, fallen trees and various objects it has picked up on the flooded banks. It was not safe for planes yet.

June 5. A special day. I repacked Elkink's trunk and had her luggage ready. I went to the village to photograph Mrs. Martin's display of skinned muskrat carcasses hung to dry in the sun. The pupils were able to go with me out-of-doors to sketch, not wearing their winter parkas. About 5 p.m. Fulton told me the surprise: "we are going on a picnic." By 5:30 we were on our way: Constable Eric Jensen, Rev. and Mrs. Marsh and David, Elkink (by doctor's permission) and myself. The men carried Elkink and put her in the boat. We slowly travelled along and so that Elkink wouldn't completely miss Aklavik's' events one of the men shot a rat. We passed the S.S. Hearne Lake still waiting for her crew to fly in. Finally we had our supper on a high sunny bank. Everything was so perfect. The sun was still high when we got back at 9:40.

Boats came and went but still no planes came until June 9. We had 45 minutes to get Elkink ready. The little John Deere tractor pulled her on the stone boat to the river. All of the children came along. We were a bit early so were able to quickly look through the school mail and gave Elkink hers. Nearly the whole town was out to see the plane so she was able to see them all. It was a large C.P.A.. plane. They packed in a great many bales of fur, then Elkink and another lady. We watched until the plane was out of sight. I felt lost.

So far, I had buried myself in the present hours, slept only when I was extremely fatigued and so it was like a bolt from the sky when Mrs. Marsh told me that the doctor had told her my sad news and she was sorry. I looked at the doctor in disbelief. How did he know? He turned away and I hurried to my room. I had earnestly felt that if no one knew, I could handle myself better and save other friends their concern. I didn't want to share and now I supposed everyone knew.

A few days later I fainted as I got up from the table. I quickly revived but heard someone say, "She's had too much. How can she do it?" Stubbornly I ignored them and carried on with my work.

We were so pleased to have winter go and the sun welcomed us to be outside whenever we could, lunches and many of our classes were spent on two big board platforms near the school. On the 14th we watched the S.S. Hearne Lake leave for the south.

ALL DAY – NO NIGHT

Woodcock was now in hospital so I helped when I could in the kitchen. June 16 was Saturday so I made 14 pies, 20 tarts and some raisin twists with the pastry scraps. Every year we got 20-pound boxes of dried apples. Some of the girls helped me take out the bits of core from the leathery slices. We added water and left them over night. By morning the slices were swollen and soft, ready to pile into the pans of pastry with brown sugar. I added a shake of cinnamon to each pie, put on the covers, sealed the edges and entertained the helpers by piercing the tops with a knife point to make patterns. Meanwhile the big bread oven was heated and the pies and tarts went in to bake. Unlike our efforts to persuade the northern children to eat vegetables, sweet pies and cakes seemed no problem. Some of this baking was reserved for a big party we held for the people who were leaving Aklavik, their terms finished. I had no desire to join them. Aklavik was my refuge and I would stay.

From a letter I wrote on June 10, 1945:

Some days I wonder, "Where in the whole world could it be this cold in June?" Then sometimes we have such a nice day, most wonderful in the world, I'm sure, for it is 24 hours of sunshine and warmth.

I have often had the whole school lately. Mr. Gibson is so busy. He was trying to plow the garden then he wrenched his back. He is one of those people whose enthusiasm exceeds his strength. When something needs doing, he does it, and quietly.

I am pleased to hear that my supply orders including the art supplies have been safely packed. I hope to paint much more this year. Thank you for the gladioli bulbs. I will plant them tomorrow with a ruler beside each so that I can chart their daily growth. The greenhouse is becoming a jungle. I have one Jerusalem Cherry with its second leaves. Also tell my sister that I planted the spider plant seeds on March 31 and this week two have come up.

We live in perpetual sunshine (June 1 to July 11) if the sky isn't cloudy. It is really very interesting. I have only one complaint – that one

cannot keep on going from dawn to dark. I never get tired and always hate to go to sleep while the sun is so bright. It is during the night hours that the Delta comes to life.

An excerpt from a letter written on the night of June 22, 1945:

I am on the very top of the Cathedral tower, sitting down as I feel safer that way. Misses Fulton, Niven, Coates and Archdeacon Marsh are also up here. We're taking snaps of the Midnight Sun. We set our cameras on a level and undisturbed place looking north, click the shutter every ten minutes for 1 1/2 hours before midnight and 1 1/2 hours after. I have Gibson's camera as well as my own. Altogether there are eight cameras. The sky is clear and blue, so close I feel 'in it'. There is a chilly wind and we are huddled in our parkas or heavy coats. I write a few lines in every ten minute interval.

When I look around I see the river, the Mackenzie (West Branch) circling us like a huge bend of blue taffeta ribbon. There's green grass and tiny dime-sized leaves on the poplar trees in the church yard. (I'm not sure but I think these trees are the farthest north in the Delta.) In the distance are the purple and white mountains. All along the river bank the white schooners are anchored.

Right at 12 midnight the sun seemed to almost touch the distant tree tops. Now at 12:30 it has started up again. During the entire night it has shone brightly on everything . . . I hope that after these 3 hours of careful watching I will have an interesting picture to show you.

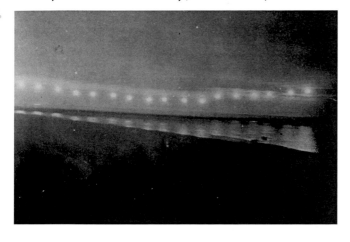

*Homemade ice cream
cones at 2/25¢ were most
popular.*

*I entered the womens'
pie eating contest.*

June 23 - 1945 Aklavik Sports Day

It was 10 past 3 when we got home from the church tower. It is at least 3 years since I was up so late!

Before we went on the above adventure to "spy" on the sun, Mr. Gibson and I transplanted cabbage plants from our little greenhouse to the garden plot near his house. We did 24 cauliflower plants, hoping our experimenting will bring some rewards. Back in the kitchen we helped slice and butter between 90 and 100 loaves of bread.

Tomorrow will be "July 1 Sports Day."

From a hectographic letter to relatives in the south:

Usually by the first of July many of the people, who hurried in to Aklavik when "ratting" closed on June 15, are already leaving again, particularly the Eskimo who leave for the white whale hunt. Hence the local Red Cross members decided to hold the annual Dominion Day Sports earlier so that more people could take part. The men declared a civic holiday for Saturday, June 23.

Preparation began. Food — bread, cake, pies, and three reindeer had to be cooked, gallons of ice cream were made from dried and canned milk. Every white woman was busy. The sports committee, Constable Carey and Mike Koziak, prepared a program and collected $200 for cash prizes.

The day was warm and sunny. By eleven o'clock people began to gather around the booths erected on the flat between the oil tanks and Douglas' store. Our school children took their lunch to the grounds.

In the booths we were soon busy selling plate dinners. On each plate we put generous slices of roast reindeer, two slices of bread and butter, a piece of pie and two pieces of cake. Tea was added making the meal for One Dollar. We sold several hundred.

At the same time in another booth root beer and ice cream were sold. The root beer was very active and many of the young boys bought it to delight in its effervescence.

In yet another booth Miss Coates and Miss Sutton sold tickets on a quilt and draws from a fish pond. The latter appeals with its element of surprise and is most popular.

Meanwhile, from the tents along the river shore to the north, and the bend to the west, the Pokiak settlement and the Hudson's Bay Creek encampments, as well as the village dwellings people came in hundreds — probably 800.

  To see that crowd was inspiring! The Eskimo of the delta, the Alaska Eskimo, the Loucheux Indians, the white people representing nearly every nationality, and the large number of people, especially children, who are a mixture of native and white, intermingled. There were the Roman Catholic Sisters in their crisp garb, other white women in a variety of slack suits and summer dresses, native women in Mother Hubbards of gay print, or parkas of luxurious fur, Bishop Flemming in his usual clerical attire, semi-native people in semi-native clothes. The children in new "store" clothes, were all grubby with ice cream and dust. Babies supported hazardously by beaded bands to their mothers' backs; Babies beneath the mother's parka, held up by a tapsy (a wide sash) and making a bump on her back; Babies in arms; Babies in baby carriages. How they all contrasted, but yet how similar they were. Everyone seemed happy, and nowhere could you have found a pleasanter crowd. "A smile is the key to happiness" and indeed these people prove the truth . You look about, see smiles and smile.

The sports went on intermittently. There were races for various age groups. Prizes were Three dollars, Two dollars and One dollar. Most interesting were the contests. In the first one about twelve men lined up on a platform and were instructed to eat two dry hard tack biscuits, then whistle. Their faces were comical as they hastily tried to swallow the dry food then screw up their mouths to whistle.

I entered the next contest. Along with Eskimo and Loucheux women. I was instructed to eat a piece of pie, then whistle or sing. My portion was a fifth of an apple pie. At "Go" I took a big bite — too big, for I was still masticating it when an Eskimo woman near me whistled!

There were tug-of-wars for men and for women, then a less popular softball game completed the events.

We reaped joy and good fellowship at the same time realizing over nine Hundred Dollars for the Red Cross.

Some of the young people danced in the evening, but we were glad to put the children to bed and find respite to open our letters which had just arrived.

There was a week left for school classes. The children had nearly all returned from ratting. I had 64 in the morning and the others in the afternoon. With Elkink away, and Mr. Gibson too busy and with a very bad back, I was really busy too. I helped all I could with the plants. It was truly amazing to see how quickly they grew in continual light.

I don't know what July will mean for me. There are no classroom classes so I guess I will have various duties. There are ten or more children to whom the school is a home. They may be orphans or for various reasons their parents can't come so we "mother" them. I am hoping to get a look at the Arctic Sea and especially Tuktoyaktuk. I am hoping to paint, too. This part of Canada is so wonder full.

A VERY DIFFERENT SUMMER

July 22, 1945. As expected, I've had a great many varied tasks, all of them interesting. Whenever there's an opportunity we try to give one another some time off. We have a little cabin out along a small creek on the other side of the river. We can pack a lunch or supper, canoe across and relax. There's a little stove made from a small oil drum, a bunk, some old dishes, a cooking pot and odds and ends. It's the "school  cabin." The hospital staff also have one in the other direction. Often we take the "permanent" children. They really enjoy gathering wood, getting the fire going and being 'like home.' Light is no problem as the sun is always up.

We've had only one rainy day. How things grow! Only a few days after we planted radish seed we ate radishes. The peas are in bloom. It seems there's no way to define a Delta summer as it seems each one is a surprise.

On July First I had the joy of picking the first sweet pea. I started the seeds in the classroom and now they're climbing about in the greenhouse. I sent the first bouquet to the hospital as they are entertaining Bishop and Mrs. Fleming. I've been able to share these delicate flowers with most of the town. I also have double nasturtiums, vividly beautiful. Many other flowers are blooming: mallows, linaria, lovely schizanthus, but the balsam and petunia aren't quite ready. I'd like to try some perennial onions and some phlox – the Bouncing Betty kind, it's hard to kill on the prairie.

The S.S. Distributor has been to Aklavik this month. Our little John Deere tractor has been busy chugging up and down from the river bank to the hospital or school with huge quantities of freight. Not long after it arrived someone said they had seen a huge box with my name on it.

The box is now in my room. Everyone is admiring my Dad's carpentry. Mr. Gibson brought a claw hammer and a screw driver and took the lid off.

The opening of the box is a sort of 'family' party here. Everything in my box is just perfect as my parents are so careful and generous. Actually I feel wealthy as the twelve cans of fruit juice are more than anyone else got! With all the art supplies and writing paper and envelopes I wasn't really surprised to see a label stuck on my door, "King's Printer." (One of the staff found a broken jar of pickles in her box.)

The last word from Elkink was that her parents moved her from Edmonton to care for her at home until they have a vacancy in a Saskatchewan sanatorium.

Try as hard as I could I couldn't hide the trouble I was having with internal pains. Each attack was worse and so sudden and sharp there was no use denying that something was wrong. The urine test showed kidney hemorrhage. The doctor said I'd have to get to the hospital in Edmonton. By then I was not resisting, the symptoms were all I could handle.

From my notebook: It was 1:15 p.m. on Friday July 27 when we whirred out on the R.C.A.F. 245 that had been diverted to Aklavik to pick me up. The pilot, co-pilot and I, out on the river – away from the Aklavik mud – leaving Sutton Woodcock, Rev. Gibson and Dr. and Mrs Hayward and children, huddling in the rain. It was pouring, like my shattered ego. We lifted easily and gradually. Aklavik was dripping – one huge drippy canvas on my easel of life.

We circled and headed south. I reclined and settled in a lying position on sleeping bags to soften my lot on the floor. I closed my eyes and told myself, "that's it. Relax. take what comes." Between severe back spasms I sat up and looked down. We flew in a stormy sky – blue, black and terrific. Rain and hail lashed the panes of the plane and pain stabbed my back so that I had to lie down and bear what I had to. Then I'd loath the thought of the lemon pie which Woodcock in her kindness had begged me to eat before I left. That pie! And I'd reach for the little box Sutton, also kind, had thrown in, just in case! once I looked to see two beautiful rainbows and was amazed when at 3:40 we lowered to land at Norman Wells. It wasn't raining.

A truck met us. Some men took me to the hospital and I was shown in to meet Dr. MacKinnon. He was stern as he gravely asked, "Where do you come from? Whom do you work for? Another teacher just came out also – something funny about that!" and he continued writing on a form on his desk and read Dr. Hayward's letter.

I was as near frightened as I could ever be – he was a Major! See his pips! He wasn't a doctor who had been at Pangnirtung? Or was he?

They put me to bed in a huge pair of men's pyjamas, after all this was a military unit and patients were usually men. The bed was so good. I felt so tired and floated off and on again to try to remember. A nurse came, a Mrs. Price, very understanding, no one could have been nicer. It seemed almost instantly Mrs. MacKinnon came to see me and I was offered orange juice, oranges and a huge supper tray to 'glance' at.

The three male patients unknowingly serenaded with their gramophone. Dr. MacKinnon proved very approachable but if anyone were to tell him so I can imagine he'd just grunt. He explained that he couldn't "wrangle" the R.C.A.F. to take me farther as there was a commercial CPA flight scheduled. The CPA agent came in ("Canute") and said, "now I'm not saying a thing but an RCAF flight is leaving shortly."

I was so very grateful. Dr. MacKinnon investigated and found that the army plane was going to be stopping at every point. So the $200 they wished to save me would be charged to the CPA. I was too weary to try to understand but I knew they were trying to help a poor sick (and penniless) person.

The next day at noon Dr. KcKinnon took me by ambulance to the airport and thence to the staff house to wait. There I had opportune time to watch the pilots eat and wonder about a woman called Minnie who was flying out, too. She was Canute's wife and going to see her 16-year -old blind son.

Finally we left, 3 women, Mrs. Pennyfeather, Minnie and I, and ten men, all young men leaving the 'Wells after a year or so. A space was made for me to lie down. I read an Omnibook and studied the other passengers. They were a congenial group, laughing and grasping their throats each time the plane bumped. And it was rough.

We flew at 175 mph – often higher than 12,000 feet to try to avoid the storm clouds. Through rain, hail and clouds, we sailed through flashes of brilliant sunshine.

St. John, B.C. The pilot said, "You all have to get out while we gas up, maybe 30 minutes." Two other silver "birds" were parked by us. We went to the depot, visited the washrooms and waited. I saw things I hadn't seen for over a year: a cultivated hedge, a lawn, a team of horses!

As we took off I saw a scattering of buildings like a village. There were farms all about bordered by trees like lace.

The visibility became poor again but the atmosphere became a striking visual show. Sun like shell fire shot into the plane from a background of rain, misty clouds, darkness, thunder and lightning. We saw a remarkable sight – two brilliant rainbows, one within the other, of intense hues with blue clouds beneath them. Even the men gazed spellbound.

We flew low and hurried to fasten our safety belts when we circled to land. Some passengers, nervous of the storm, were alarmed. A forced landing? Could it be Edmonton? It was.

It was 9 p.m. in Edmonton. Through pouring rain we hurried to the depot. Several bright bits of wives or girl friends waited there. When one lad from Calgary who was kindly helping me laughed, "Look at Paul!" [Paul was one of the men who had grown an immense beard during his year in the North.] I replied, "but don't laugh!" We all smiled as Paul's wife found him in the crowd.

The Calgary lad was met by his brother who had a car. They offered to take Mr. & Mrs. Paul and myself to our destinations.

It was exciting driving through the brilliance of a city even in the rain. They left me at a hospital.

I went in. A petite Sister was behind the desk. She calmly eyed me. I told her my purpose and gave her the letter to Dr. Davison. Seeing that I was exhausted she led me to a small waiting room . . . I lay on the lounge for what seemed a long time drifting in and out of sleep when my eyes opened and I looked around – a Crucifix! I must me in the Misericordia – or some place. Such a mix-up. I was too tired to panic. Finally a nurse came in. "We can't take you – you see, T.B. patients all go through Dr. Davison's Clinic and Dr. Baker gets permission for them to enter the San."

I blurted, "But I don't have T.B. . . .

Then I heard part of a conversation coming from the hallway. The voice of the little Sister: "But we can't send her away. It's 10 p.m. It's raining. And she is sick."

So I became #127.

Finally, I can drift away and rest.

Not so. A perky young red-headed intern appeared with pen and note board. I wished he'd go away. But he kept up a barrage of questions. On the fifth time he asked, "You are pregnant?" I tried to laugh. "Now don't go getting convulsions" he added. His examination was probably meaningless, a student assignment, and fortunately I never saw him again.

I was turned over to the care of a Kidney Specialist, Dr. Conroy, a welcome change.

The following weeks passed a day at a time. War was over but not over in the Pacific. Medical staff was still short-handed but I received gentle, efficient care, test after test, treatments, cystoscopies and I thought I was much better. The nurse said, "No, you weigh only 81 pounds and there's infection somewhere."

That symptom led to much more investigation. I was helped up off the bed but unless held I had no sense of balance. The black and white checked floor tiles seemed to float up. I noticed that unless very close to the nurses, I couldn't hear them. The hospital seemed uncannily silent. Instead of improving each day, things got more complicated. My left side got stiff and ached.

Finally another verdict, "You have polio, Miss Harrington," the nurse wrote on my note pad. Not being able to hear made things hard. A new doctor brought a medical brochure for me to read.

I determined I'd still defeat the problems and would pull myself around the bed to keep my legs moving. I was just skin and bones and I determined to eat my meals. I did every exercise I could think of to keep moving, although I could scarcely breath. I think I had a moderate case of polio. The nurses were so kind and I'm sure they must have put some sleeping medication into my evening meal.   I slept better.   I could focus my eyes on the only thing I could see from my window – the end of a lilac shoot against the red brick wall.

August 7, 1945 St. Mary's Ward

There is a wall and some lilacs
Just round green leaves that grow;
And iron steps throw shadows
Across the dark brown bricks in row.

I stretch and yet I see no more,
The pattern is so plain;
There, it is gone and I must wait
'Til sunshine comes again.

They bloom again
The lilacs by the old brick wall
Deep golden blooms
Tho' it were fall.

The iron steps ascend
And yet ascend again
Shadow steps for busy fairies
Dancing, leaving this terrain.

Nothing else — a brick wall,
Some steps and lilac leaves
Ordinary, commonplace, a refrain
Stories the sunbeams tell again.

One nurse was especially devoted to my care.   She was on leave from a Moravian mission in Labrador, staying in Edmonton with her mother.   On her time off she came to write on my note book, telling me about her work, and then helping with my self-imposed physical therapy.   One afternoon she came on duty early to bring me some sweet peas from her mother's garden.

I had a lot to think about.   My family didn't know that I wasn't in Aklavik.   Now what am I going to do?   The doctor said, "We'll have to decide next week."   I hoped I was better, a slight bit, sometimes I heard some noise.   The auditory technician frequently came to test. My nurse wrote, "Deafness isn't a part of polio!"

Before the week was up I had made up my mind.   I would get better.   I would make it somehow.   I couldn't go home.   I couldn't even get there.   I would go back to the School.   I could help in some ways.

My nurse helped me send a letter to Mr. Gibson telling him I'd get back by the first of 'September. I wrote to my parents and my nurse mailed the letters. I didn't mention any details to my parents except to say that I had good care and was much better. I was. I could look in the direction of a sound. I could walk if I had someone or something to hang on to.

It was late in August and several of the doctors came in with my nurse. She had a small blackboard and some chalk to write their conversations. I read that they couldn't help more. I would need a wheelchair. I would need care and '"We'll see what can be done. Don't worry." I asked about my bills. I knew the School had no insurance. "We'll figure that out tomorrow," and they left.

August 26, 1945. A letter came for Miss M. Harrington. "A plane leaving tomorrow morning for Norman Wells, 8 a.m.."

Now that the time had come, I had my first doubts that my decision was right. Could I? About the time I was most fearful, my faithful Moravian appeared. She wrote, "It's my day off. I'm getting you ready." And she did. She found answers, "The hospital will send your bill in the mail. Doctor Conroy will see you later." Later she made sure I ate a good dinner and after I was tucked in she wrote that she would see me in the morning. I slept well.

Sure enough when I had my breakfast very early she was there. She dressed me in my own clothes that I had come in, all fresh and clean. I had been well dressed for the flight so I had some heavy melton cloth slacks with wide elastic bands at the ankle. She pulled them over my long legged under pants, then I was surprised at what came next. She pulled things from the bag she had brought – cucumbers, tomatoes, apples and put them in the legs of the pants! She knew they would be kept from freezing there.

Almost before I knew it, I was in a taxi headed for the airport. Suddenly I remembered – Money? I had no money. The taxi man shook his head. Had the nurse paid for me?

At the airport I was soon helped into the plane. They already had my ticket. All I could do was smile wanly. Such kind people.

At Norman Wells I was helped out and realized that one of my helpers was Knut Lang, a trapper living near Aklavik, and also returning. I had met him and realized that he was a very shy Danish bachelor, much respected in the community.

A little truck took us to the Staff House as no plane could fly to the Delta where there was a snow storm. A cheerful little lady was the housekeeper at the Staff House. She was used to taking care of any people stranded in their journeys to the north. She fed them well – provided cots and cupboards for the men, mostly pilots, in the upstairs. I had a small place downstairs and was soon resting.

We couldn't fly the next day, either. I so wished I could hear but she seemed to know my disabilities. I wished I could help her. Finally she came down stairs with a box of socks, some balls of yarn, scissors and needles. She wrote: "They have holes. Men, they get holes in socks , throw them out. I wash and dry for time to mend." Well, I could darn socks and I did with short spells of energy most of the day.

The next day was much the same. However the weather was clearing. Maybe tomorrow. Apparently there was a smaller plane that might be able to fly Mr. Lang and me to Aklavik if there wasn't' too much of a load.

August 29. The kind housekeeper refused any of the fresh food I had in my pant legs. She helped me dress and I could tell she said affectionate things which I couldn't hear. Mr. Lang took my case and held my arm to help me get in the truck and to the plane. There we had to be weighed. He weighed exactly three times what I did. But there was space for us both. The pilot picked me up and handed me from the pontoon to his mechanic in the plane. Mr. Lang very kindly put a jacket he was carrying around me.

I had very warm greetings at Aklavik and since there was a good snow covering, I was pulled on a toboggan to the school. I am sure it was shocking to see me, so thin and unable to hear or stand. I could only guess what my fellow workers must have thought!

BACK TO SCHOOL!

Letter to my parents, September 16, 1945.

Some mail came in on a chartered plane so I had your August 19 letter early. You didn't know then that I had been sick. This mail which is to leave next week will probably be our last until the ice is hard — late in November.

I am well enough to do my classroom work and, as usual, find great joy in it — perhaps even more pleasure than usual for I so nearly didn't get back. I am so thankful to be here and to find my new class of little ones, mostly Eskimo, with happy faces, all eager to "do school."

There are 25 beginners so far. Very few Loucheux are beginning as they expect to build a new school at Fort McPherson next year. They are enthusiastic about it and are continually giving money for that purpose. They claim that for them from up the river this delta area is very unhealthy. It is damp and cloudy here so often, perhaps they are right. However, there is more T.B. at Fort Good Hope than in any other place in Canada and it is even farther up river.

Thank you for the larkspur seed. I shall plant half of it outside and keep the other half for cans next spring.

I was amazed to see the garden when I returned from Edmonton. Seeds were just sprouting when I left 5 weeks before, but when I returned lettuce, kale, parsley, chard, beet tops and other greens are being used. The cabbage plants we nurtured in the classroom produced about 30 cabbages — hard and firm, as big as our head. That is all, except 4 small pails of potatoes about like spools and marbles, mostly marbles. In the greenhouse there are about a dozen green tomatoes and one marrow.

I was sorry to learn that your hopes for a good crop had been blasted by drought . . .

The leaves got pretty here this fall — all shades of yellow with an odd red one on the lower bushes. They are all gone now. Nearly every day since I got back (Aug. 29) we have some rain and snow. The rain, so far, dissolves the snow and we have M U D — all except the mountains which stay lovely in whiteness.

There are many new people in Aklavik — the HBC manager and his wife, the R.C.M.P. Inspector and his wife, a corporal and his wife, constables, RCCS men, etc. So far I haven't met any of them. I have been devoting my time to things in the school..

In my classroom I have a regular Plant Conservatory. The seeds you sent have developed so nicely. One, Thumbergia alata [canary-eye vine], is climbing all over. However, as the days shorten I expect the annuals will slow down and die.

I have had the entire classes so far (76) But Rev. Gibson expects he can start helping with the senior pupils tomorrow. I have enjoyed their lessons after the busy primary work.

The W.A. and Brownies are in my charge again.

I have been reading the book, "Madam Curé." Like she did, I'll end my letter saying, "I embrace you tenderly."

Mary.

P.S. I wonder if I could borrow 4 or 5 stamps? I do not know how my bank account [in Conquest, Saskatchewan] is (or if its is!)

Meanwhile life's changes for me personally became routine as I carried on with my classroom and whatever else I could. Rev. Gibson put his ingenuity to work in building a mobile desk/walker that enabled me to get around unaided anywhere on the ground floor of the school, despite my lack of balance. The care and thoughtfulness of my fellow workers couldn't have been more kind. And the children – they were extremely sympathetic, especially the

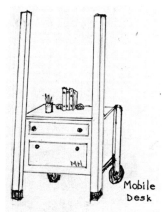

Mobile Desk

older girls who vied to walk, one on each side of me, and hold my arms firmly. Maybe it was because I was concentrating on lip reading in my teaching of English pronunciation that I felt I was hearing a little.

At the same time I am sometimes over-powered by a huge wave – a crushing dark wall of grief. Perhaps I am not completely occupied by daily occurrences, it sweeps over me. I am lonely. I am alone. Of course, it is self-pity – this is to be my life. I can no longer look forward to the planned future, sharing a life as all normal people seek. But self pity? Well, it can be fought – get busy, I thought, get busier. Think of others.

November started off with the sun shining briefly above the southern horizon. It was a crisp, beautiful day. The amaryllis in the classroom has a swelling pink bud. With my new resolve to prompt me, I offered some help when I saw Mr. Gibson going about looking fatigued after being up all night taking John Doe's night watch responsibilities on top of his own (John Doe had gone off on a hunting expedition).

Woodcock asked if I'd go for a walk with her. I went up the stairs on all fours and got warmer clothes. We met Bill Vehus who had just averted a real emergency by getting the power plant at the hospital working again. We went up the little path to where Mr. Hayward, the doctor's father, was working on the new Mission Laundry building. Then we met Mr. Campbell whom I was so glad to see. The walk was so good for me and Woodcock said, "Thanks for coming with me!"

At recess I was glad to see Mrs. Hayward and Helen. They had brought the R.C.M.P. Inspector's wife, Mrs. Kirk, to see us.

That evening we went to see the Gibson's new baby, Linda, a little doll. We told the Gibsons about the Community Hallowe'en party. I had gone to the party as a shabby old reprobate and had been attacked on the street by a real "reprobate." Luckily I wasn't alone, was rescued by a witch and a fairy and provided all with some good laughs.

Ice cutting on the river is the village harvest. The ice, at 12 inches, is the perfect thickness.

We had a Hallowe'en party for the children. They really delighted in pretending, believing in super non-natural things. The staff helped each one to have a costume. The staff also appeared – Sutton was a witch, Fulton a negress, Robinson was Bo-Peep, Woodcock, Williams and I were a family. After the children played games and pretended they needed to guess who we were, we went to the hospital to visit the patients. Jimmy Husky, a patient, said something to me which Woodcock wrote on my slate: "I dress up too. I be a sick man."

The children had a party supper: buns, cookies, ice cream and jelly with orangeade to drink.

After supper, Rev. Marsh came and pleased everyone by showing Miss Robinson's coloured Kodachromes, the first time many of us had seen coloured slides.
One Saturday Sutton, Powell (hospital Head Nurse) and Mrs. Hayward asked me if I would go to our Cabin. It would be my first trip there and although we were dressed in cumbersome parkas, we were not cold. The snow was hard enough on the river that we could walk on top and I had support on both sides. Coming to the trail through the willows to the cabin, Sutton and Hayward carried the bags of food and Miss Powell pulled me on the toboggan. Cooking was slow but gathering sticks and getting the little barrel stove warmed up was part of the party. It was all fun. I stoked the fire. We had tomato juice, cooked some bacon, warmed up cooked potatoes, had muffins and an orange which was still a treat from our boat supplies.

When we got home we were immediately met with an ominous sign:

**"Be Careful of lights,
both engines stopped,
ours frozen."**

This was a serious problem in such a big building and daylight so short. We were all armed with candles and flashlights but the danger of fire was ever on our caution list.

I really hadn't need of my serious resolutions to keep busy. It was time to prepare for Christmas – our letters to go out on a plane, if one came; our Christmas concerts for all; our thousands of donuts and gingerbread cakes to be made and frozen; invitations out for dinners; the Brownies and Girls Aid all demanding seasonal programs; everyone needing more recreation, play Monopoly, sing, etc.

At the Loucheux W.A. in the library at Marsh's house we had a beautiful evening by candle-light. Beside Rev. Marsh and Mrs. Marsh, Susie and Mrs. Husky, Vivian and Gladys Koe, Mrs. Carmichael, Charlotte Vehus, Ruth and Mrs Greenland, Julia Edwards, there were Williams (the hospital kitchen supervisor) and I who took the cake.

Sometimes, if it's not too cold, I "escape" to my classroom. The Amaryllis blooms gorgeously and the Morning Glory still produces delicate and sky-purple blossoms. Beside my Christmas letter I am working on a real Northern Primer. I need material that really belongs in the Arctic – not like "Dick and Jane" in their far-away "outside" place. So, page by page, I use my hectographs and the beginners are building up their own books, so proud that they can read each page.

Our Book

see airplane
go up

Jim works

We learn to talk,
We learn to write,
We learn to read
English.

Aklavik, N.W.T.
1945···· MH.

Jim

Anna

dog

Top Left: Kitchen Break (The Bread is Rising)
Top Right: Rub a dub - three boys in a tub
Middle: A Tidy Dormitory
Bottom Left: Eric and Fred out "Ratting" in March
Bottom Right: Wash up for Juniors

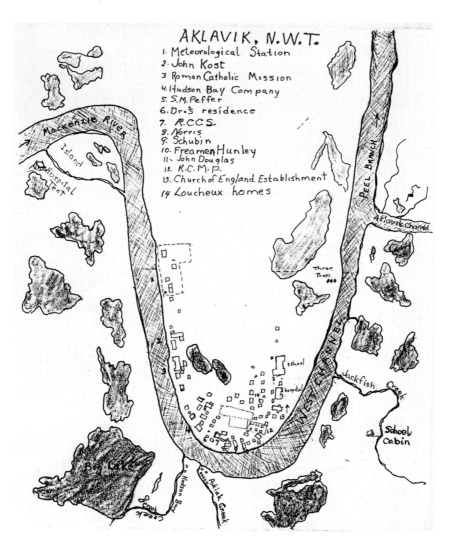

AKLAVIK, N.W.T.

1. Meteorological Station
2. John Kost
3. Roman Catholic Mission
4. Hudson Bay Company
5. S.M. Peffer
6. Dr.'s residence
7. R.C.C.S.
8. Norris
9. Schubin
10. Freamen Hunley
11. John Douglas
12. R.C.M.P.
13. Church of England Establishment
14. Loucheux homes

In the early history of fur trading in the Delta the coastal Eskimo travelled far inland to trade at Fort McPherson. There they were enemies of the Loucheux Indians. Consequently, when a trader set up only 69 miles by water from the coast they stopped there on the west branch of the MacKenzie River. "Aklavik" they called it – they had seen "brown bears there"

A HECTOGRAPHIC LETTER TO FRIENDS

Aklavik, N.W.T.
November, 1945.

Dear Friends

     The latest local news is that the spruce branches are laid out on the new river ice to make an airplane runway. That means it's time to prepare a Christmas letter.

     I shall tell you about Aklavik. Its size and components usually surprise newcomers. I know I was surprised particularly to see everything look so attractive and well painted.

     I drew this map from a small aerial photograph to show you how Aklavik is built within one of the countless bows of the West Channel of the Peel River, a tributary to the Mackenzie River. The entire surrounding area is a mass of lakes, creeks and low lands which nurture spruce, willows, alders and a few birch trees, all of which are diminutive reminders of their relatives farther south.

     The placement of the buildings may not be entirely accurate but I hope to give you an approximate impression.

     Arriving downstream by boat you start at the left of the diagram where the hospital staff have their tent. It is a picturesque spot with a splendid view to the mountains and affords a pleasant place for leisure time.

     The first buildings are what has been called "the Farm" but are fast becoming the "Met Station." Dr. Livingstone, a formerly resident doctor, built a barn and other buildings comprising a farm. Since his departure a year ago the value of such an enterprise at this latitude has been doubted and left to neglect. An out-of-town man has rented the second cow and has the goats. The last cow has been eaten. The barn has been sold intact. Government carpenters are presently erecting buildings for the new meteorological station. We are kept in close intelligence of this transition by our last year's Girls' Supervisor, Miss Niven, who married the head meteorologist.

     The buildings of John Kost come next. One is a striking old log hotel. I expect it is the only structure of its type down here. When Mrs. Kost and her brother were also here they ran it as a hotel, restaurant and store. Now only the store (trading post) is in business.

Next comes the Roman Catholic School, Hospital and Brothers' House. The school had about 60 pupils last year. The Hospital has fifteen beds.

The Hudson's Bay Company comes next. Their buildings, look immaculate with white walls and red rooves. One house was new a year and a half ago. The manager, Mr. McLeod, his wife and small son, Mr. Simpson, his wife and son, and other clerks comprise the staff.

The street that turns northward from the Bay is called "Main Street." The General Store and Hotel of Stan Peffer are built along it. Peffers have the only truck in town but it can run very little in the summer because of mud and little in the spring as then there is no need for it, in fact when it could run in the winter it doesn't have any need either. Peffer's Hotel is the centre of our Community activity. It is there one can get a meal for $1.00, see a very old film for $1.00, or dance for nothing. I saw "49th Parallel" recently. It was in 3 or 4 reels and went off regularly despite good sound effects . . . but the Mickey Mouse reel just never got finished. Some of the white people and many of the natives gather to dance in the evenings. The dance steps, I believe, would be called "Oldtime" outside. The staff at Peffer's is made up of a little round cook, two white waitresses, one member of the large Eskimo family of Kagliks and other native help. (By the way, a good dishwasher can earn $110 a month.)

The other side of Main Street has only some of the Royal Canadian Corps of Signals' power houses except at the corner where Dr. Hayward, his wife and three children reside.

Passing farther along "'River Street Drive" the R.C.C.S. buildings are next. They have had Canadian Army Engineers in for two successive years constructing two fine homes and modernizing things generally. At present they are remodelling the large radio room.

Norris, a white trapper lives next and while in town his family serves meals.

The adjoining building with warehouse behind is Schun's store. Mrs. Roberts manages it. Mr. Schun also has stores elsewhere in the north. It is a very busy place when the Eskimo come in to Aklavik. Mr. Roberts has a caterpillar tractor which he uses for jobs hauling wood, etc.

Freeman and Annie Hunley live next where they have a restaurant.

Annie, a great cook, also sells bread and other home baking.

Neighbouring is the house of Pauline and Doug McNiece. They have a new baby this year.

The next rectangle on the map is John Douglas' store where Doug is the clerk and manages the Post Office there, too. There's a real kayak hanging up on the front wall above the door.

The compound with 7 small buildings is the R.C.M.P. headquarters. In the enclosure behind, their dogs are kennelled.

The large fenced area beside the R.C.M.P. yard is the place allotted for Protestant graves.

All of the buildings from there northward, facing the river, are of the Church of England. From the south to north they are: Mission House (Archdeacon Marsh, Mrs. Marsh and their 3 children), All Saints' Cathedral, All Saints' Hospital (three nurses, a nurse-aid and native help), the new laundry, the Principal's residence and All Saint's School.

The buildings behind are chiefly dwellings of the Loucheux people which they use when they are in town. Some of the new ones are frame but the majority are log and are being mudded up now for the winter.

North of the school, "Grover," an Eskimo helper at the school lives. He has a quaint little shack that looks as if it were made from packing boxes.

The farthest north is the pretty cottage of Mr. & Mrs. Rawlings, former school employees, now trapping and working locally.

Every year Aklavik changes greatly. Few of the white people, excepting those married to native women are permanent residents. The rest of us are here for varied terms. Thus each fall finds some old citizens missing and some new ones added. Altogether it is a neighbourly, congenial place to live — an opinion agreed to by all.

On my map I have marked a few other places of local interest. If you walk north from the school over the trail through the willows you pass by the "tin can dump" and finally come to "Three Trees" — a terminal for our walks. There you see empty wiener cans and the charred remains of many camp fires. Only one of the 3 trees remains.

Across from the school, in view from my window, is the mouth of "Jackfish Creek." We have a small log cabin along on the creek bank. Last Saturday some of us went over for supper. The walk across the river and between the frosted trees bordering the creek was delightful. Then, gathering dry wood, getting the fire going in the little barrel stove, frying bacon and making coffee was fun. The stove only has space for one cooking pot at a time, so we eat one thing at a time.

South of town there are two creeks. On Pokiak there are about a dozen homes belonging to Loucheux or Loucheux-white families. I used to go there last winter for Sunday School. This year many of the children come to Day School.

There are only two houses on Hudson Bay Creek but during the summer Eskimo pitch their tents and camp there for several months.

At the school this year we have 90 children registered in residence and 13 come to day classes. The majority are new; 39 of my class of 60 are beginners. More than half are Eskimo whereas last year they were in the minority. So far this year we have had epidemics of whooping cough, mumps, chicken pox and stomach 'flu. It is only now that classroom attendance is regular.

At the time I write, we lack four staff members — a laundry matron, a girl's supervisor, a senior teacher and male help. Rev. Gibson teaches seniors when he can and, fortunately, other members of the staff are able to carry on most school activities.

Have I written about the garden? The plants which we started in the classroom, moved to the greenhouse and then to the garden produced a few very fine cabbages. We had lettuce, beet tops and other greens for a short season. There was one cauliflower and one vegetable marrow. The tomato plants did not thrive outside but from the few which we left in the greenhouse, we have a dozen green tomatoes.

The flowers were more prolific. Sweet peas and nasturtiums in the greenhouse produced a profusion of bloom from July until late September. Only transplanted pansies and poppies developed outside. Many varieties I maintained in the classroom as house plants. In this way a gladiola gave us two pretty spikes. The balsam and amaryllis are blooming now. If "flowers are the earth's smiles," we are well rewarded.

Our radio has new batteries but we still could not hear the Northern Messenger last week. We haven't heard any world news either, not since our September mail.

HECTOGRAPHIC CHRISTMAS LETTER
TO FAMILY AND FRIENDS

I have enjoyed my second Christmas at Aklavik. As in all the years since I started teaching, Christmas was preceded by weeks training the children for a concert. This year I had 66 but I found parts for only 61 as the other 5 come to school only half days.

The 12 smallest girls sang about Santa Claus to the tune of "Jingle Bells" — the tallest, in the back row, sang the verses. The little girls in the front row twisted and squirmed and sang so spasmodically that it turned out to be a humorous beginning to the program.

The next 12 girls were poinsettias, with white dresses upon which we sewed green stems and leaves. They wore little yellow caps and their corollas were huge and red. They did various exercises to the waltz, "A Sweet Bunch of Daisies."

We sang and dramatized "Good King Wenceslas" and I was pleased that we could have the conversations in solo. The trees (girls concealed behind spruce trees) stayed on the stage for "Little Red Riding Hood." The latter walked in the woods, listened to the robins [children] sing and watched the rabbits [children] hop and play. The part of the wolf was vigourously acted by a new boy who is 15 and knows very little English. He really could bark, howl and growl. One pupil brought a real wolf's tail so we pinned it to his overalls. With cutting, sewing and pasting Shredded Wheat boxes and attaching bits of old fur I constructed a head-piece (we had 5 kinds: wolf, wolverine, muskrat, beaver, lynx). It was truly a curious looking thing. The effect of the wolf's appearance on the audience was interesting, some were terrified while others shrieked with laughter.

Then my juniors had a shadow play of Dr. I Cuttem in his office doing an operation.

Our chorus was a carol, "The Birth Song of Jesus." As Rev. Gibson had to substitute with the Seniors, he had no time to prepare numbers so other staff prepared four pretty drills. We completed the program with a pageant.

The rehearsal was on Friday and the final was on Christmas Eve. A large crowd of Eskimo, Loucheaux and white people attended. Then the supervisors took the children up to bed with snacks and we served tea, doughnuts and cake to the visitors. [Whenever we served tea one person followed with a jug of cold water as many native people don't drink hot tea.] Several visitors helped to be sure no one was missed. It was over by 11 o'clock and time for those who wished to leave for the midnight service of Holy Communion. Miss Sutton and I remained on duty and hung the gifts on the tree in readiness for the morrow.

Christmas Day found us rising at 7:30, turning on the lights and watching as the children dashed to their towel hooks, got their stockings and ran back to their warm beds. All those tousled black haired little girls in their long soft nighties digging to the very toes of their stockings was an unforgettable sight. They pulled out various things — all of which had been sent in by outside churches' auxiliaries in bales. Our matron and her helpers had done a marvellous job of Mrs. Santa Claus.

Miss Sutton and I went with the Confirmed students to make their Christmas Communion. As we approached the Cathedral it was beautiful with the lights shining from the colourful windows, stars filled the dark sky. The service also was beautiful in the quiet holiness of the church.

Back at the school there was scarcely time for the staff to get their stockings, pulling out soap, a new towel, a comb, white thread and other needful things. The gong went and we all joined the children for a joyful family service in the big dining room.

Sutton, Woodcock, Mike and I helped serve the children's dinner. They had roast reindeer, mashed potatoes (a special treat as we were unable to get a fresh supply this year so these were a gift from the hospital's supply) canned tomatoes, green string beans, gravy and Christmas pudding. They sat in families or relative groups and really seemed very happy.

A joyful service
in the dining room.

At 2 o'clock a former All Saints employee, Mr. Rawlings, costumed as Santa Claus came for the children's tree in the centre of the long front hall. The faces waiting eagerly for their turns lit up as each name was called. Then while they investigated their parcels we went to ours in the sitting room. It was almost like home.

Everyone went out for walks. The moon was shining as it seems to all winter. The children had a picnic supper in their playrooms while we had our dinner. This year we had two of their dining room tables placed end to end. I made little favours with gum drops and tooth picks and we decorated a little tree in the middle of the table with gum drops. Our guests were: Mr. and Mrs. Boxer, Rev. and Mrs. Gibson, Constables Storey and Thue. Altogether there were 16 of us.

Gumdrop table favors '45

We feasted on stuffed reindeer hearts, canned peas and corn, potatoes, plum pudding and mince tarts. While it seemed that we were all seeking a different life in coming to this far-away place, we were still making great efforts to carry on our old traditions.

After dinner it wasn't long before we gave in to the excitement and tiredness of busy days and retired early.

The next day some little girls inquired, "Christmas, when?" When I replied, "Christmas was yesterday," they said, "Oh! How quick."

Now I am spending the main part of each day cleaning in the classroom — a really thorough cleaning which the busy days with classes won't permit. Many students visit with family every day, the rest holiday here. Two new pupils have arrived since I started writing this, this afternoon. That brings my enrolment to 68 and the total residential enrolment to 94.

I have omitted to tell you of the most beautiful of all our Christmas gifts. It was a gorgeous sky — very vividly red during the mid hours of the day. There was no wind. It was all that I needed to bring me that feeling of serene happiness and well-being I had been seeking

All Saints Cathedral

Behind the Altar a painting of Christmas with northern people.

Left - Right
Rev. Jim Sittichinli
Rev. Ralph Gibson
Archdeacon Marsh.

A NEW SCHOOL YEAR BEGINS

My second year at All Saint's School was less of a novelty. While many things were now routine, others, because of new people in the community and changing happenings, made the year full of interesting times.

I began with 67 pupils with good attendance. Despite having to carry a broken left shoulder in a sling and being unable to walk unaided, I found the children's learning a rewarding experience. I could see that my approach was being successful, the children and I were both learning. Day by day the sun shone more into our classroom. From being a bright red area at the Southern horizon, the days had grown from colour to light. Illiteracy was fading like the Arctic winter nights.

Choosing a more ambitious theme, I began to paint in earnest. With "Angel Heads" by Reynolds as a guide, I began moving some of my pupils' faces to my canvas. And I began collecting some local stories from our older native people.

Our night watchman, John Doe, told me a story. He sat by the kitchen table between his nightly rounds to tend the furnace and check the school. If I worked late I could make some hot chocolate for us both and as he talked, I would jot down the key words he used.

Social life in Aklavik went merrily on. The regular clubs and organizations prospered with new help. Everyone's birthday also merited a party. We also had another serious epidemic of 'flu.

Finally, at the end of February, after a long delay, a new staff member, Marjorie Neales, arrived to take the senior students. She had worked at Chapleau School in Ontario with the Gibsons and Sutton for several years. Her arrival was none too soon as it relieved Rev. Gibson from teaching just when he was urgently needed to solve the water supply problem when the pipes froze.
The Fort Norman Hospital burned down and some of the patients were flown to our hospital and school. Now I have 69 students and find it difficult to move my little portable desk around in the classroom.

When ratting began on the First of March our afternoon class times were changed to 1:15 to 3:00 to allow time for the senior students who wanted to go ratting after 3:00 p.m. Staff who were willing took groups of senior girls to trap across the river on lakes designated for school use.

I was immediately keen to take one group of girls and Agnes Martin, Barbara Esau, Bertha Moses and Sophie Okalasuk were anxious to go with me and help me walk. Neales, Robinson and Jessie Bonnetplume also took groups of girls. The senior boys went on their own. Ratting was one activity where we weren't the teachers – the students knew it all.

My birthday, being at the beginning of March, I was in for a surprise. The tail of the first muskrat caught was a very special morsel and always given to the best friend of the trapper. At supper I was surprised to have the girls serving the staff table come in singing "Happy Birthday" and present to me  a plate with a shiny, black, boiled muskrat tail on it. Of course, it made a memorable birthday!

HAPPY BIRTHDAY, Mmay

1. *Little girls carefully open up a push-up on the lake.*
2. *"Oh, we caught a rat".*
3. *Sophie calls. "Oh, it's alive!"*

1. *Bertha Moses and Minnie investigate their trap.*
2. *Bertha and Agnes Martin see a rat.*
3. *The push-up must be closed to keep it from freezing.*

Quoting from my diary: *. . . a beautiful day, snow on the branches, blue sky and mountains. We passed through the Lagoon and portaged to Big Lake. Jessie's group was at the near end so we went to the farthest end. Agnes Martin had some pushups staked. Her first one had a rat frozen in it. I chopped it out, minus the tail! Then she re-set her trap while I went to help Sophie. We caught 3 rats within 15 minutes in Sophie's traps. Altogether the children had 14 rats. [I never knew if my birthday gift was the tail I had chopped off.]*

On Saturday I went again with the girls. Bertha got a rat. Agnes' trap was sprung. Sophie's pushup was frozen and it took us a long time to get her trap chopped out. We went daily to "rat" until the traps weren't catching anything. Meanwhile in the evenings the girls had skinned their rats, put the skins on stretchers and hung them to dry.

Later we sold them for $2.25 per skin.

Enjoying every day to the fullest, I still had one dread: I had heard that it was being suggested that for the benefit of all concerned I should not spend another year at Aklavik. True, I had had some illness but had missed fewer days than several others. Good friends were nevertheless concerned that if I stayed, my health problems could prove fatal, leaving my position vacant. They thought it would be best for all concerned for me to obtain a change of venue. But I felt my health was improving and that my work was becoming increasingly effective. Finally a letter from the School Commission eliminated my worry. It read in part:

"Thank you for your consistently good service to our Mission.
We are pleased that you will continue."

I stayed up late to prepare an order to Eaton's. Eaton's store in Winnipeg set up some very helpful services for workers in our northern schools. A special shopper was assigned to each of us who wished the service. My shopper had my parents' address as well as mine. She would shop not only for me but would also shop and mail gifts to my family. Likewise she would accept requests from my parents and send their gifts to me. Postage was free. I would pay by a cheque on my Saskatchewan account.

We had some warm weather just before Easter and ceilings everywhere wept down upon us. The "Drip, Drip" verses I had penned in 1945 came to life again.

At Easter the town was full of
people and there was much
visiting, selling of furs,
buying summer supplies and
going to church. Our W.A.
sales were very well

RATTING Sunday

collection plate

patronized. The church collection plates on "Ratting Sunday" have
slowly become more sophisticated. Several years ago the donations
of freshly prepared muskrat skins overflowed the plates: this year
only a few appeared but many crumpled bills took their place. When
possible the Delta people are very cheerfully generous.

The Easter week over, the dog
teams with toboggans well
loaded, pulled away, leaving the
population of Aklavik to settle
back to normal.

Classes started again. On
May 2, when the first wild
ducks flew in, the excitement of warmer spring days spread. We had
forgotten about the mud until it again stuck on our shoes. Run-off
water at the sides of the river ice prompted some trappers to begin
their shooting of muskrats.

Flu struck again in May but the children seemed less ill than in earlier
epidemics, probably because their general health was much
improved.

The weather was very changeable. After a few warm hours it could
turn cold and snow. Sometimes flocks of little birds got stranded and
sought shelter around the school. Rev. Gibson used some of our
classroom storm windows to reconstruct the greenhouse.

On the grass in front of the school there were several wooden
platforms. A warm spell tempted us to go there for a class of writing,
drawing or just talking. The sun was so warm. At least twice we made
hurried dashes back inside as a sudden wind whipped some winter
back into town.

Some of our staff are to leave this summer. By June the First I had finished five little paintings the community had commissioned me to paint as gifts for: Nurses Powell, Brooks and Beech, Misses Fulton and Robinson. Neales, Sutton and I took the paintings to Mrs. Gibson where we decided which to give to whom. Then we made cards and wrapped them. We had just finished when in rushed Jimmy Husky, "Big Smoke in this power house." It was 10 p.m. The generator had burned. No lights. Thankfully, it is June and the sun is doing its summer job. Except for requiring electricity for some appliances, we won't complain while the generator is being replaced.

Throughout the spring all eyes were on the river. A big crack appeared, water was high on the river shores, but the ice stayed firmly in place. The shore waters provided streams for traffic as the current was quite strong. Rev. Gibson showed all a new skill – he lassoed a runaway  scow that was floating by and tethered it to a huge driftwood log on shore so that the owner could retrieve it.

Finally, on May 26 the ice moved out. Right on its departure a HBC vessel, the "Watson Lake," came down from the Liard River. Mike Koziak of the school staff hurried to the dock and bought some fresh food to share with us. (Oranges, 8 for $1 or 10 for $1, Grapefruit 25¢ each and fresh eggs 75¢ each.) The same day a real snow storm blew in. A box of grapefruit had been overlooked, froze and was thrown out. The native children, thinking they had a windfall, gleefully used them for footballs.

At the school we began having bees to prepare for the Red Cross spring campaign. First task – collect bottles for root beer. The bees really hummed – social times. To make the root beer, Ms. Kirk, Mrs. Simpson and Mrs. Chapman helped Fulton mix the ingredients and extract. Byers and I washed bottles. The Corporal bottled. Capping was done by Sutton, Neales and John LeBell. When the evening was over we had 375 bottles to leave to ripen.

Then on June 1 I received a blow in a letter from our Commission:

"We regret, you must go out this summer."

With a heavy heart yet determined mind, I went to see my Principal, Rev. Gibson. Then Sutton helped me go through a fierce blizzard to see Dr. Hayward. I needed grounds to ask the Commission to change their decision. Both Rev. Gibson and Dr. Hayward felt I merited their help and quickly wrote to the Commission.

With so many hours of June sunshine, my disappointments vanished like the snow and for a while I refused my fate.

I took my class outside to draw and to write. We used oral English constantly, each one having a turn to tell a story or describe something. We made use of the wooden platforms where we could be out of the mud.

Inspired by the spring, Rev. Gibson decided to enlarge his small garden space. He cut and lifted the grass sods. I and some of the children helped by shaking the sods to save the soil, then put the grass into a compost pile. Both Woodcock and I, farmers' daughters, shared Rev. Gibson's ambitions and were delighted by the rapid plant growth. By June 14 the marsh marigolds were blooming in the marsh near the school. Pussy willows bent in the breeze and birds were everywhere. Our school bell was in a free-standing tower just outside the dining room windows. We were pleased to see a pair of robins nesting in the tower near the bell.

Marsh Marigolds

Nest

And, like the wonder of spring, word came that minds in the Commission were changed. I would stay in Aklavik after all. Saying goodbye to old friends who were leaving, both colleagues at the school and village neighbours was so much easier for me as we welcomed new ones.

REPORT TO FRIENDS AND FAMILY – TRIP TO MCPHERSON

The end of June: Emptying and tidying of desks; returning well-worn readers; giving out report cards; the usual school closing, — but not the same for me, for instead of feeling the sadness of departure, I was one of the crowd — wrapped up in excited anticipation of going with the children to McPherson. Perhaps it was the children's holiday bags bulging into odd shapes by my classroom door or perhaps it was because I had spent a few moments planning my own holiday bag — trying to decide whether my old reliable ski pants, or the blue slacks whose three buttons had dissolved in the wash, would be preferable; and then, a uniform for Sunday, films, and oil paints; comparing notes with Eleanor who was not only packing her bag but the food rations too; a big turkey supper provided by Mike to celebrate his birthday; and by ten to eight we were on the beach boarding Lazarus'  schooner, stowing luggage into the barge and waving good-bye to the friends on shore.

We were a curious cargo: Mr. Gibson, our Principal, Lazarus Sittichinli, John Joseph, Frank, Thomas Njootli, Thad Harris, Mrs. Francis, her family and yelping dog, Mrs. Blake, about 25 children, Miss Greening, Eleanor and I.

We pulled away into the indescribable beauty of an Arctic summer night of clear sunshine. Even the smallest children loitered on deck to watch the nearness of the mountains and reflections, until Mr. Gibson reminded them that they must seek rest among the conglomeration of quilts, parkas, and bed roles in the tent on the barge. They slept talkatively and small wonder — soon — Home — Home.

Around midnight the engine pump stopped working and the murderous mosquitoes pounced on us from the shores. Even after we were on the deck in our bed rolls with head nets and mosquito bars, we found no respite from them. From then on they were the bane of our trip. "Skeeter Skatter" and "Stay-Away" were of little use because while you attempted to unscrew the bottle they chewed on your hands. It was a common sight to see people trying to eat with a sandwich or cup inside their head nets.

During the first day we travelled slowly. Miss Woodcock and I made food for the children who, alternately, lolled around in the heat or shivered from the cold rain. When it rained the cabin leaked in a multitude of places even  after the men had covered it with a tarpaulin. So you see we enjoyed the spice of life (variety).

We arrived early the next morning at Fort McPherson. Consequently there were few to greet us; but the children scampered down the catwalk and to their homes. During the day we were able to attend the services and visit with the Dewdneys (the resident missionary and his wife). We slept at Dewdneys that night and really appreciated the luxury of beds.

On the following day, July the First, I was glad that we were not ready to leave for Aklavik. In the afternoon I did some charcoal sketching from the rectory's mosquito-proof porch. The Loucheaux people had a feast, eating together on the grass. Then the sound of gun-fire called us all to the cleared grassy heath in front of the Hudson's Bay store for the annual sports.

First, a long rope was brought and the women grasped one side while the men took the other. They pulled and the men's side won. No cheers. Apparently this broke a tradition – that the women always win – or else the men thought it well to let them – so a few strong men transferred to the women's end of the rope. They pulled again. This time, cheers for the women!! There was a candy scramble for the children (with the adults getting the most candy). Then followed different races for the various age groups. It greatly amused me to see how the Chief would collect some money then direct a few events until his funds were depleted, then collect again. When we had been entertained by both a men's

J U L Y 1 9 4 6

S P O R T S D A Y

The Church

Tug-of-War

and women's hard tack eating contest wherein the contestants included the Roman Catholic priest and Anglican clergymen, there seemed no more need for sport and the crowd dispersed to the community hall where a sign over the door read:

DANCE TO-NIGHT 11 PM. — 7 A.M.
GIRLS NOT ALLOWED TO WEAR PARKAS
SIGNED JOHN MODESTE

Many of our crew left us as they wished to dance. We went on board and they joined us when they tired of it. Dewdneys had lent us a double width mosquito bar so we put it on the front of the barge. Greening, Eleanor and I spread our bed roles under it, killed off the mosquitoes that had ventured in with us, and finally slept well.

We returned via the Aklavik Channel, a very scenic river of many turns, clothed in gracious reflections and closely guarded by the quiet mountains. We stopped to load cordwood from piles that had been purchased by the school and piled on the high bank of the river. While the others worked hard throwing the wood down and then loading it, I fought mosquitoes, sketched, mixed and served lime juice to the thirsty moilers.

It was six in the morning when we reached Aklavik. A flying boat and two other airplanes were at the shore. Only this week I was talking to Thomas and he said, "It was a good trip to look back at."

A BUSY SUMMER

After our return from Fort McPherson, the days just flew by. I filled in wherever I was needed. A group of Coast children (Ruth, Lena, Rosie and Jimmy) left on the schooner "Only Way" with Owen Allen. Then only 5 boys remained at the school: Andy Carpenter, Walter Possana, Fred Wingnik, Elvin and Tommy Tucker). The S.S. McKenzie River arrived at 3 a.m. on July 8. Trunks came for staff who had flown in earlier and trunks left for those flying out this summer.

Boat staff unloaded the ship's barges and stacked the freight on the shore. Their purser was stationed there and each person or place signed off with him before their boxes could be released. Each time a boat comes in some of our staff are very busy claiming freight, hauling it to the school on the wagon behind our little John Deere tractor, storing the boxes and checking invoices.

Mrs. Harvey and children (Dr. Harvey will replace Dr. Hayward) arrived from Fort Norman so Mrs. Hayward and the children stayed at Gibson's and Dr. Hayward at the school until they left for the south. Vic Oke and Mrs. Oke and daughter, Grace Anne, came to work with us and temporarily stayed at the school. Miss Sowden, an English lady who for many years had worked in the Canadian Arctic, took Miss Fulton's place as Matron of the school.

We tried to keep the children who didn't go away busy and happy. We took them to two shows at Peffer's, "First Love" with Deanna Durbin and "First Beau" with Jane Withers. If possible someone would take them somewhere each day. When a Fairbanks plane missed the landing strip and cracked up in front of the hospital, we all hurried down to see what happened.

Mosquitoes were very bad on warm days. I tried to keep them off my hands with "612" and wore a head net when I painted out-of-doors.

Sometimes the backs of my hands were black and the canvas became quite realistic with insects stuck in the paint!

Jim Edwards and Rev. Gibson had some work to do in Tuktoyaktuk converting the Mission House into a church. They decided to take the Mission boat, the "Messenger." Marge Sutton, Woodcock, and Williiams were chosen to go for a holiday. I was given the interesting job of helping in the hospital kitchen. With the cooks from both the school, Woodcock, and the hospital, Williams, away at Tuk, the hospital especially needed some help. The Matron asked, "Will you fill in for Williams?" I had checked on the daily schedules as listed by Willy before she left. Taking on her job meant from 5 a.m. 'til after supper – meals for over 50 patients, the nurses and the other staff. Me? There was no one else so apparently unemployed. And when one is asked to volunteer, does one refuse?

Most days went along splendidly until one morning the dish boiler presented a problem by not boiling. Regulations required all patients' dishes and cutlery to be boiled, then washed. That morning it was noon before the breakfast dishes were finished.

Six native girls were always employed to help the hospital cook. They were a great bunch of sturdy young women who could do as they were shown and guided. I wasn't used to this and soon complications showed up when I failed to supervise every detail.

The Matron was very patient with me but I did have to watch the cooking supplies very carefully. All the essentials came in on the boat only once a year. So we had to plan and ration for a year with some left over in case next year's boat was late. After a few days I was feeling less bewildered. The breakfast of huge pots of cooked cereal and jugs of re-constituted dried milk; the snacks of jam on huge biscuits; lunch of nutritious reindeer stew filled with dried vegetables; supper of spread bread, jello, dried fruit and tea, all seemed fairly simple once I knew how much. The girls served the patients and took smaller amounts to a dining room for the nurses and staff.

Every other day the girls put two huge metal tubs on the kitchen work table and divided a 100-pound sack of flour between the tubs. Into each went one cup of salt. We had gallon jugs of warm water in which we dissolved sugar. I needed to watch this for the girls loved sweet things. Six cups were needed for each 50 pounds of flour. We had a brew of liquid yeast which we reserved from day to day and added six cups for each tub. The liquids were added to the flour and it took great strength to stir with the huge wooden spoons – combining the ingredients to make a good dough. The girls could never estimate the amount of fluid needed and when to dump the dough onto the table for kneading. I still see them, each wearing a big apron made from flour sacks, their sleeves rolled up and long black hair tied back. I would pinch the dough to determine its readiness to be heaved back into the tub, covered with a clean old quilt and left to rise. Depending on the warmth of the kitchen, it was from two to three hours later that the dough had pushed the quilt up like a mushroom top. Then the girls kneaded it down, dumped out the batter, cut it into chunks, shaped loaves and later baked it.

One morning as I was planning soup for lunch and the girls had the bread at the "rising" stage, I felt the kitchen getting cold. The day, although in August, was cloudy and snow flurried about. I immediately checked the huge kitchen range – no flame. The fire was out. The hospital, a few years previously, had replaced the wood-burning ranges. A tank of oil sat outside and oil came in through a pipe to the stove. It hadn't gone out before and everyone was sure the tank wasn't empty. Our native caretaker had never had to fix the stove but he went away and soon came back with the church Archdeacon, whom everyone expected could do everything. He was armed with a huge wrench. The clock was getting close to 12 – no soup. The bread was rising despite the cool kitchen – no hot oven. Matron came through with a meal saver – gallon cans of pork and beans donated to the hospital by the U.S. Army when they closed their camp on the MacKenzie River at the end of the war. Regardless of what a dietician would say, cold pork and beans, crackers and water to drink made a most memorable lunch on the wards.

But what to do with two huge tubs of soft bread dough? "Let's give it away," I suggested. We chopped it into cushion sized pieces, wrapped each up and the girls ran to different houses, the

school, the tents, to anyone who could cook it either as bannock on a pan over the fire or in an oven.

As one of the girls came back she called, " Dey say tank your, 'ary much."

Fortunately, the kitchen stove was running again by evening; the patients hadn't suffered from the beans; and the "cook" hadn't been fired! Or can volunteers be fired?

I still required help to get around except within a room where I could move from object to object, e.g. tables, chairs, etc. I got "taken" back to the school at night, then brought back to the hospital early in the morning. Often I stayed late to bake big pans of cake and cookies for mid-meal snacks for the patients. I always had time at the school to water the plants and practise the hymns on the little organ for the following Sunday.

Dr. Hayward and family, the Marshes, Fulton and Robinson left via Fairbanks. No one replaced the Marshes that summer but Harveys from Fort Norman replaced the Haywards.

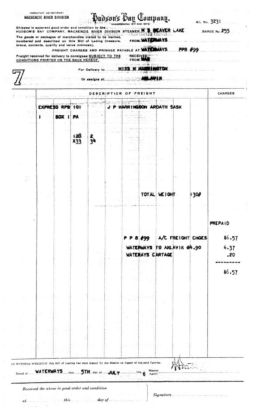

Letter home August 16, 1946:

Dear family,

S. S. McKenzie River chugged in to Aklavik about 8:15 this morning. As the day went by I learned that there were no freight bills for me so you can imagine how pleased I was the next morning when, among the freight was a big box for me. We found the bills later but by then I had a hammer and was taking out the nails. Believe me, the boxes you send are the best nailed of any that reach Aklavik — and the contents are better, too!

I finally got Mr. Gibson to help me finish taking off the lid. His eyes popped when he saw the fruit juice. I have saved and saved what you sent last year — thinking that it was limited and so handy when someone is sick. So thank you for the nuts, dates, cocoa, chocolate, etc. and all the work that packing such a box took.

The newly appointed Superintendent from the "Department of Education for N.W.T.", Mr. McKinnon (formerly of Melfort and Ottawa) is here. He spends a great deal of time here inspecting and asking questions so that he can help us get materials, money and favourable criticism in Ottawa.

On Monday some of us went 12 miles by boat then walked toward the mountains. We picked enough blueberries for 18 quarts and 6 pies, also 5 quarts of red currants. The mosquitoes were BAD!

I feel especially well this fall — so different from last year

SCHOOL STARTS AGAIN

Letter home, September 3, 1946

Dear Mother,

I have your Aug. 17 letter today. I was sorry to hear about the drought and crop depreciation.

I have a few flowers to give away every day. It has snowed several days but miraculously the frost has held off. I can boast of a big bunch of Chinese larkspur (from your seed) on my desk now.

I've had a few days break, staying with Niven (now Chapman) who was on our staff. They have a good view of the mountains and I had time to paint. I am teaching her to crochet and to cook. Then I took two of the Coppermine Eskimo boys who couldn't go home, to our school cabin. (It is across the river along Jackfish creek.) It is a very old log cabin 8' X 10' with grass growing on the mudded roof and stunted spruce trees growing around it. Some staff took us over in the boat and left us to stay all night.

I put the boys to sleep on the bunk and I slept on blankets on the floor. Mosquitoes and spiders tormented me but to see how much the boys were enjoying the camping was worth it. The next day I let the boys learn how to light the fire (they haven't the wood at Coppermine) and to cook while I watched and sketched. They had a wonderful time!

Mr. Hayward finished building the Day School at Fort McPherson and returned to Aklavik. I gave him my room and moved to the chesterfield in the staff lounge. He's so much like Dad and I am really glad to see him. However, he had to go to the hospital yesterday to have a major operation for some type of hernia. He is quite ill.

School opened today. The hospital is X-raying everyone. Two of my beginners have had to go to hospital.

So many have wished to come to school this year that we have had to turn some away.

Oh, I wanted to tell you that when at the cabin and I gave the boys some tomato juice and chocolate, one lad said we ate, "just like eaters in books."

We're lucky with our garden this year. We're eating cabbage, cauliflower, lettuce and kale.

Excerpt from a Letter to a sister, September 16, 1946

My dear sister,

. . . We have 95 in residence and expect 5 more as the regulations for this school allow only 100. So many more want to come. About 20 pupils live at home and come to Day School. They are either white or half-white.

We are having the strangest weather. It hasn't stopped snowing for days. Already we have more snow than all of last winter. The leaves are still on the trees — great masses of golden foliage showing through the white snow. The old, gray river goes crawling by.

The summer went so quickly. I painted my room ceiling and walls; helped about the school, slated the blackboards, painted walls in the classroom.

This week we went about a mile to pick wild cranberries. They grow in the moss under the willow trees. Since there hasn't been rain recently the moss was dry and we could crawl around. We picked several big pails full.

Yesterday several big flocks of geese flew over in their V-formations going south so we know the ice is forming at the coast.

I have some plants blooming in cans on my desk — 4 snapdragons, some lobelia, butterfly flowers and balsam. The larkspur and poppies in the garden are frozen stiff.

We have had another epidemic of TB with 5 deaths in one week. The government is paying for mass lung X-rays. Our hospital is doing between 30 and 40 daily. If any positive films are seen, then the person can be isolated in hospital to keep from spreading the sickness.

I have one little Eskimo boy that just can't sit still. When I asked him why he wiggled so much in school, he said, "I'm not used to having a desk over my knees."

Excerpt from a Hectographic letter to friends & relatives. September 21, 1946.

Dear

. . . I don't think I told you about our garden, the new one beside the Gibson's house.

The snow has killed the plants and frozen our cabbages. While still frozen we harvested them to store in the ice house, to be used as needed. Boiled from the frozen state they are good. Many of them are larger than we grew at the farm. Also we had around 40 heads of cauliflower. The summer turnips got as large as grapefruit and can also be kept frozen. The burning bush grew about 16 inches high and was soft and green. It never turned red. I had some pretty bouquets of larkspur. Only the blue and purple varieties bloomed but they were

beautiful. It was like some of your garden had moved into ours!

The men will leave this week for the reindeer kill. They take the boat and barge to the herding grounds. The government allots so many to be killed and places such as our school are allowed a certain portion of the harvest. It comes to about 40 cents per pound. The main herder stands with his gun as the reindeer are herded past. He shoots the ones he thinks are full-grown stags. Each purchaser has a marker the herder attaches then the recipients know which ones they can buy. Some of the carcasses are skinned, all are gutted, the hearts and livers packed to be brought home. The natives value highly the heads and usually get them before others can.

For my part I will be glad to have fresh meat in our meals. I will have more energy.

Thank you for the seeds and the onion sets.

Letter to a sister, November 1946

Dear Sister,

Sutton and I are in our 3rd year — two of the longest serving on the staff. Miss Sowden, Matron and Miss Jones, Boy's Supervisor, have returned from furlough and serving elsewhere. The new laundry for joint use by the school and hospital is in operation in its own building which it shares with the lighting plant. Removing the big washer from its former room at the school has made the room more accessible for our private laundries and the children's baths. With fresh cupboards and paint it is an attractive room.

Another change is the use of the strip of cleared land in front of our mission property as an airfield. In summer wheel planes and now in winter small planes on skies have landed there.

My work continues much the same. Eighteen day pupils make my class larger (76 on the roll). They are an excellent bunch and a rewarding challenge. I've been lent a set of "Dick and Jane" readers which help with the Day School pupils who have been "outside" and can relate to them. Some of the bigger boys (13 - 15 years) are doing well with the fret saws . . . sent me. We use wood from boxes as our plywood is too heavy.

The older girls delight in making model parkas, and even party clothes for dolls. They teach the younger girls. I've been donated beads to pass along for their use.

Besides these activities, I've been trying to play the organ for some of the church services. I wasn't surprised when on Sunday the Archdeacon apologized for not having shown me where the light switch was — he thought I'd been playing in the dark!

All Sain Ts School,
Aklavik, N.W. T,
Nov. 28. 1946
Daer Santa Claus
I like a air plane please
Santa Claus I wund how
are you Sainta Claus for
my Shovel and for
Book and my Ball Santa
Claua
GoodBye Santa Claus
Herschel Hratunn

all Saints sckool.
aklavik, N, W, T,
nov, 28, 1946,
Dear SantaClaus,
Thank you for the doll
From last year,
The children are hoppy
at school.
I am uery hoppy at
school too,
I want a little doll
Please,
Ruth Wingnik

CHRISTMAS 1946

From a letter to my parents, December 22, 1946

Dear Mother and Dad,

Here it is almost Christmas . . . I hope you still have Jap oranges for the toes of our socks when I'm home in '48. . . .

The fur prices are down about a third lower than last year. (A white fox was $22.00, now it is $15.00.) Sadly, while commerce has advanced in the north and our stores are well stocked (we are not rationed) the skill of money management is unknown to native people. The stores have stacks of tempting fruit cakes, candies and toys. Even I was tempted: I bought a play table and two chairs for my classroom. The set was slightly damaged, a bargain at $1.00. The children will really enjoy it.

Our darkest day is gone and we look for a bit more light each day. A few, like myself, never notice the days as dark and gloomy. Many others are depressed, grumbling and yearning for sunshine. I don't miss it, yet I'll cheer when the first rays brighten our mid-day.

Happy New Year!

1947
THE SAME – BUT SOME DIFFERENCES AND SOME "FIRSTS"

The annual Loucheux New Year's Feast was at Jimmy Husky's house this year. Everyone was welcome but usually children didn't go. Neales, Woodcock, Gibsons and Jones went. When they returned, Rothwell, Sutton and I took our turn. From the RCMP, Kirks, Jewett, Scotty and others were coming, others going. It was a generous buffet. There were pans of cold roasted caribou, boiled Arctic Char, pots of bubbling caribou stew on the stove, big jars of sweet pickles, bowls of white lard and thick slices of bread as well as other foods donated by the Hudson's Bay Company. I ate cold meat, pickle, an orange, apple pie with cranberry sauce – a very delicious meal.

We started school classes again the next day. It seemed almost a rest after the pace of holiday social life. This year whenever Miss Sowden, our Matron, had a day off or was busy with other activities, I moved in to take over the dispensary and health care, which I really enjoyed. One of our new students, 15-year-old James Gordon, a shy boy with very little English, came to see me about a painful sore on his lower back. His cousin, George, came with him. I asked James to push his pants down so that I could see what the problem was and then turned away, busying myself on the other side of the room to try to reduce his embarrassment. He had a large, angry looking swelling on his buttock. I asked him to lie down on the examining table which he did without a sound. After sterilizing a scalpel I lanced the swelling. In the process of cleaning the wound, I extracted quite a large sliver, an inch long and the diameter of a match. In all of this probing James never even squirmed or spoke. After bandaging the wound I showed him the sliver and asked, "How did you get this?" James frowned. He, too, was surprised and shook his head. "Maybe sleep on floor at Alex." (Alex was his uncle, the father of George, and had taken the two boys to his home for the holiday. Many homes had few beds so sleeping on the bare board floors was a common occurrence.)

The health concerns of dispensary care also involved doling out to each child a daily dose of Vitamin D. In summer, cases of Cod Liver Oil in gallon cans, came in the supplies. By the time it got to Aklavik it was often quite rancid and strong but, we were assured by the medical people, still 100% viable and quite likely to be relished by Arctic children used to rancid seal oil. But it wasn't relished and the children thought of all sorts of ways to avoid taking it and swallowing. By the time I arrived, the previous Matron had devised a way to ensure they got this valuable vitamin. As the children were dismissed from the breakfast tables, they exited the dining room single-file through a side door. There, beside a table with the big can of cod liver oil, a jug and a long-handled tablespoon, stood the Matron. She poured oil into the jug then as each child appeared she poured a spoonful into the child's open mouth. The recipient had to say, "thank you," which he or she couldn't do without swallowing the dose. As the school days passed, the whole process of about 100 doses took place quickly. The "get it over with" feeling helped. When I was substituting, we approached it as a game. (I could recall my childhood and the dreaded castor oil!)

When the first Saturday of the new year came, it was my day off and I went visiting about town. First the hospital patients: then McLeods where Mrs. M. let me give baby Keith his bottle. At Harvey's all of the Christmas toys were brought out to show me. At Bell's they were washing the walls of their new house after a disastrous mis-function of the oil burner. And so I spent my day and at each place there was talk of longer light in the noon time sky.

I continued to be called upon to "do" the ladies' hair. This year more of them wanted permanents. Pauline got a supply of the kits so the others bought them from her. Then, when I got an early invitation for supper I suspected what might be my rôle. It was like a playtime chemistry kit – new to me.

From my diary of January 11, 1947 at Chapman's

. . . By 2:05 I got started on her hair. I was a little concerned – especially as the first curler fell out before I had the 4th on. I finally realized that the instructions had omitted, "after you use a roller, apply a clamp." That helped. From time to time the baby needed tending, or the oven turned down, or something else caused my hostess to jump up. It was 4:30 before I could apply the magic fluid to the 28 rollers and set them sizzling. It was rather fun but a very evil smelling price for beauty. The rollers got very hot and smoke-like steam filled the room. She got a headache so even though they were still warm, we took the rollers off!. Fun and games – at least her hair hadn't come off! Right after supper I shampooed and set it. Her hair was a mop of tight blond curls.

January was the month to work on all the requisitions for supplies for the next year. It took time and careful forethought, especially for newcomers. Beside food there were all the other details not available in an Arctic trading post; clothing, cosmetics, gifts, etc.

From my diary, a typical day.

Because Miss Sowden was tired and sleeping in, I had dispensary. Shirley Iglijuk has a dreadful, weeping skin trouble in ears, neck and scalp. Little John is 103.6°. Many others have a digestive 'flu. Miss Hockin [Hospital Matron] came to see John. I'm to give him hypos of sulfa every 4 hours. (sulfa is our only antibiotic, a discovery from the present war. It is a very fine white powder which has to be dissolved in sterilized water and cooled.)

Very cold weather. If the wind blows on my classroom's end of the school we can't sit and work there, so often I get the big boys to push open the folding doors to make the playroom available for games, singing exercises and relays. A plane that came in on January 13 was unable to leave until February 1 due to the extreme cold and strong winds. It would not have left even then except for a medical emergency. Constable Thue, travelling by dog team at the coast, had been storm bound and had frozen his feet. Fortunately Miss Hockin had had special training in arctic nursing in her Eastern Arctic work and provided excellent preliminary help but if the Constable's feet could be saved he required emergency help in a city hospital. (Despite the extreme cold, the pilot was able to take off. We heard later that Constable Thue's feet were saved by the medical people in Edmonton but he did lose some of his toes.)

During the first week of February the weather was very cold, staying lower than -45°F (-43°C), the lowest was -62°F (-52°C) on February 5. To make things even colder, we had cutting winds. The fuel oil which was fed in to the hospital cook stove from a tank outside had become almost solid, requiring a supplementary system of heating the pipeline in order to get the oil to flow.

To help shorten the dark nights many people were involved in a cribbage tournament. When any two of the players could meet, they'd play a game and enter their scores. One evening I went to Boxer's with Neales. While Neales and Marge Boxer played, I knit and made lunch. Boxers lived across the river and on our way home I enjoyed the winter moon which, like the summer sun, travels in a circle above the horizon. That night the Northern Lights were very active and even though I had a frozen nose I really enjoyed the walk with Neales. (Another thing I noticed was that when the full moon is at its closest to the horizon it doesn't appear round but out of shape like a soft balloon.)

The sickness, especially among the school children, continued for many weeks. Fever, nose-bleeds, heavy colds, as well as digestive troubles were severe. Many got infections in the slightest skin cut or disruption such as a needle prick when sewing. For that staph problem we heated up a strong solution of Epsom Salts and water and the infected part was soaked in it. We had a collection of small jars which we used for fingers. Many people in the village were also ill.

Sowden and I had several children on the four-hour sulfa injections. The fevers often reached 105° but the hospital could take no more patients. If we could keep the dormitories warm we kept the children in bed, otherwise they were better dressed and resting. Keeping them well supplied with fluids was my special objective. I tried several things such as cooking dried fruits like apples or prunes and straining off the juice. One that helped many was when I tried making egg nog. I mixed milk powder and a little egg yolk powder, dissolved them in water and added sugar and vanilla. One day Sammy Smith who, when well, was a very precocious lad, called out, "Miss Mayee, more that Ice cream juice!" I knew he was getting better. But many were very seriously ill with very high temperatures. Sutton was off work for a long time so we missed her help in the kitchen to make soups and other tempting nourishment.

Meanwhile other activities such as ratting kept any waking hours very busy. The children needed hair cuts so badly that Rev. Gibson finally lent me his electric clippers.

Four girls who had recovered were very helpful with the school chores. When they begged to set some muskrat traps I felt it would also be good for me to get away from the coughing, the bathing, the thermometers, emptying pails, etc. so right after the 2:30 afternoon sulfa injections, Bertha, Ada, Rhoda, Sophie and I left for the lakes across the river.

Bertha had a live rat. The trap was broken but she caught the rat in her mitts. Rhoda had one frozen, Ada had one toe, Sophie had one foot. The traps were cruel. A red fox came to play on the lake. We had seen a set-off fox trap, so in play the girls set it again. I was home for the 6:30 sulfa work but before the next one, a town lady came for a permanent! Right after the 10:30 shots, I was asleep.

Almost miraculously I slept well. The alarm clock's ringing didn't even seem to bother me. But what did was the almost daily news of losing some one we had hoped would be better. By mid March many were better but some just stayed very ill for an extended time. Some day, we hoped, there'd be a better medicine.

ALARM CLOCKS

by Mary A. Harrington

I like to wake up early
And hear the alarm clocks ring;
There's one that starts with a mighty threat,
And one that begins with a ting;
One that calls not far from my walls
Is a linguist from stranger clime
It minds not a bit – but shouts with gall
To get you up on time.

And some there are that get choked with a pounce
And some are allowed to scold;
It seems the best to spring with a bounce
To keep them from being bold.
As long as I hear these alarm clocks ring,
I know I'm not getting old
For I feel the urge to laugh and sing
And jump out in the cold! !

All Saints School, Aklavik, N.W.T. March 1947

By the end of March the sun was strong and the warmth caused the annual "drips" in the school. Fortunately, however, they were not as bad as previously. Mr. Gibson made flats for plants in my classroom. We planted more seeds that needed an early start. The amaryllis were magnificent again.

Our good friend, Shorty Wilson, borrowed a team of four dogs and toboggan from Jack Andrews and came to take Neales and me to the cabin. Fulton walked ahead to break trail. It was amusing as the dogs seemed so illiterate, "Gee" or "Haw" meant nothing. It ended up with Shorty walking while Neales and I rode in the toboggan laughing. Once there, I endeavoured to help chop up some willow branches for the little stove. Shorty showed me how to hold the axe in one hand and the stick in the other. Looked easy. I tried his technique but hit my knee. "Nothing much," I declared, and it wasn't until I got home that I looked. The two pairs of warm pants and the long johns all needed mending; my knee needed some adhesive tape!

Hectographic letter to friends, Spring, 1947

All Saints School,
Aklavik, N.W.T.
Spring, 1947.

Dear Friends:
    This, May 25, is a radiant day with only a slight breeze to ripple the water at the edge of the river. The main ice remains sparkling white over the

established river course but as each day
sees the water rise higher, it nears the
time of break-up. In the trees and
sheltered places, traces of snow are seen.
Many birds — ducks, geese, swans,
robins, blackbirds, plovers, snipes,
seagulls, terns and flocks of little
sparrows etc. have returned and make
glad the drab willows with their carols.

Callas
Aklavik, 1947

Two of the big calla lilies are in bloom in the classroom, lovely blooms although too late for Easter. We had the south windows in the classroom full of plants and seedlings, but since the greenhouse has been kept heated at nights the plants have been transferred there. To me the greenhouse is the most interesting place in town just now. The sun shines nearly all night, consequently the plants grow exceptionally fast.

One little corner of the greenhouse was empty so I took some rocks that I had collected from here and there on the trip down river and I am making a little rock garden.

Aklavik is not only advancing in the seasons but with them. I think that I have mentioned the mud of Aklavik — so it is like announcing a victory to say that we have conquered it. During the finer days the men have been laying down sidewalks. Each property owner was given the lumber and responsibility of putting it down. Now we can start at our door and walk to the farthest end of town!

197

The radio station here [started by volunteers] has been licensed to broadcast. The men at the wireless station operate it in their spare time. It is decidedly local and I think that listening to one hour would give you a fairly good survey of Aklavik in general.

Once a week they read Delta news, individuals send messages to folks out of town. On Sundays the Roman Catholic and Anglican churches broadcast services. Mr. McLeod has one hour of classical music, while the remainder of the programs are requests from a collection of 150 records.

During the busy Easter period they broadcast from the hotel and restaurant, detailing an Eskimo dance, an amateur hour and a quiz program. The programs must be wholly entertaining for those dwelling in camps throughout the Delta.

There are not many muskrats this year and the price is less than a dollar. However, the trappers should still be able to manage if they are careful.

I had several pleasant trips over to the school cabin before the trail melted. It is a restful spot away from the busy school life. I enjoyed the different views as we followed the trail along the creek with the tall spindly evergreens reaching like mulleins into the sky.

Finally, the school pupils seem well. The boys had a piece of ground already dry enough for a soft ball field. The girls were able to procure a few beads and have been enthusiastically making little broaches of various shapes and sizes.

We had our annual Sports Day on Thursday, June 19. It was 40°F and a strong wind blew off the Arctic ice, causing the dry silt-like dust to fly in all directions. In the booths we had to cover everything but even then . . . . (can you picture lemon pies with gray meringue?)!

I went down to the sports about 2:30 and helped sell ice cream cones until nearly seven. We sold them at 2 for 25¢ until near the end, then to sell the last freezer, they were offered at 3 for 25¢. The day was so cold that I couldn't understand how the people could eat so much as well as drink ice-cold root beer. Of course, the natives all seemed to be wearing the same clothes as they had for the winter.

I took some snaps as various ones came to the booth, but I did not get out to see the sports events.

Mr. McKinnon, our School Superintendent, has just left after

PLAY TIMES

1. *Brownies*   2. *Sliding*
3. *Play House*   4. *Swing and Sing*
5. *Snowman*   6. *Snowball*

spending this week here and in the Delta. He is very interested and keen in his work for education in N.W.T., a congenial and enjoyable visitor.

We held the first Teachers' Convention ever held in the N.W.T. On Friday morning there was a knock on my classroom door. When I opened it there stood Mr. McKinnon and Sisters Douso and Sowka from the R.C. School. They observed and talked nearly all morning, then went to Miss Neales' classroom. After noon dinner we went to their school. They have about half as many pupils and teach in a much different manner than I am used to. After school was dismissed at 3:30 the five of us discussed education — imagine that — away up here!'

The competition I instigated in my woodcraft class for the boys was judged by two pilots, Doug Ireland and Morris Danes, in on a waterfowl survey being undertaken by an American wildlife group. James, Alex and Taddit won in the senior class, Woodie, George Gordon and John Francis in the junior. For winning first prizes, the judges gave James and Woodie their first plane rides. James reported, "Gee, my stomach, it's tickly."

Carved from scraps of wood with pocket knives

Bi-plane   Grumman Goose   1st Prize James G.

2nd Prize Woodie E.   Model Contest '47

Miss Hockin judged the girls' sewing. (They were making dolls and dressing them.) Bertha Moses and Helen Wingnik tied for first, Rosie Firth was second and Annie Roberts was third. Miss Hockin and I took them all down to Annie Hunley's for lunch, and to the store to buy some new materials to sew.

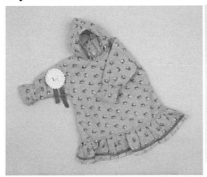

Our first visit to our cabin in the spring found it in a deplorable state of mud and water which had dripped through the roof bringing the soggy corrugated cardboard through, too. I got up on the roof to push down

The children see the river in flood but they draw what they "see" there – beaver, boats, etc.!

the snow that was left. We worked hard then cooked our bacon for sandwiches. The spring days seemed even more invigorating this year. Every spare moment I obtained help to get to the greenhouse or somewhere to sketch. Later someone always came to help me back. (My sense of balance was still such that I was unable to walk unaided.) There was also lots of incentive in the classroom to work well and quickly so that we could all go outside.

 Spring break-up was very exciting with ice jams and very high water levels. At one point the water covered the air strip in front of the school. A twin-engine Associated Airways plane landed on the field of mud, bogged down, went up on its nose and fell back again, greatly damaged. Unhurt, the aviators got out of the plane but as they attempted to walk to a drier spot they lost their boots in the sticky mud. After exactly two weeks, the drying winds had dried up the strip, the men had repaired their plane and they flew away with a roar in a cloud of dust.

A C.P.A. flight brought Miss Robinson back from her furlough. It also brought Dr. Tickle, a dentist, for the summer. Another plane, on June 22 brought Mrs. Kirk with her baby son and Corporal Bayne and family.

Some of my class have had little gardens in cans by our classroom windows. Now we've planted them in our own little garden in front of the school. I hope the children see some good results.

TO FORT MCPHERSON AGAIN

Probably because I was least needed at the school and Saturday was my day off, I accompanied Mr. Gibson, Mr. Oke and Miss MacDonald R.N. in taking the Loucheux children back to Fort McPherson for the summer. As Dr. Tickle wanted to include them in his schedule before we left, he worked all day on their teeth. It was 9:30 in the evening, June 17, before we got away.

From my diary:

Fulton, Woodie, Robinson, Neales and Rothwell stood on the shore, arms clasped in defiance of the chilly breeze. Mr. Hayward, sad that he's not going, helped to push us off.

It is my first time on board the "Beacon," and am pleased to find it so roomy and the engine so quiet. As soon as we got away from town we put the 25 children to bed on the floor of the cabin. (See chart and names.) They, understandably, seem to find sleep hard to overtake. (But it was easy to kick, yank the covers or say, "I can't go to sleep.")

Taddit Francis	Charlie Snowshoe	Annie Robert
William Koush	John Francis	Minnie Robert
Robert Alexi	John Nerzyoo	Margaret Stewart
John Blake	George Kunizzi	Sarah Teya
Neil Robert	Abraham Vittrekwa	Ellen Snowshoe
Neil Vitshehh	Effie Neyando	Agnes Modeste
Woodie Elias	Emma Robert	Mary Modeste
John Ed Snowshoe	Bertha Robert	Beartice Kaye.
	Ellen Alexi	

Sleeping arrangement for children on the Beacon, June 1947.

At 11:30 Little John is still awake. Miss MacDonald is in her sleeping bag on the fore deck. I can see Mr. Oke at the wheel. Lazarus is with us but I do not know the names of the other men.

Well, about 2 a.m. the rain chased MacDonald in. I went out and gathered a few perishables. Then the water started to drip in a few places. Margaret Stewart was quite sick (she had 5 teeth extracted with a general anaesthetic yesterday). Regularly through the hours I was signalling, "Get down," especially out of consideration of the ones who did get to sleep.

Finally around 5 a.m. we arrived at Fort McPherson. Many people were out to meet us and to claim their children. We met many parents for the first time. We all went to Dewdneys (Rev. and Mrs.) for a brief snack and back to the boat to sleep. MacDonald and I had the

Stateroom at one end of the Beacon – very comfortable. Mr. Oke and Rev. Gibson just slept on blankets in the galley

After a late breakfast at Dewdneys we visited Miss Herschel at her school [built last year by Mr. Hayward]. At three we went to an English service. Mr. Dewdney preached, Mr. Gibson read the lessons.

After dinner we went to visit the HBC Carsons. MacDonald and I visited the Veneltzis whose daughter, Bella, had died of the 'flu at Aklavik.

We left McPherson in the rain and travelled to the woodpile at Irish Coulter's place by 4 a.m. The barge was already loaded but not correctly. The men all helped to rearrange the logs and we were soon on our way.

At supper time we arrived at Aklavik. Mr. Forward, Miss Sowden and Mike, with the little green tractor, were standing on the bank.

SUMMER VISITORS – AND EXPLODING PUMPKINS

Mr. Hayward has been working steadily to construct the new mission house for the Cathedral incumbent. It seemed nearly finished when, on July 1, Woodcock and I went to see him. He had a Canadian flag flying.

Mr. Forward from the Toronto office of the School Commission spent the beginning part of July in Aklavik. I gave him a painting and he ordered another. Later I sent it but never heard from him. Of course, I never enclosed a bill. I learned a lesson.

On July 8 the "Messenger" with Rev. Jim Sittichinli (also known as Jim Edwards), Mr. Hayward with all his tools, and the four Wingnik children, left for Tuktoyaktuk.

In Aklavik we were getting a steady stream of visitors. They included Alex Stevenson from the federal Department of Resources and Development and Dr. Levey who stayed to examine eyes. He had Marshall, his son, with him. Only those who had prearranged appointments had their eyes examined. The Leveys left after just two days.

As a small monetary activity the mission took on the dismantling of an old barge that was left by the flood. While we enjoyed the challenge of nail pulling we were also able to enjoy being out in the

sunlight and seeing the many aircraft that were landing and taking off from the river. At one time, lined up along the shore, there was an Army plane, Mike Zubko's BRD and a Stinson. Another plane landed and brought Mary Elias a Loucheux church lady from Old Crow.

The pleasant summer days were sandwiched between times of very cold winds and snow storms. The greenhouse was a shelter for sweet peas, stocks, etc. but what we'd started outside just sat there. The mosquitoes weren't at all affected by the spurts of cold: at the first return of warmth they were hungrier than ever.

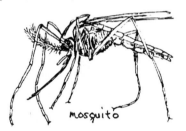

On July 14 the "Hearne Lake" arrived with three barges loaded with our freight. Neales helped me join the crowd at the river bank. Miss Sowden who, from previous times in the Western Arctic, renewed acquaintance with the Captain and caught up on the river news.

It was enlightening to watch the school freight being unloaded – it was like a preview of next year's meals. First came 20 huge bags (cwt) of sugar, then many cases of cornflakes (for Sundays?) etc. Our boxes from home, newcomers' trunks and, along with it all, the general excitement in the air were invigorating.

A few days later the S.S. Mckenzie River blew its loud steam whistle and pushed around the bend. It brought two new staff, Miss Snuggs to replace Miss Sowden as Matron and Miss Lau to assist with teaching. The fresh foods were then unloaded and came to the school on the wagon behind our little green John Deere.

Everyone helped. My job was to check the fruits. I picked over lemons first (9 bad out of 300). Then oranges (26 out of 440). Not bad, I thought, for all those weeks on the river.

On a special barge was a big pile of unusual boxes. The Canol staff quarters at Norman Wells had closed their big mess hall and made a deal with the Mission to take much of their food stuff still in stock. The boxes contained gallon cans of war-time rations from the U.S.A., e.g. very spicy hash, stews, wieners in salty brine, canned vegetables, etc. As the little tractor arrived back at the school with each load, Mike and Sutton removed the boxes so that the heavy cans could be identified and carried more easily. The storage room was a small area in our cellar where the frost didn't penetrate.

One fine day at noon they had just removed the boxes when lunch call came so we went in to sit, rest and eat. Meanwhile the sun shone. After lunch, just as Mike reached for a big can of pumpkin, it exploded. And before we knew what had happened there were more huge bangs. I was just coming out from the school and stared in amazement. Pumpkin pie filling covered everything including Mike and Sutton! (Dare I laugh?)

One of the native men picked up the garden hose. The water was cold but it not only cooled the cans (and saved some pumpkin pie fillings)

but it washed some of the excess from Mike and Sutton so they could get indoors to change clothes.

Mike was soon out working again but I took a while when Sutton came out of a bath, to reset her hair and tie a scarf over it.

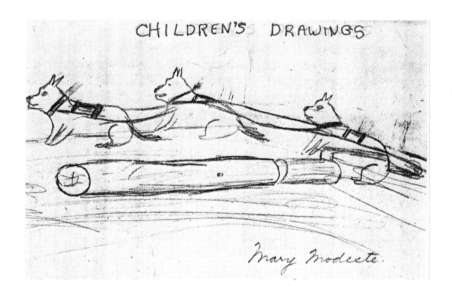

THE DREAM IS REAL

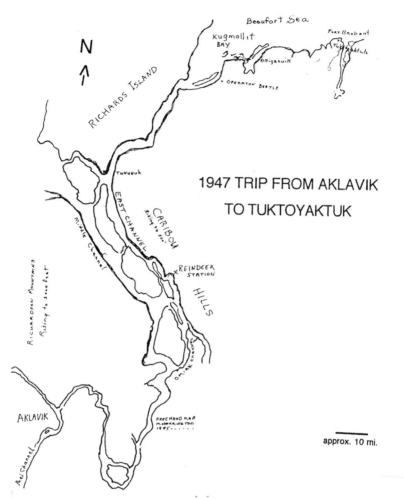

1947 TRIP FROM AKLAVIK
TO TUKTOYAKTUK

approx. 10 mi.

On July 19 when I heard there was work I could do in Tuktoyaktuk, I decided to take my last chance to go there. But I would have to find a way and pay for it. I had been officially declared a Civil Servant, A Day School Teacher, under Federal contract. However, my School Commission contract still had one more year. Since my status seemed in limbo, unlike Neales, Jones and Rothwell who had been approved to go to Tuktoyaktuk, I took my own initiative and went to see the officials at the S.S. McKenzie River. Purser Harold Gaskell and Capt. MacDonald assured us that if we could afford the cost, they could take us.

```
Trip................$10 + 15% tax, times 2 for return
Berth ............ $1.75 per night
Meals ........... $1.25 each
```

The ship was going to stay 1 to 3 weeks and that would make the cost about $100 each. We said we could take a tent and food supplies to camp. The trip was recorded (i.e. booked).

I had to be at the dentist's from 2 to 3:30 because the type of filling I needed had to be done in intervals. Then final packing, Neales and Rothwell added more for me, we had supper, got our mail and left with our letters in our pockets. Mr. Gibson wasn't around and I was unable to notify him of my decision, which I regretted.

Shorty Wilson came with Dave Jones' truck and took our grub and luggage. We walked on down and just in time to get up the last gang plank. Our food boxes nearly went astray but we finally got all collected. There was quite a crowd to see the boat off – and us, too.

We left Aklavik at 8:25 p.m. but, since we were conscious that this trip would be our only chance to see the "real" Arctic we had dreamed about, we were determined not to miss a thing. Neales and Rothwell sat on chairs on the deck until they found it too damp and cold.

First we travelled along the Aklavik Channel with its many bends and turns. There were often brilliant rays of sun bathing the river banks in bright bronze light.

Rothwell and Neales were in room #10, Jones and I in #12. Mrs. Figgures, whose husband was the HBC factor at Tuk, and her six months old baby, "Freddie," and Constable Scotty Stewart were also passengers.

By morning we were travelling in the Umiak Channel and I was glad to learn that the Reindeer Station was still to come. Miss Jones seemed to have slept well but I was too busy looking out the windows. There was a man on board trying to fashion sandals with coiled rope because the stewardesses were finding the hot floor made their feet swell. Our main floor is above the huge furnaces that heat water for steam power to turn the paddle wheel. The galley is also down below but the stewardessses work on the main floor.

The S.S. McKenzie River was pushing three steel barges, the centre one being a large house barge. Altogether the barges carried a record load of 800 tons of freight.

1 p.m. We saw the Reindeer [Caribou] Hills which were very interesting, with trees between the ridges and here and there a lot of bright colour. As we passed close to the Station we saw several individuals waving to us.

We had dinner at noon: tomato soup, roast beef, potatoes, turnips, and apple pie. Then my companions went for a rest while I sat on deck watching the pale, treeless Richardson Mountains to the west. They rise 2000 feet above sea level and are our first truly Arctic scenery.

One of the women passengers was down on the lower deck, talking to the deckhands. Her voice came up to me, "What I'd like to see is a real Eskimo!" I heard Victor Stewart reply, "Here's one right here" – pointing to Tommy Ross, Allan Koe and one I didn't know, sitting nearby. Now she is expressing herself "very incredulous" that the moccasins one of the men was wearing were decorated with porcupine quills.

The day went on – cold in the wind so we stayed in the saloon and talked to other passengers. Intermittently I read, "Magnificent Obsession" by L.C. Douglas.

We saw the Caribou Hills dwindle into mere gray knolls and evergreens completely disappear. We got lodged a bit on several sandbars but manoeuvred off and travelled more slowly.

Earlier we had seen one of Mike Zubko's planes overhead. After supper a CPA plane circled and landed. Herb Figgures came aboard to join his wife and Freddie. Marg. Greening and Dr. Tickle waved from the plane's window.

When we got near Kittigazuit, we tied up to a flat island sandbar as the water was rough.

The "Hearne Lake," and the "Watson Lake," are also here, the former with a bent rudder from struggling with the sandbar. We heard that a plane is also stranded on the sandbar. There is an "Operation Beetle" project being built near here.

<u>8 a.m. July 21/47.</u> I hurried to get dressed as the ship was moving but by the time I got to a window we were back at our mooring. One of the barges had been taken to the Beetle site, which is said to be the site of the original reindeer camp in 1935. Captain MacDonald went off with Captain Elyea on the Hearne Lake to take soundings and wind readings. The farther north the Delta waters flow, the more they slow down and drop their heavy loads of silt. Safe navigation routes are always changing.

We left our mooring at 2 p.m. and watched all day for white whales. The scenery is a monochromatic gray. Kugmalit Bay of the Beaufort Sea is very shallow and required careful navigation. Then through the dull scenery, like a phantom, we saw the S.S. Hearne Lake ahead. We saw barrel buoys and, what we had read about, pingos. We passed Whitefish Station with many schooners and several tents on the shore.

Approaching Tuktoyaktuk, Pingoes

We were pleased, indeed, to arrive at Tuk at 8:30. As we got closer, we saw the S.S. Fort Ross on shore being repaired. The "Lady of Lourdes," the R.C. Mission boat, was at anchor. We saw racks of whale meat drying here and there. Then we saw a crowd gathered at the shore where we met Rev. Jim Sittichinli and Mr. Hayward. The Wingnik children whom we had at the Aklavik school, came running to greet us. We finally went to the "Messenger" with Jim and Mr. Hayward. After having tea and/or cocoa with them we went to visit Rev. Thomas and Susie Umaok. We went to the church on our way

back to the S.S. McKenzie River and our last soft beds for a while.
The "Hearne Lake" had some barges stuck on the beach as the tide
was out but the Captain was anxious to leave. The "McKenzie"
worked hard to try to pull them off into deeper water but it was in vain.
We disembarked before noon to set up our camp and visit our Aklavik
boat, the "Messenger."

Miss Jones and I cooked bacon and eggs for Jim and Mr. Hayward
who lived on board while May (Rothwell) and Neales brought up our
luggage. In the afternoon I sat in the new school and started a painting
looking across the bay to the village.

At the HBC store an American artist, Kihn, was painting a portrait. I
found his technique very interesting and from then on kept looking
more closely at faces around Tuk.

After supper the tent had to go up. Some local youths helped us set up
the old white canvas tent just above tide line on the rocky beach. With
no trees or even sticks available, they wound the guy lines around
rocks and also stabilized the tent poles (which we had brought from
Aklavik) with rocks. There was no floor, just rocky bumps to spread
the blankets on. We soon found out that this location was a sanctuary
for the millions of arctic mosquitoes, along with the many loose sled
dog puppies that had easy access under the sides of the tent.

"Tuk" was an annual gathering place where the Eskimo came to hunt the beluga whales. The whales came there each year just as the char were leaving the mouth of a nearby fresh-water creek. (This was also the village's summer source of drinking water.) Tuk was a small place but since the summer is short, and the days long, it was busy.

I finished my painting after the tent was up and we four walked along the beach gathering stones. Three planes came in: R.C.A.F once and C.P.A. twice. One brought Joe Thorpe to fix the Fort Ross's stem.

The insects seemed to rest during the midnight hours and we were able to sleep a little. Early the next morning I heard the hammers as the men began the day's work on the school. I was really glad to get up and go to the Messenger for breakfast. May and Neales did the cooking while Jones and I walked to the point. While I chatted with Bob Cockney whose descendants were part of the Fiji Islander crews of early whaling ships, he had some quite pointed questions about me: "Why would you be nun?" "Why you not have husband and family?" "Why you work so hard with 100 kids? One or two no work." After so many questions he finally paused just as my companions returned from the Bonny Belle, the Cockney schooner, I barely had time to reassure him that I was not a nun.

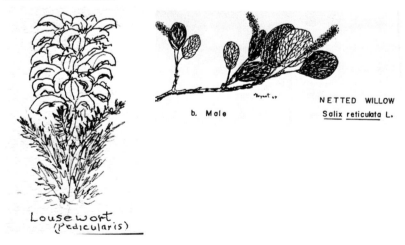

b. Male

NETTED WILLOW
Salix reticulata L.

Lousewort
(Pedicularis)

After dinner I worked on the school, tacking the big rolls of pink fibre glass insulation into the walls as far up as I could reach. The dust from the batts caused a very itchy rash and I decided to get some gloves on my next trip to the HBC. Meanwhile the other staff rowed to an Island. They brought me some wild flowers, willow twigs and Pedicularis.

The carpenters took a mid-afternoon rest so, to be quiet, I got Neales to leave me on the cemetery hill where I had a good view of the S.S. McKenzie River in the bay. I thought the scene interesting. It was to be the last trip of the big paddlewheeler to the sea. Also, since the crew had two live cows left of their fresh meat supply, they tethered the animals between me and the shore. They added a rare touch to an arctic scene.

 It was very hot and I was really plagued with both mosquitoes and other insects so it was a relief to have Neales come for me. We were invited to go with the Messenger, taking Thomas Umaok as a guide, to get fresh water as it came from a creek. They filled barrels on the deck by bailing with pails tied to ropes. Once again the insects attacked us.

Later, just before midnight, Artist Kihn and his wife came to have tea with us on the Messenger. As we talked we could hear deck hands unloading freight from the "McKenzie River."

The romantic sound of rain on the tent's roof roused us about 5 a.m. We scrambled to move things away from the walls of the tent. It was hard to get back to sleep so Jones and I went early to make breakfast. Then as the rain had stopped I went to sketch in the beautiful early light down by Susie Umaok's muktuk racks.

Later on Jones and I cooked a meal: 2 herrings, a whitefish, potatoes and jam. Each time we ate with Jim and Mr. Hayward we took contributions from the school supplies that we had brought with us.

The afternoon was eventful. The carpenters were resting, the day was unusually warm. We walked across the spit of land and noticed some naked native women bathing themselves and their children in the sea water. It really looked inviting. What could we wear? Just to get into the Arctic water? The others had shorts and blouses but I hadn't brought any. Jones offered to lend me her extra pair of pyjamas so in we went. First warm. Then cold, but if you plunged in, it was fine. We went back nearer shore and had a grand time. I decided on one more swim. And I kept going. The water held me up and I aimed for an ice floe ahead. The edge of the ice was ridged and hanging with dripping icicles. With great effort I got up on top.

1. Rothwell, Neales,
Harrington and Jones
A memorable swim
in the Arctic

2. It wasn't too cold
near the shore
Rothwell, Me, Neales

It was then I realized I had gone a long way – everyone on shore looked so small. And I could see I had got scratched on the rough ice. Maybe the ice was moving farther away? That was a frightening idea. I was shivering so plunged back in. Going back was harder but I made it. Everyone was laughing – Jones' pyjamas that I had borrowed stretched in the water and every stroke I made caused the legs and sleeves to flop around me.

I realized how really foolish I had been when Mr. Hayward quietly cautioned me about the venture. It had really worried him to see me so far away in the cold water.

Jones and I decided to do some baking in the Messenger We had brought some fresh apples. I made 4 apple pies. Jones made some biscuits which, because I had the little oven full, she took over to Susie Umaok's oven. We added cans of beans to the supper menu and it prompted Jim Sittichinli to say, "We eat like rich people."

We had scarcely finished the washing up when Jim announced that Thomas was returning from the whale hunt. We could hear the "punt, punt" of the motor. As I threw the dish water overboard, his vessel came round the point. I had a film to put into my camera , then we dashed.

The whale was a large white beluga and to me, as the community gathered and pulled it away from the boat to the shore, it looked like a great ugly shape of soft rubber. It probably weighed nearly 1800 pounds. Only the tail seemed to have design or beauty. The half-inch slits for eyes were ridiculous!

Before long, more people had come from the village to pull on the rope to get it fully on shore.

Thomas, the hunter, cut a piece off the tail. Bob Cockney cut off the head. There were thick layers of white skin and blubber (fat). I stayed to see the inside, clearly more interesting than the outside.

Neales and May left, (May Rothwell did not like to be called by her surname) Jones moved back after she was sure I was supported by a few empty oil drums. The whale had a heart much bigger than my head. It had a big meal of fish in its stomach and, sadly, a three-foot long fetus.

ulu

Each part was carefully cut away with the women's ulus and carried away in pails. The final mass of entrails was thrown further down shore to a howling bunch of dogs. The women took over the butchering but not before everyone was offered a small piece cut by Thomas from a flipper. I watched the others as they took it off the ulu with their

Thomas Umaok and Bob Cockney return

Neales helps to pull

Neales helps to pull

Harrington and Rothwell

Harpoon wounds on Beluga

HARVESTING THE BELUGA

Bob Cockney and Rev. Umaok begin the butchering

Susie renders the blubber to get oil - uqsuq

Entrails are fed to the dogs

lips. I did, too. Then I chewed, and chewed. It looked like a piece of hard cooked eggwhite but it was like rubber with an oily taste. The harder you tried, the more it seemed to bounce your teeth apart. I thought the local people swallowed it whole. Fortunately, I was able to quietly drop mine into the sand..

Neales came back again and thoughtfully brought my pencils and paints.

As I painted a bit further up the shore one of the whalers asked if I would like "go whale catch, morrow 4 a.m." "Oh yes, I would!"

So I had a unique early morning experience, dressed in my warmest clothes, wrapped in a tarpaulin, travelling out to sea until the hunters saw white backs moving in the waves. They then slowed down and while one man moved the boat closer, the other stood poised, harpoon at the ready. It all happened so quickly the whale was secured after another harpoon was in his thick skin. We got back to shore before noon.

I was, for once, very fatigued, and although a dozen or more children were waiting to have school on the beach, I took a rest. In an hour they were still waiting near the tent. Some of our school girls had taken over my rôle and were selling things (empty boxes, tin cans, etc.) in our make-believe store. That is how education works. Ruth Wingnik had brought home the little book I had made in school and she was "teaching."

That evening the S.S. McKenzie River had a party – everyone at Tuk was invited. Not knowing northern etiquette, we went at 9:30. The Saloon was set up for a party but no one had yet shown up. Then the Kihn's came. They entertained us with some anecdotes of their experiences. Finally everyone came – the Figgures, the Fort Ross crew, Sedgwicks, Mr. McCauley and all the native people. Most of the late arrivals had to look in from the deck as the Saloon was packed. The pilot played the violin, a deck hand the guitar and the party began. Nearly everyone danced. I nearly got left in the middle of a quadrille but I got into the ring again without falling. The brass stripping between the sections of linoleum flooring was a bit of a hazard but even the sombre Lieutenant was soon enjoying himself, as happy as a college freshman. Maybe it was the punch of ginger ale, Coke and rum served in a help-yourself fashion.

We had waltzes , etc. an old time menu of fun. The engineer had his camera and was taking pictures of various groups. The dances were sandwiched between songs by Tommy Ross and Scotty Stewart. Jim Sittichinli called the square dances.

Finally, at 2 a.m. we were directed to the dining room for a buffet – a table loaded with beef sandwiches, ham, tarts, etc.

Next followed the speeches. Captain MacDonald related how this boat – S.S. McKenzie River – started in 1907 (40 years ago) and that this party marked its last trip. Lieut. Brooks was brief – said it was his pleasure! Mr. McCauley was also a man of few words. Mr. Gaskell said one word – "Thanks." Captain Brayshaw – a speech of wit to match his red face; Mr. Sedgwick was a nervous wonder and Mr. Figgures declared he was a new man. Since I hadn't tried the punch, I enjoyed everything immensely

Then we all crowded into the Saloon, crossed arms and sang, "Auld Lang Syne" and the National Anthem. The voices resonated into the beautiful Arctic skies. What a party!

The next day the village was quiet until about noon except for me and my gang of children. I could hear them waiting outside the tent. As soon as I dressed we went to the sandiest part of the beach to do our numbers in the sand. Using a finger or a little stone for a pencil we did counting, adding and even some "take aways" – all with learning some English words. We did action words: walk, come, go, take, bring, etc. They seemed to learn so quickly.

There was some more I could do to help in the school. Jim and Billy were putting ten-test on the classroom ceiling and asked if we could put the insulation in the floor before it was boarded over. There was more I could do after Jim showed me how to place the boards for nailing.

Saturday was overcast and windy so we didn't expect our boat to leave although it again made a try to pull the Fort Ross off the shore. The tide is erratic at Tuk – never very high, occasionally very low. This week-end it seemed never to come in far enough. When first we saw the S.S. McKenzie River moving, we had hurriedly packed our bags which we later had to unpack to get a sleep.

The picturesque Anglican church in Tuktoyaktuk. Built by the people of drift logs.

July, 1947 After Sunday Service
Rev. Umoach in robes
I am at the central corner of the church.

The Ministry July 27, 1947
L to R
Rev. Jim Sittichinli,
an Eskimo Lay Reader,
Rev. Thomas Umoach,
the resident clergyman

Before we retired we tried to make the rounds to say our farewells. My children grew into quite a group before we had gone far. They kept saying, "Stay, stay. No go". They were learning English, and happiness, too.

Lying in wait for sleep I listened to Tuk. It was never quiet. Dogs tied to drift logs near the shore howled. Terns and gulls cried. Hordes of mosquitoes droned. Only when I heard a bell, I realized I had gone to sleep. It was Sunday, July 27 and Thomas Umaok wanted to see us all at his church.

The little church is made of logs – all gifts from as far away as the British Columbia forests, delivered free by the mighty MacKenzie River, the water road to the Arctic. Only the chancel of the church is furnished. There are three planks on blocks for pews. Thomas took the service in Eskimo, Jim read the lessons in English. When the planks were full, the others sat on the floor. There was no organ but the singing was pleasant. When we heard the tunes we could find the hymns in the syllabic books.

We had just returned to the Messenger when Jim Daye came in to say that the work boat was coming for us. We dashed to our tent, packed and pulled the tent down. In 15 minutes they were rowing us back. We went aboard at the galley door. At 10 to 2 we left Tuk.

When we were several miles out to sea I saw a man in a row boat – was it Mr. Hayward? Every day he rowed out and back for a nostalgic memory of his Newfoundland boyhood.

We settled down again in cabin 12. What luxury! From the window I could see the white whales cavorting in the waves. What wonderful memories they had given me.

By the time we reached Kittigazuit the sea was calm. As we neared Operation Beetle, the men reported that the barge we were to have picked up empty was still loaded. As soon as we arrived our crew and the RCAF staff (together 50 men, 3 of which are American) began work. The RCAF had unloaded five tons in six days but there were 270 tons left. They had two bulldozers but the steel construction bars, pipes, etc. were

Pulsatilla seed stalk.
Crocus seed head

Moneses uniflora
Pyrola

223

very heavy.

After 9:30 May, Jones and I walked up the hill and saw the camp sites and some wonderful scenery. We even saw the old Reindeer buildings. I gathered some flowers, finding among others, pyrola, yarrow and daisies, not to mention the fluffy seed balls of crocus. In the afternoon we went up again. This time I had my paints. I got left on a high point overlooking the northern tip of land. When, after two hours, Neales came to help me back to the ship, I had a painting which looked like a setting or background for an active stage play. Maybe it was.

In the evening our walks took us along the shores looking for interesting pieces of driftwood. A plane came in with Olden, Post, Cowan and Stevens so I sent a note to Woodcock who was visiting at the Reindeer Roundup. Another plane soon landed. It was an RCAF plane sent to evacuate a steel worker who had a stomach ache.

Cranberry and Twinflower

By morning when we got up for breakfast we were moving carefully along the East Channel watching for the Reindeer Station to come into view. It did at dinner time, so we finished our meal and went ashore. We went straight for the hill on the left. The birch trees were beautiful, their leaves golden. I was surprised as we climbed to find twin flowers growing among the cranberries. The hillside was riddled with ground squirrel holes which helped our footing. I stopped part way up to sketch the view.

Later I descended the hill by myself, mostly in the sitting position. We went to visit Mrs. (Marie) McGinnis. Her brother, Andrew, and Barbara Sedgwick were playing with a pet squirrel. Our short visit was enjoyable as we

Arctic Ground Squirrel

quickly exchanged news. They had recently had a visit from Miss

Oldenburg. They also knew that Miss Sowden, our school Matron, had flown out. We'll not see her to say farewell.

At 10 a.m. Wednesday, July 30 we were in Aklavik. The usual crowd was down to greet the McKenzie River. Sutton and I hurried to the school to let Dr. Tickle know that the boat was in. (He was booked to go south on it.)

The following summary with drawings was sent to friends at Christmas.

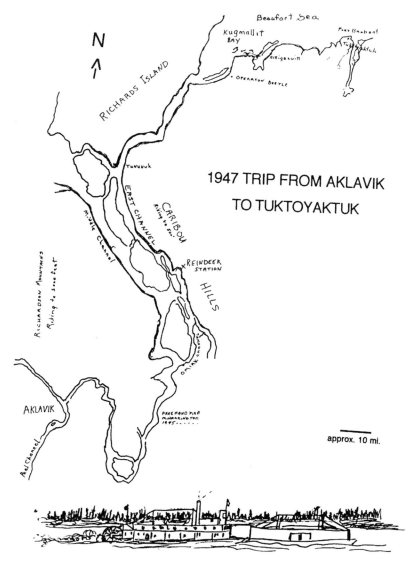

1. July 19, 1947. Aboard the S.S. McKenzie River. Left Aklavik in the evening, headed north. Prepared to stay up as long as we liked. Sun clothed alders in the bronze-gold light. Cold wind on deck so we went to rest around midnight.

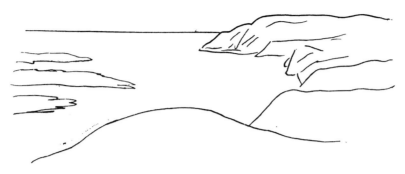

2. Saw the Caribou Hills dwindle into mere grey knolls and the evergreens completely disappeared. Stopped at mouth of river where we left a barge for the new advanced radio and Loran station being erected by the Army.

3. Passed the "Point of Land" into a monochromatic grey scenery – the Kugmallick Bay of the Beaufort Sea and felt that we had reached the Arctic Ocean. Watched the water in vain for white whales to appear. Strange little mole-like hills, [pingos] like miniature dead volcanoes, were of great interest.

4. Arrived at Tuktoyaktuk in the evening. Went ashore to see Mr. Hayward and Jim Edwards who were building the new school. Next morning they helped pitch our tent near the almost erected building.

5. Church of England, picturesque log building, still being furnished. Shepherded by Deacon Thomas Umaok, native Eskimo, so short of stature that the lectern towers above him.

6. Saw Thomas and a helper return from a whale catch – a "day's work with a whale of a catch!" Approximate weight 1800 lbs. Watched cutting of it on the beach: thick layer of skin and fat removed. Dark meat – has a fishy taste.

7. Whale's tremendous coating of skin and fat cut into pieces and hung in the sun until time is found to boil it outdoors in a barrel. Skin is severed from blubber and called "muktuk," resembling the hard boiled white of an egg – in texture and taste. The blubber is rendered and consequently becomes the offensive "ookshuk."

8. Aklavik mission boat anchored in cove below our church and Thomas Umaok's house. Mr. Hayward and Jim Edwards live on the Messenger and while at "Tuk" we used the boat for our "tuk" shop and cooked the meals.

9. On our return trip saw white whale momentarily appear among the waves. Spent several hours at the Reindeer Station, where the staff in charge of the reindeer herd have their residence. Saw no deer as they were herded north for the summer round-up. Climbed up on the hills for beautiful view. The hills stretched off into a barren land where the moss, the chief food of the reindeer grows.

10. The next day we were home.

SUMMERTIME DILEMMAS AND DECISIONS

The 1947 garden was a mixed success but the greenhouse was beautiful from spring until late September. The frilly petunias were especially successful. Eleanor's (Woodcock) wall flowers gave a delightful fragrance when you opened the greenhouse door. Even the straw flowers matured. By the first of August I was able to take bouquets of sweet peas and nasturtiums to friends. On one occasion when we had special guests to share a gift of fresh pork chops, I added the table centre of flowers and a seldom used salad bowl full of curly green lettuce. Every new mother got a bouquet of sweet peas.

By mid-August we had enough lettuce to share with all the town women. The growth was slowing but the quality was excellent. Knowing winter was approaching, I took spare moments to add soil to my house (classroom) plants. In September the greenhouse plants bloomed profusely. The more flowers I gave away, the more we had. On September 14 Eleanor and I picked 14 bouquets of flowers. The windows on the greenhouse were moved back to the school windows and only the plants I could save for a while were brought indoors.

Without the garden, I had a few more spare hours which soon got taken up when I was asked to type up the "Eskimo Records." It was a 270- page hand-written list of names, church affiliation, births, marriages, deaths, etc. Many pages also had information on the reverse side of the form. Typing was laborious for me but at least I could work from a chair. I began on August 5 and it was mid-September when I finished.

At the same time I was trying to complete my little primer, using 60 Basic English words, with drawings to accompany each page. I had my jelly hectograph, a special indelible pencil and paper. I could print two pages at a time on the hectograph, then the jelly had to sit over night to allow the imprint to sink. After doing this several times the pan had to be warmed to allow the old ink to move to the bottom, then left to jell again. It was a slow process. I had hoped to produce over sixty books. Each beginner would have one and it could be taken home. The little characters on the pages were local people engaged in local activities. From the very first pages it was a great success, meaningful and a source of pride for each child – they felt that they were in it.

The staff made several day-away boat trips to Red Mountain. Some climbed while the others went only as far as a good berry patch. The biting fly problem had diminished on the higher levels where a slight frost had hit. The frost had also improved the flavours of the berries. Beside the natural source for Vitamin C, these trips were great outings before winter set in. Nearer home, the children and I could still find a rewarding harvest of cranberries in the moss and lichens.

*Climbing
Red Mountain*

Meanwhile I was having some decisions to make. The Commission wrote wanting to know if I wished to leave. There was still one more boat to go south. I hadn't considered it, since I was not ill and I had a four-year agreement. The letter set me wondering if they wished me to go and if I should go. I was now officially the government-paid Day School teacher. Did the Commission think the government would sever this group of pupils from the school? I didn't know what to think. Just in case, I packed my trunk, with reluctance. The decision weighed on my mind until the last boat left for the south. My trunk and I hadn't.

This year my class would be smaller. Nominally my junior classroom was for the beginners up to about the grade 4 level. Once students had reached that level they were supposed to move on to Miss Neales' senior room. There the students spent half days in the classroom and half days doing and learning domestic tasks, kitchen, laundry, mending, wood cutting, etc. in preparation for their lives beyond school. I had been holding back some of my more progressive and academically inclined students to ensure that they received full time academic advancement. The longer I could keep them, the faster and more they could learn. They were in a home-like atmosphere of all ages, useful for me, but also in their school-to-home adjustments of family and languages. Perhaps I was also selfish in that I really enjoyed the older students and seeing their progress was extremely rewarding. I privately felt that the extra hours they spent in my room were of greater advantage to them in the rapidly changing social environment in which they would be living than those spent repeatedly darning socks, scrubbing floors, cooking, cleaning, etc. Partly as a result of that attitude, by the beginning of the 1947-48 academic year I had about 70 students to Miss Neales' 40. The discrepancy also had the very unfortunate result that Miss Neales may have been hurt by the thought that I considered myself the better teacher. I was very sorry about that because we were good personal friends. Rev. Gibson, as Principal of the school, had both the authority and the responsibility to make the change but it was a bit of a wedge in our congenial endeavours.

It was not that I lacked things to do. I still had about fifty students, counting the beginning Day Pupils. Corporal Bayne's little boy, Jimmy, started. He was a happy little blond boy with big blue eyes. The other children all wanted to be near him. One day not long after his family got a new baby sister, he came to school, threw off his parka and boots and rushed to tell me, "Miss Harrington, I don't feel wicked today. I am too tired. I had a bad night when baby Margaret cried and woke me up!" So then followed a classroom talk about what Jimmy said, some new words.

As the days went by I was mentally and emotionally trying to sort out another dilemma. "Outside" when on our way north, friends teased us about catching "Scarlet Fever," referring to the R.C.M.P. At that time I wasn't likely to become infected, I had a "permanent" attachment and felt a life-long commitment. The war changed that and here in 1947 I was getting that "dreaded" disease! Among the many friends with whom we worked, one became more special to me than the others. We shared some community interests and most of all the need to have a special companion. Many of the younger unmarried men about town were often visitors at the school. They often provided help to carry out our Aklavik events such as Sports Days by coming to assist our staff with preparations: planning, ice cream making, doughnut cutting, root beer bottling, the choir, films and skating. We all benefited from the friendships and co-operation. However, to a few these contacts became more deeply personal and that was natural.

My friend and I shared many similar goals and long conversations at first. Then I began to feel that our hopes were diverging. Would I stay and join his? I began to see my married friends – happy and secure, housekeeping, loving their babies and friends. I began studying a few unmarried friends – very philosophically determined to continue their careers but often unhappy. Which road would I take? Neither seemed for me. I needed time. We went to shows, the local parties, we worked well together on the committees and work groups in the Aklavik Activity Association (AAA) that had been formed to include native and white folk to construct a hall. But I could not see further.

The garden, 1947, in Rev. Gibson's Yard.
Foreground - Head lettuce, other plants are cabbages

A big event for me – on August 29 I walked alone from Gibson's front gate to the head lettuce patch. After two years of trying – often alone at night so I could fall safely in the snow with no one to see me – I had walked alone! Another important date was a month later when I walked to Pauline's house alone, falling only twice, and not hurt! Being very cautious after that I just walked in the moonlight on the sidewalk where the fence was near to catch if I needed it.

WINTER SETTLES IN

As the ice began to form at the river's edge, Aklavik said "au revoir" when the last boats left and the planes stopped flying. At the school classes were settling in and, dictated by the calendar, routine events followed those of the previous years. Provisions, stored hurriedly, were being sorted and stock taken. In unpacking some of the Canol windfall, the Matron found whole cases of "Rum Extract," 48 little bottles in each case. And 60 pounds of Bay leaves!

While the native enrolment was quite static, I had new day pupils whenever the parents brought them. I gained Elizabeth Firth and Ephriam who, I was forewarned, was "a little tiger." There were difficulties for me with both non-English-speaking and English-speaking students at the same time. The latter required much more attention, always "finished" and ready to move ahead, whereas for the native children, just watching and listening for the first few weeks kept them busy.

While 1947 had its highlights, there was one very low light. Ice cutting was being done but the watery holes left in the river's ice cover didn't freeze over as well in the milder weather. We were just sitting down for supper on October 28 when John Doe rushed in, "Two babies, she die, she drowned." We learned that little Ronald McNiece and Lee Hunley, both aged two, cousins, had drowned in an ice hole. For all of us, for the entire community, it was a big shock. A tragedy for the town. Their mothers, Pauline and Annie, sisters, had come north together to work in the Kost restaurant. They stayed, married, their sons were born the same month, two years ago. Apparently playing together in the snow in the fenced yard they had wandered off and down the river bank. The search found them, their bulky winter snow suits holding them up at the surface of one of the ice holes. Frantic efforts couldn't revive them. Everybody wanted to do something. There was nothing, except support for the parents. All meetings for the evening were cancelled. I spent the late hours making paper lilies and wreaths for the little coffins. We hurried to do baking to take to the homes.

For the sake of our other children we had to have a fun time over Hallowe'en. We helped them make costumes and dressed ourselves. We gave prizes for the best self-made masks. Then after parades and games, children and staff ate "incognito" at a buffet supper in their dining room, ending with ice cream.

An incredible report came to us that on November 1 the ice had gone out on the MacKenzie River! Apparently because of the milder autumn and heavy rain farther south, the thin ice hadn't held as the surge of water came along the main channel. Before long, however, extremely cold temperatures stilled the waters again.

The school children and the Aklavik community were in good health this term. The older boys in school were excited about the contest we had last year when the two winners got airplane rides. This year they all were anxious to try again and spent as much time as I could allow working in the corner of our classroom where we kept a table and the tools. Sometimes I listened in and marvelled at the rate they had leaned to use English. Several of them easily covered basic arithmetic in fewer than two years.

Mid winter brought even more social activities, more parties, more dances, and skating on the river ice where the young men had cleared a rink. Usually the moonlight was beautiful since in clear weather we saw it for 24 hours each day. Quite a number of the native people joined us, skating and playing games on the ice. On milder nights the old record player worked but when it gradually slowed down, someone wound it again. After a few episodes, we gave up on it and we would sing.

For Christmas entertainment I had my juniors do a series of nursery stories with Old Mother Goose sitting high up (on a ladder) in a huge shoe which I had constructed. "The Cat and the Fiddle," "Little Boy Blue," "Bo Peep." "Red Riding Hood," "Three Little Pigs," etc. popped in and out of a hole in the toe to do their parts. It turned out very effective and to my great relief, the shoe stayed in one piece until the last act when the wolf tripped on the shoe lace! The shoe collapsed and left Mother Goose (Martina Martin) sitting on her ladder among the rubble amid thunderous applause.

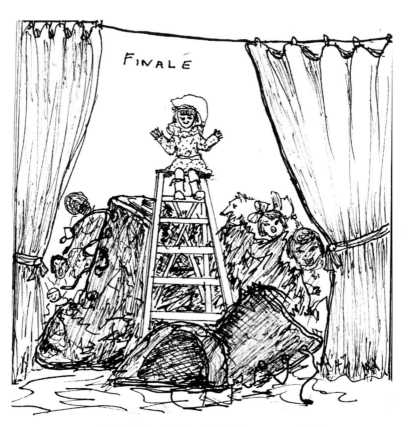

FINALÉ

Tuktuyaktok
Dec. 30th 1947

Dear Mary Harrington
All Saints School
N. W. T.

Dear Mary.

Very thanks for your
welcome letter. The people in here had
a very happy Xmas. Everyone is all
well and happy. except Lily Jonah's
wife, Mr. Philip nogasak, and Jimmie's
little boy is sick. at Xmas we had
a feast the H. B. C. manager gave us
the feast, we had feast in Day school
house after the noel. After the feast
we had the husky dance in the Day
school house. I send my best wishes
and also send a Merry Xmas to
Archdeacon Marsh, to James Edward
and to Mr. & Mrs Jones and to all
The staff at aklavik.

May God bless us all
till we sheet again.

From your helper

Deacon Thomas nuwook

1948
CHANGING TIMES BRING CHANGING ROLES

On New Year's Eve there was a big community dance to get ready for the next year. Many dances were novelties. In one, the contest was to see which couple could blow a balloon the farthest. Ward Stevens and I got that prize. The dances included "Drops of Brandy", jigs, a handkerchief dance and many rabbit dances (polkas). When the supper dance played, I had supper with one of my good friends, Stan. Then, when the dance in the community hall was over I went with Ward to Peffer's to welcome in the New Year again. There the dance went on 'til 6 a.m., truly a lively beginning for January 1, 1948.

The winter social life was more active than ever. The largest party was probably the one we had at the school to say farewell to some and to welcome new people. Now that planes came so frequently there were often changes made in the RCMP and the Signal Corps. Even in the January darkness the CPA flew reindeer meat from the Reindeer Station. Some local native people began to use charter flights to get to and from their camps. Mike Zubko's Air Service was based right in Aklavik and very busy.

The Community Hall was supported by natives and whites equally so many events were held there. At the same time we often had people bring to the school films that the children could share. The radio station (CHAK) broadcasts coming events and often described them afterwards. There was now a Trappers' Association that broadcast announcements of upcoming meetings and subsequently the main decisions concerning hunting and trapping. That seemed to involve more people. Sometimes I went across the river to baby sit for Mrs. Boxer so that she could visit in town. Her husband (Bert) was out at his trapping camp most of the winter but she kept in touch by sending messages through CHAK.

Besides teaching, school duties, dispensary, Brownies, Women's and Girls' Auxiliaries, choir, organ playing, manual training etc., I had a new chore – regular charts to fill in for the federal government concerning the Day School pupils. The charts were hard to understand so I went to see the federal administrator, Albert Cottrell, to ask for help. The School Commission also had required forms but they were just attendance and I was used to them.

Mrs. Kirk came to see my paintings. She and the Inspector commissioned me to do two paintings. I was always happy to have a canvas on the go for spare moments!

The weather was becoming extremely cold at the end of January. Fortunately we didn't have wind and the buildings were warm. On one occasion the heavy snowfall was blown into huge drifts, which delighted the boys. Their game was to run and jump into a drift. If the jumper disappeared he was a winner.

Deep snow Divers, Aklavik

Along in March many visitors dropped into my classroom – the plants were blooming, the boys' woodwork and the girls' sewing, as well as our wall charts and decorations were all on display. If a visitor came during class times, I would ask the students to be hosts, to answer questions, especially on their own work. Surprisingly they never hesitated and were sometimes quite entertaining.

On Thursday, March 11 Marge Sutton went with me to the Signals' Station to send a short-wave radio message to Boxers at their out-of-town home telling them that I'd leave for their place at 5 p.m. Friday, weather permitting. I had planned a venture!

I would walk and snowshoe out to visit Marge Boxer, Bert and the two little boys at their trapline camp. I wanted to see if I could. How far? Someone said it was ten miles but I thought they were just trying to deter me.

Friday was clear sunshine, -11°F. At noon I packed a few things into the haversack I had made and left my travel clothes ready on the bed. At five I supervised my cleaning jobs, and dressed quickly – I was off amidst the children's queries, "Where you go?"

After the rush it was refreshing to be out, warmly dressed, striding confidently in the bright moonlight. When the trail entered the willows I felt less secure, there were so many shadows! My feet snapped some twigs! The trail was less travelled. For some time I quickened my pace and thought of other things. Then from far off I heard the jingle of dog harness.  How could I meet a dog team on such a narrow trail in the snowy woods? Get off the trail. I did as soon as I could. Then I stood and waited. The team stopped before it reached me and Bert Boxer called out and turned his team. He had come to meet me.

Donald Greenland had hitched a ride with Bert although his own dog team, driven by his son, Garnet, was following behind with an empty sleigh. Apparently Donald preferred Bert's team and had jumped in, uninvited. Bert told him he was turning back with me and that he'd have to ride with Garnet.

Boxers' Cabins

We had a good ride through the mouth of the Aklavik Channel, along the Jameison and over the portages. The dogs knew they were going home. Marge had just skinned 13 rats in 35 minutes and had supper ready. Ward Stevens had been staying there but had gone back to town. Little Donald (4) said I could have Ward's dinner. Marge and I slept in the outer bedroom, an addition to the big cabin. Bert and the boys, Donald and Teddy, stayed in the cabin.

<u>Saturday</u> Bert went out in the -32°F weather to check his traps and lifted them. Marge showed me how to take the dried skins from the stretchers and how to put new ones on. We strung them on a line near the ceiling. Bert was doing some skinning but I didn't ask to learn that!

Bonnie snares a rabbit.

After lunch Donald took me out to see his snare and we were both amazed – he had caught a rabbit. We took it back to the cabin where it could become tomorrow's lunch. There was a small hill down to the frozen river so we had fun sliding down on the toboggan, walking up dragging the toboggan and doing it all over again.

In the evening Marge gave me my first lesson in chess. By then little Teddy had got over his fear of me, a stranger, and chose to sit on my lap.

<u>Sunday</u> Was an easy day for Boxers, since the traps had been pulled

Somersault on the river bank.

and there were no rats to skin. I took the boys out to play. They were used to the cold and snow and liked to slide. Another game was to somersault down the hill. Naturally I could do that, too, but a few times and I felt really dizzy. We re-set the snare and went in.

The plan was that Bert would drive me part way home after an early supper but company came so I stayed for the night and we got up before seven next morning. The wind was in our faces and I'd have really frozen except that I was sitting well wrapped in a sleeping bag in the carriole. It was 7 minutes to 9 when Bert dropped me off at the school. Of course the children saw me coming and had lots of questions. We made it into a lesson. I sketched a moon and some one walking. They told me what caption to write, then I drew a cabin and a lady with 2 boys. I drew a rabbit in a snare, boys sliding on a hill, boys somersaulting down a hill, and each sketch needed a caption. They really enjoyed the morning. While the senior students could almost write them appropriately, the beginning students drew pictures. After recess and their arithmetic lessons they made pictures and captions for me of one of their own ventures.

No wonder the children and I belonged to one another. We enjoyed it.

Towards the end of March there was great excitement around town when the doctor's igloo (Quonset Hut) burned down. Dr. Harvey used the igloo for this office, health matters as well as native concerns. The water hose from the river froze so little could be done. Many records burned but copies for most were likely in Ottawa since, with frequent air service, all reports now went out as they were prepared. On one of my recent walks I saw four aircraft; Mike Zubko's Cruiser, CPA's "BVH," "ATZ," (Fairchild) and "DON," a Taylorcraft which was flying prospectors.

The School Superintendent, Mr. McKinnon, came to Aklavik at Eastertime. He was always a welcome visitor and guest. With his visit we held our second Teachers' Convention. One morning we faced a fierce north wind to go to observe at the Roman Catholic School. They showed us a dormitory as well as changes in the classrooms. At 3 p.m. Sisters Poulin and Douso came to visit us. I was not sure that the Sisters really understood enough English to comprehend our discussions but all the teachers tried to put forward topics that would let Mr. McKinnon understand a bit more of the Delta life. We hoped to advise him as he would be setting the new curriculum patterns.

Aklavik was once again struck with a 'flu epidemic. Before we realized it, most of the children were in bed sick. The place was a continuously hacking noise of coughing

From my Diary: *Apr. 4. Sunday. I had an annoying cough yesterday. I may have a touch of the 'flu, at any rate have some minor aches, an unusual touch of laziness with a temperature of 102.4. I got up to take my evening duties. Now 93 children are sick. Only Lily Rhoda Kolinyek and 4 boys are up. I won't give in as most of the staff are also down, as is most of the village.*

By the 10th most were getting better again but we kept hearing that one of our older people had died. Daily a plane brought in patients and took improved ones home. I never got really ill. I was soon able to complete a set of india ink drawings of the wrought-iron candlesticks and candle brackets at the church. Bishop Fleming had asked me to do them and send them to Toronto.

From my diary, Apr. 26. Above freezing, 40°F. Classes in a.m. Went ratting with Anna, Ada, Annie Abel, Bertha Moses, Lena, Ruth, Rosie and Barbara. Set 6 traps on the first girls' lake. Set 2 on little lake. Deep snow. Lovely wind in the trees. I watched snowflakes and ravens. I still hung on to some 'flu and weariness but nature rejuvenated me undeniably.

The next day we got three rats. A new Day student, Dorothy Cook arrived. There was word of more deaths: Maurice Mitchel and Old Pete. By evening we were in the midst of a raging blizzard.

<u>May.</u> The Delta area is a fascinating place, not only the ever extreme changes in the weather but the lively social activities of the inhabitants. If only a few were well they still danced, visited, played bridge, etc. I saw my special friend nearly every day. He respected my plea for more time. I had such a difficult decision that had to be finalized soon. It wouldn't be easy. Sometimes I was sure: when I left the north I'd go to university, I'd immerse myself in studies, there were so many areas that stirred my curiosity – mostly the natural world. Then I'd see my friend and once again, the problem.

I'd been bringing branches of willows indoors. In only two or three days the "pussies" opened and I could share them with others. One day I had an excellent study of some pine grosbeaks. The greenhouse was planted and the early sweet peas were up. On May 13 a very

Robin

worn and faded robin perched on our fence. The seagulls were sitting around on the snow waiting for open water. I took my "ratting" girls out to market their pelts in a modern way – estimates, bills, grading, etc. They got $2.25 average for each of their 22 pelts. The boys had 23 rats but they were offered only $2.00 each. It all turned out well, however, when Miss Lau, who wanted a fur jacket, bought the boys' rats for $2.25 each, the same as the girls had obtained.

May 14. Marge Sutton and I, dressed in ski pants, jackets, rubber boots and carrying our pack sacks, made a trip out to see Marge Boxer. The ice on the channels and creeks was strong but soft. The days were long and we arrived before

Marge had got to sleep. We had one full day with her and the little boys, enjoying the freedom of quietness, playing with the boys, listening to the "Patients' Party" from CHAK Aklavik. On Sunday we were on our way back by 6 a.m. There was no wind, lots of clear sunshine and best of all, the trail, having frozen hard overnight, enabled us to get back to the school in two hours. We heard and saw grackles and blackbirds.

By the middle of May we received reports that the ice had gone out at Norman Wells but here at Aklavik the only open water was a small patch by the HBC. The Snowy Owl that I saw was turning brown. Many small sparrow-like birds had arrived but not finding dry nesting sites, had laid their little speckled eggs on the ground as they sat and waited. The children frequently brought me

SNOWY OWL

eggs that they had found on one grassy place in the yard. Numerous flocks of migrating geese squawked and honked as they flew and circled overhead looking for resting places to nest and swim. I had the rock garden ready in one corner of the greenhouse. Spring was late but surely on its way.

Five days later, on May 21, the streams of water on both sides of the river's ice were rising. Our men took one last chance to pump water and fill the cisterns then went over to the ice in the jolly boat, disconnected the engine and pump and put them into the boat. Then, pulling the pipeline behind, they returned to the shore.

From my diary. *At noon I walked into the willows past Rawlings. The wet snow came up to my knees, I got wet but did not care as I saw many birds – grackles, sparrows, tree sparrows and one perky little white-crowned sparrow. My boys in their woodworking group finished their boats. At 4:30 I went down town and stopped to speak to Mrs. Kirk and Brian. My friend called me and invited me to the dance. The dance was over by one but we talked until nearly 3:30 a.m.*

An Anson aircraft came in and landed on the ice in the middle of the river. Besides bringing in employees for Peffer's, it brought a supply of fresh food. Eleanor Woodcock and I went to the store and bought: 7 oranges $1.00, bananas 20¢ each, tomatoes 80¢ a pound, oranges and apples 15¢ each and cabbage at 75¢. Just seeing food that hadn't had to be soaked over night, food that we didn't even have to cook, was a good re-vitalizer for our enthusiasm. In the evening after church several couples, including my special friend who had been at church for the first time, came to the school for lunch and to work on a big jigsaw puzzle. Seeing the emerging picture of mountains on the table reminded me of my scholarship to the Art School in Banff. I had been allowed to defer it until the summer of 1948 but now it would lapse. I wouldn't be there.

On May 26 I saw dozens of birds – plovers and longspurs were everywhere. I have changed the children's feelings about birds. When I first came to the Delta their impulse, as soon as they saw a bird, was to kill it. A bit of hard mud, a bit of ice, the use of catapults, anything to strike the bird. Now most of them would tell me at once, "There a bird. See," and I often heard the older students admonish new children not to hurt the birds. I have found creatures familiar in the Arctic very useful in arousing use of new words, conversations and even stories and songs.

By May 28 the water had risen extremely high. The men in town were constantly busy moving things to higher ground. They were

SPRING FLOOD

Going to school

Scott's house

Sidewalks afloat

Boats are isolated

Off to school

continually checking their boats, for even those that had been on the high banks all winter were apt to float as the water reached them. Some boats were already floating towards the oil tanks. Fortunately the Mission boat, the "Messenger," was still dry. I had been asked to make a stencil of its name. The situation now reminded me that if I didn't use it now, I might not be able to later. So I left the other watchers, returned to the school, got the stencil, paint, brush and some tape. It didn't take long to do.

By noon on the 29th of May the ice moved. The sweepstake was $145.00 of which the winner, Jim MacDonald, got half – the rest went to the AAA for community use. The water kept rising and many of the village residents were up day and night.

From my diary, *Sunday, May 30 Men very busy. Children up early and at the windows. The water is rising rapidly. Children play by our front walk in a canoe. Six of them turned over into the shallow water and mud, causing a good laugh (and the day in bed!). After Sunday School, Marge Sutton and I walked Bonny Bell home – also we wanted to see the high water. Boats, barrels, boxes, etc. were all afloat and, in canoes, many men were trying to redirect them to more secure places.*

Diary, *May 31. Rain has changed to snow. Water is at our door, sidewalk is afloat. Some of town, e.g. Pauline's, Freeman's, is cut off. They've moved out to be safe. Ed. Scott's house is up to the chimney. Water is in Boxer's town house. Mike took some of us across to the Pokiak Channel and we saw Scott's house-top in the whirling water. Our sheer pin broke so, in that rapid flooding river, we had a hard time to paddle back to shore. The police boat was out and they seemed to be keeping an eye out for our safety. Dodging flotsam in the strong current was a real problem.*

Mike from our school went out ratting every night, as many of the residents here did. He shot about 35 rats per night. Early in June I enjoyed a memorable night. At 5 p.m. I went in the boat with Mike. We saw mink playing on the river bank, a huge raven's nest in an old spruce leaning over the river. In some places there were snowdrifts 16 feet deep but flowers already blooming a few feet away. We got home again at 2 a.m.

Everyone was trying to help the flooded people. We started in on massive laundries to wash clothes and bedding that got saturated with muddy water. Scott's was the biggest job as all of their possessions except one had been inside the house. The surviving article was Massey's (Mrs. Scott's) wedding dress which was stowed in a ribbon-tied box up on the highest rafter under the roof.

Many of my annual plants were already blooming. Before I went walking with Marge Sutton today I cut the snapdragon blooms to take to Mr. Campbell who has been very ill.

June 12. Other signs of the season: the dentist, Dr. Tickle, is back; the ratting season closed on the 10th; the whooping crane research team (Allan and Smith) from the United States is here; four buyers are vying for pelts at the trading posts. I had finished the two paintings for Kirks, so delivered them, wondering if I'd ever see them again. [The two paintings had taken me about 500 hours to complete and netted $100.]

June 18. My first day of Summer School for Day pupils. Five came the first day. The next day, 10 more. I set the time to be from 4 p.m. to 8 p.m. to accommodate the local habits. We started off with basic English and soon I would be able to grade them. I hoped we would be working together for at least a month.

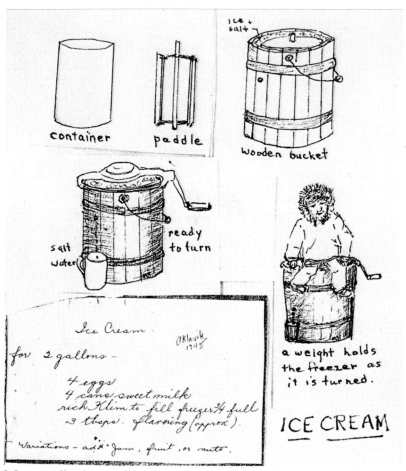

container paddle

wooden bucket

salt water ready to turn

a weight holds the freezer as it is turned.

ICE CREAM

Ice Cream (Aklavik 1945)

for 2 gallons -

4 eggs
4 cans sweet milk
rich Klim to fill freezer ¾ full
3 tbsp. flavoring (approx.).

Variations - add jam, fruit, or nuts.

My contribution to the annual sports day was organizing the making of ice cream. On June 23, before opening my classroom I had been all over town collecting ice cream freezers and ladles and enough ingredients including the sweet condensed milk which was supplied by HBC. That evening, after 8, many volunteers came to make ice cream while others made pies.

The Sports Day, June 24, 1948. We couldn't have had nicer weather. We had school class in the morning. My helpers in the busy ice cream business were Wally Storey and Marge Sutton. We also sold the root beer. The next booth sold pie, doughnuts and coffee. Mrs. Roberts had a fish pond. Miss Lau and Mrs. Carson had games. After expenses we cleared $700.00 for the Community Sports Association and satisfied a lot of appetites. I got back to the school by 7 p.m.

Nearly everyone, except two of us on duty, was at the evening dance which lasted until 4 a.m.

<u>Friday, June 25.</u> An exciting last day of school for the residential pupils. We cleared desks, books, etc., played and I explained the written reports that would be given to the parents. My beginning Day pupils were also there in full numbers and I was hoping that the full-time students would pass along to them the enthusiasm and enjoyment they got from our school. I started on my end of June register when Ward Stevens came and I went with him to release three muskrats and feed the Boxers' dogs. There were a few mosquitoes but the evening was truly lovely.

With the end of June many phases of school life terminated. The "Beacon" left with the Fort McPherson children. Some parents who had been waiting in Aklavik for their children and/or their relatives' children, took them off for the summer. And I seemed to have come to the end of my indefatigable source of energy. For several days I did as little as possible.

My Day School class was expanding and we decided to begin at 3 p.m. which extended their days to 5 hours, 3 to 8. They were all native people — not all children — who were in Aklavik temporarily, mainly to take advantage of summer employment when the boats came in.

I was glad to be left to take over the dispensary and various health concerns as they arose. For some time John Andrews had had a high temperature which bed rest hadn't remedied. During the War, medics had begun to use a synthetic compound called "sulfa" to treat bacterial infections. As soon as it passed the Health Research requirements it was made available to the northern medical people. It

came in powder form at first and we dissolved it in sterilized water for injection by hypodermics every four hours. John slept a great deal and didn't even wake when I gave him his night time shots. Some of the patients showed reactions to sulfa but he tolerated it.

July 1, 1948. Down town was observing the national holiday. I was feeling energetic so scrubbed some of the classroom and held my classes between helping John Andrews who hadn't really responded to the slow sulfa. His temperature stayed quite high. The evening light on the cathedral lured me to the beach with my paint box. Looking back from the beach, with the bright colours of the roofs and the pale new leaves of the poplar behind, the scene was very impressive. I worked quickly. That was fortunate as Pauline and Mrs. Kirk, with 5 tourists in tow, hailed me. I gave them a tour of my classroom and the main parts of the school. They seemed to find every detail incredible, not what they had expected in the Arctic.

After they left I dressed to go with Marge Sutton and Marge Boxer to the native dance at Peffer's. There were 5 Husky drums, very entertaining. We joined in the women's rôle in the dances, stepping in the circle slowly to the beat around the story dancing man in the middle. I hurried home at 2 a.m. to give John Andrews his sulfa and encourage him to have a large cup of cold fruit juice, his head was so warm. I went back for a few more dances. A bilingual native translated the dancer's stories orally for us. One was a ptarmigan arguing with an Arctic Owl. One's imagination in interpreting his actions made it a lively production.

My classes turned out well and attendance was good despite all the activity that occured in the village throughout the nights. Each evening when I was wishing to finish, my students were very reluctant to leave. The days were consistently pleasant and warm. I was very pleased to visit Captain

The Dance
OwL AND PTARMIGAN FIGHT

Naylor here on his way to Tuk with the S.S. Pelican Rapids. (He had been our 'understanding' Captain on the S.S. Distributor in 1944.) I was also happy to spend some times alone in the bush when I searched for and found a little orchis (a kind of wild orchid). I went to Kirks who were packed to leave and paid her for some surplus tanned moose hide she wanted to sell. They paid me for my paintings. Ward Stevens visited and because of my questions, lent me some plant and bird books.

The Kirks left on the 7th and the village seems to be slowly quieting after the departure of people and boats. On one task after another I closed my books: the W.A., the Brownies, the choir, and so on, soon it would be the lid of my trunk.

Whenever I found time in good weather I haunted the woods. I found <u>Moneses</u> <u>uniflora</u>, etc. The mosquitoes were in swarms and multiplying. I saw two brown cranes to add to my blackboard list and <u>Listera</u> <u>caurina</u>, I thought. I took a lily to the Sisters and repotted my classroom plants. More people were asking me for paintings. My days were long but with my Day Classes now down to 8 students, I felt we were making great progress. The Eskimo learned English, at least the basic form I taught, very quickly and with such good humour. One day I had a dental appointment and arranged with them to put on an "English" visit for me to listen to when I returned. It was a great surprise. They chose the girl with the best English to be the teacher (me) and the rest played the students. She welcomed me, "Hello. Glad you come. Sit down." Then each one read some of my (our) new book. She added, "Questions?" and she got some. Then they sang a song with both Eskimo and English mixed. The tune was good. I closed the class with prizes for all before I left for a trip to the Reindeer Station.

one-flowered Wintergreen   Listera

REINDEER STATION

We left Aklavik about 1:45 p.m. on the "Ram" pushing a large scow. The eight school boys who remained at the school for the summer were on board:

Steven Bonnetplume,	Sammy Smith,
Charlie Supee,	Joseph Urvena,
Alec Illysiak	George Gordon,
Moses Amayok	Walter Poasanna.

Other passengers were:

Mr. Gibson (our Principal)	Len Brown
Charlie Smith	Pauline McNiece
Westaway	Owen Allan

Owen Allen's wife, Martha, little Renie and their new baby.

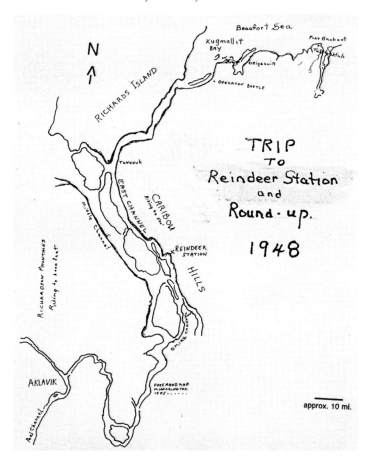

We went via the Peel Channel, Aklavik Channel, Schooner Channel, the Napoiyak, crossed the MacKenzie (Middle Channel) to Umiak and thence to the Reindeer Station, arriving at midnight. We had had a little engine trouble just before we crossed the MacKenzie so we were over an hour late.

Lorna Post (wife of the Station manager) and Marie McGinnis (wife of the Station Engineer) and some men helped us ashore. We ate some lunch we had brought and Lorna took us to our beds.

During the night rain and strong winds blew in. We had planned to rise at 7:30 but it was nine before anyone stirred. I tried to help make the boys' breakfast. After we had all eaten, Mr. Gibson and I did the dishes.

In my diary, July 20, written at 10:45 p.m.:
Day is over. All day it was foggy, windy and dull. I haven't been out-of-doors. Needless to say, I found things to do like making a huge batch of cookies in Post's kitchen. Right at noon a plane, a Cessna, arrived from Flin Flon with Mssrs. Plumers and Dodd, sportsmen on holiday. Mr. Dodd talked about Flin Flon and told me he knew my uncles, Harry and Charlie Kelly. The visitors shared our lunch and left, despite the storm, for Whitefish Station.
In the evening we knit, read and lunched. Marie McGinnis came over to join us at Post's. When she went home, Pauline and Westaway went with her. I am going to bed at 11:39, hoping the weather will clear overnight.

Wednesday and the weather was even worse. No one got up 'til after ten. After helping with breakfast, I went to the boy's cabin. The boys and I decided to climb the hills. Half way up the clouds opened and the rain poured down. Soaked to the skin, we hurried back.

There was no hope of travel so we passed the time reading, talking, playing games and trying to see out the windows, checking to see if the pier had floated away. I went with Marie McGinnis to her house where I met Mr. Brown and Dick Vokototh, an entomologist, who knew my brother Joe. To pass the time we had a big game of rummy, using three packs of cards.

The next day remained windy but it wasn't raining. The ladies all needed their hair done and I also had time to make some pies. In the evening the wind dropped a bit so the "Ram" loaded its 22 passengers (8 boys, Mr. Brown, Dick Vokototh, Lee post, Charlie Smith, Len Brown, Felix and his wife and girl, Owen Allan and his wife and baby, a native called Andrew and Rev. Gibson) and left with its scow.

Left on our own at the Reindeer Station, we had a restful evening talking and knitting.

Friday was a miserable day again.

From my diary:
I went up on the hill anyway. I went away back over the barren land, land like I had never seen or felt before. It was level and seemed to stretch for ever. I saw cranberries, blueberries, yellow pedicularis (louse wort) and other plants. I looked around and could see no landmarks. Feeling lost, I followed my steps in the moss and returned to the house. In the evening I returned, carrying my paints and located half way up the hill. The Reindeer Station was comfortable in the trees below. I was so totally immersed in this unique geography that I was up early next morning, lit the fire to warm the house and went back up to finish my painting. ATZ flew in, landed, left again.

By lunch time I was ready for a meal so decided I'd better leave the hill for an hour or so. When I went up again with Pauline and Westaway, we continued to the very top and I painted looking north. The fog and mist kept rolling in, making it wet and cold. My hands were numb but the scene was colourful and interesting. The plane returned at dinner time, bringing Messrs Fraser, Prescott, Boyes and the Pilot, Cameron. Ward Stevens came later by canoe, towing a smaller canoe.

Then the men poured drinks and we women went over to Marie McGinnis' to knit. Everyone found some place to spend the night.

On Sunday I had breakfast with Marie McGinnis and Cameron. Then we went down to the river to watch Fraser, Boyes, Marie, Pauline and Lorna fly off with Cameron to Aklavik.

From my diary:
Ward Stevens and I went by canoe to the first lake. He portaged the canoe and we paddled. The beaver he had seen last fall have deserted and we saw only a bit of an old lodge. It was lovely on the lake. We found a few plants. As we returned home we met the S.S. Radium Queen with barges of oil on its way to the Lorran Station. I watched Ward press his botanical specimens.

Westaway and I cooked dinner for Lee, Ward and Prescott. The plane returned from Aklavik. Boyes remained but they brought Miss Hinds, the new teacher from Fort McPherson. Mr. Fraser was holding a conference at Post's so we went to Marie's where Miss Hinds and I also spent the night.

Monday, July 26 From my diary:
The men left on the plane, flying off into a beautiful blue sky. When I went up on the hill, Miss Hinds came too. My sketch was rather poor and not the usual fun as Miss Hinds talked continually of her travels in Sweden, Lapland, New Zealand, Australia, Saskatchewan, etc. An amazing woman but I missed my inspiration that nature's beauty moving onto my canvas creates, the inner therapy I've needed all my life.
It was 4 o'clock when we came down to the Station. Westaway was a kindred spirit – acting on our mutual dare, we went down to the river by the pier, shed some of our clothing and jumped in! It was cold, invigorating to say the least. How many miles are we north of the Arctic Circle?

There was a violent storm overnight. We were pleased to find the sky clearing when we arose at 7:30. This was to be the day we were to fly to Kidluit Bay. We waited all day for ATZ. Lorna couldn't contact either Aklavik or Lee on the short wave radio. I had used nearly all of my knitting supplies and was tired of idleness. Pauline and I took a long walk, up the hill, past the ice well (which was built into the hillside), through the glade, along the top and down the front. The bake apples are turning yellow and the cranberries, red.

Albert was coming in from fishing and I was curious to see his catch. He had a number of crooked backs and whitefish.

ATZ came late and stayed only long enough for Albert to move the Cat (tractor) to the point as the S.S. Radium Queen was scheduled to pick it up and take it to Fort Good Hope. Then the crew left for Aklavik.

Early the next morning we flew away to the Reindeer Roundup.

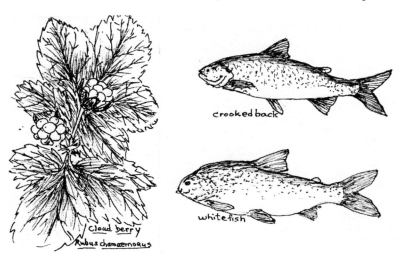

crooked back

whitefish

Cloud berry
Rubus chamaemorus

REINDEER ROUNDUP

It was only a short flight from the Reindeer Station to Richards Island where the roundup was taking place. Because of a good supply of lichen (primary feed for the reindeer) and frequent winds to reduce the biting fly torment, the reindeer were herded to Richards Island to produce their calves each year.

We descended to the plane's pontoons and to the temporary dock, up the bank to the tents. The herders had a series of corrals about six feet high built of wooden planks. The largest corral funnelled in to a smaller which opened to the smallest which had an exit gate.

The Corral
1945
(simplified)
M.

The herders spread out in two groups, walked slowly on each side to gently herd the animals towards the open, large corral. When they came near, each group picked up the long yard-wide strip of burlap that was lying ready. It made a wall barrier to direct the animals into the corrals. Now the first animals in the herd entered the large corral. Slowly some entered the next and some the last. The veterinarian and his assistants waited to select some young males which they castrated. The testicles were thrown into a pail. I heard later that they were a special delicacy.

Another group of men were the branders. Their work was to grab an animal, throw it on one side and stamp a red hot iron on the animal's right, upper leg. There was a puff of smoke and the smell of burning

hair. Then we could see a six-inch blackened "8," a symbol for 1948. Last year they were identified by a "7," but now, a year later, those "7"s had grown over and were very difficult to see. Unlike the southern Alberta ranches where the brand identified ownership, these brands distinguished the animals from caribou and also indicated their ages. Once branded, if not slated to be castrated, the animal would be allowed to exit from the last corral.

The scene was a turmoil of churning animals, still bearing their winter antlers, some bellowing, all trying to escape, milling about. The clicking of hooves made voices hard to hear.

Around noon the cooks at the cook tent had a big table piled with pots of food, especially freshly cooked reindeer, potatoes and gravy, large pan fried bannocks and pails of lard to spread on the bannock. Westaway asked about the meat which was very tender and they told us to eat all we liked, "some young animals get to die when the big ones get too many together." Indeed, we saw some calves, injured, which were humanely put down.

Up beside one of the tents was a mature reindeer, completely undisturbed by this yearly event. He, "Lazy" was a pet, raised from a few days old by one of the children of the main herder, Mikkel Pulk, a Laplander. They told us that Lazy would pull the carriole in winter. To "drive" Lazy they slipped light ropes around the base of his antlers and by pulling on one rope or the other, could direct Lazy to turn. The children had a little cart they said he would pull but, maybe because he was lazy in the warm sun, we didn't see him work. He didn't object to being petted or having his ears scratched.

The roundup continued all day with most of the herders spelling one another off. Finally the veterinarian had to stop to rest. He had no replacement so quit to have a nap. Eventually the herd was branded, some, deprived of their testicles, limped away and everyone stopped work to eat bannock and jam, drink cold tea and rest in the shade of the tents.

Before our plane returned, I had collected some plants, especially arctic cotton (<u>Eriophorum</u>), which grew in many low places.

ARCTIC

COTTON GRASS

<u>Eriophorum</u> <u>callitrix</u> Cham.

HOME FROM THE REINDEER STATION, JULY 29

There was no lack of things to do in August. So many of the staff either left or were going away on short trips whenever they could before the next term began. Helping in the kitchen was always welcome. Entertaining visitors was a major activity. When Rev. and Mrs. Garbett, Toronto, arrived from Whitehorse, they brought news that Sutton and Woodcock were working at the Whitehorse Inn awaiting boat accommodation south. The Garbetts stayed for a while and I was all set to leave when they did. But Ward Stevens said a government plane would have space to include me. After all, I was a federal employee, too, and, since the Commission was responsible for returning me to Edmonton, it would save it some money. I was not idle: besides meeting the new Dr. Callaghan and his wife Margaret and substituting for Matron Snuggs, there were many community activities.

After a heavy snow storm on August 28 the weather cleared on the 29th so I had one more turn to play the Cathedral organ and say another farewell to friends. There was still no word of the Barclay Beechcraft that was due to come and leave Aklavik on the 30th. I didn't dare give way to my feelings. It wasn't so much the village of Aklavik – as Ward Stevens said, "It's a miserable muddy place" – but the wonderful days in my classroom, the precious welcomes in so many homes, the many generous friendships, etc. There were feelings of being a vital part with others in a special way, an overwhelming emotional package to leave behind. I cut as many of my flowers as I could and made one more trip to pass them to folks who would soon be part of my past.

It was 8:15 a.m. August 30 when we left Aklavik.

FROM NORTH TO SOUTH, 1948

My notes from a little black note book:

Left Aklavik August 30 at 8:15, in a Beaver aircraft. Had dinner at Norman Wells. Saw others I knew there, including Dr. Tickle and Dr. and Mrs. Dalani. Was taken to see the greenhouse – tomatoes, cukes, Utah celery in good stalks by the row outside. Very pleasant. Doctor drove us in the ambulance to the plane.

Flew to Fort Norman and let Gloria Baton off (RCCS' little girl). Arrived at Fort Simpson in heavy rain before dark. Pilot couldn't see. He said, "For all I know we're flying upside down." Reassuring!

I went up the hill to HBC and asked for Craigs. They're in England. Met the relief agent, Mr. John Keats. He took me to the house to meet Mrs. Keats and daughter Jean (15). They are from Montreal, formerly of Labrador. Had supper with them and their clerk, John Ford. After supper we went to meet Rev. & Mrs. Bell and 5 little Bells. Very pleased to see our Sally Ezia, our former Aklavik student who worked at Bells. Bells are from Saskatoon so we had a happy evening. Mrs. Keats and I returned to her home through darkness, rain and mud. I had a room upstairs. A big old rambling house.

As we travelled southward I sat in the front with Gordon Cameron, the pilot, to the left. This was his first flight with the new "Beaver" as it had just come from Toronto on Saturday – CF - GIX.

I have noticed more autumnal colours along the way than there were at Aklavik. Gardens at Simpson are wonderful.

Friday The alarm went at 6:15 but as I saw rain everywhere I shut it off and slept again. Mrs. Keats called me at 8:15 when Cameron called. I dressed, ate and literally slipped through the mud to the plane in 15 minutes. Stan Copp, Vic, the game warden and Cameron were sitting in the plane waiting. We flew blind for a while through the rain. Saw Fort Providence, then landed at Hay River. I had an excellent view of Hay River and noted that it seems to have grown since 1944. I thought of Nurse Neville and noted a bare spot where the big old school had been. We stopped on a little snye by the oil tanks where some barges had been sunk to form a convenient dock. I liked it there, gently warm and pretty. I saw a flock of real crows (not ravens), some bulrushes, some raspberry canes and so I began to feel that I was approaching home.

We picked up another man and more baggage and flew into

the rain again.

Saw some holes in the earth like sunken cones or upside-down pingos.

[It was my first experience with karst (sink holes).]

Followed above the tractor trail.

Fort Smith. Arrived about 2 p.m. We pulled GIX in beside ATZ. They unloaded and Cameron, Mush and I came up with Frank McCall in the Jeep. The CPA office was closed so we went to the hotel. Then Stan Copp directed me to the Rite Spot where a woman of the plump friendly type, with a mass of curlers around a pretentious hair band and a short-at-the-back dress waited. She served me cold beef, fried potatoes, tomatoes and lettuce plus an orange, for 85¢.

Then I came back to the hotel and waited.

It is strange to hear the trucks and cars go by. The telephone rings, the cash register dings.

While going for lunch I saw the new school being built, a new apartment house for government people and the liquor store nearly finished. I went back to the hotel and while sitting writing in came Sgt. Abraham and Constable Davidson. So good to see the Sergeant again. He took me to the house to meet Mrs. Abraham and Gweneth again. We talked and had tea. The CPA weren't leaving 'til seven so I prepared to stay to help them eat roast mallards.

Then CPA said at 6:35 I had to leave with Stan Copp in the taxi to the airport.

Flew off southward at 6:45. Flying pretty rough in the big DC2. Had lunch.

Landed at Fort McMurray for 5 minutes. On to Edmonton by 10:55 p.m., September 3, 1948.

Part 2

— and then some

AND THEN SOME

SUMMER 1955

The Pas, Manitoba to Aklavik, N.W.T.

Sitting at our small kitchen table in The Pas ordering groceries for a year, I was ticking off items on our order forms from the Hudson's Bay Company Wholesale Supply in Edmonton when my neighbour dropped in. She had heard we were leaving and going to Aklavik in the Arctic. I told her I had been there previously and knew we must order enough supplies for a year – and then some in case the boats were detained. She sensed the enormity of my task and asked, "Well, what a job! How can you tell how many loaves of bread to order?"

Yes, how?

As a child I used to go with my Dad to a mill in Harris, Saskatchewan to trade good clean wheat for ten 100-pound bags of flour. If a big family needed ten bags of flour, I figured five would be more than adequate for us. She marvelled that I knew how to bake bread.

We puzzled over the instructions requiring only full case lots. In order to get items such as pepper, for example, I had to order a complete case, which sometimes meant 12, 24 or 48 similar items.

The initial payment was going to be high. In the few days we had to make arrangements, the difficulties were all worked out.
First one of my sisters loaned us the money to pay for the order.
Secondly, since we had so recently begun to furnish our little house at The Pas, Manitoba, we had little in it. The things we absolutely needed could be shipped to Aklavik, others could be given away except for a new chesterfield and chair set which we shipped for storage at my parents' farm in Saskatchewan.
Finally we managed the sale of our little house.

Our just-two year old Tommy was no problem at all as he busied himself playing happily amidst the disruption, eating green peas in our garden and playing with the baby bunnies that Joe had salvaged on one of his field trips in southern Manitoba. Joe was working long days wrapping up his four years of work in Manitoba so Tommy and I took the train to stay with my parents until he could meet us and we could begin a new venture – his appointment with the Canadian Wildlife Service as Resident Mammalogist at Aklavik.

Summer 1955. Tommy plays gently with a baby bunny. Joe saved the not-yet-born of a Jack Rabbit killed by a car. At home we raised it to maturity.

September 5, 1955.   From Edmonton to Aklavik – and all in one day – with a husband and a two-year-old son.   What a different journey from the one recounted in the beginning chapters of this book!

Joe & Tommy standing in the mud by the DC3 that had brought us to Norman Wells, September 5, 1955.

We travelled from Norman Wells to Aklavik in this DeHaviland "Otter' with Stu Hill, as the pilot.

Since travel to Aklavik was so very different it was reassuring to find after nine years there were still some familiar things to see.   The Anglican Mission buildings were much the same except that the Archdeacon's house was finished and the Sittichinli family lived in the old one.   Peffers remained intact but there was a new Day School and a Federal Administration Building.   Where I had wandered to find plants and taken the children to pick cranberries and to see the birds, the land had been cleared.   Tiny houses were here and there,

1. *Traffic on our street.*
   (Kerr's house in background)

2. *Joe and Tommy*

3. *The inside of our back door.*
   (We have an ice pick!)

4. *Tommy on Joe's "Eliason"*
   motor toboggan.

joined by a narrow board walk. Indeed, our assigned home was one of those buildings and very close to us, a little larger one was occupied by "Moose" Kerr and family. He was the Day School Principal. The little roads near our house were bordered by deep drainage ditches.

The houses were called "512s" because of their size (512 square feet). Sitting on pilings above the permafrost, with small windows and insulated walls, they were designed to resist the Arctic cold. We found that in winter if a drop of water fell to the floor it became a coin of ice so we soon fitted our footwear with heavy felt insoles.

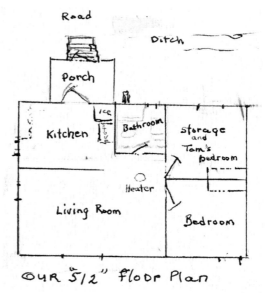

OUR "5/2" floor Plan

The government had supplied the basics – a single and a double bed, a chesterfield and one chair, a drop-leaf table with four chairs, built-in kitchen cupboards, an oil burning kitchen range and a small oil burner in the central spot near the doors to the four rooms. The cupboards had the bare essentials for cooking and some odds and ends of dishes. Fortunately I had packed a barrel of dishes and some cutlery.

It didn't take long for us to settle in with only our hand luggage but when a late boat brought our books, supplies and all our boxes of food supplies, there was scarcely room to move. The men helped Joe to line two inner walls of one room with shelves for the boxes: Tommy's single bed and a small dresser filled that space. A double bed, a dresser and a trunk filled our room. The living room occupied a quarter of the house and the last quarter was divided for the kitchen and bathroom.

The government had built an administration building in the main part of the village where Joe had an office and work space. We did have electric lights, the bulbs hanging from the ceiling. The village generator burned oil which came in from Norman Wells on the summer barges.

In one corner of the kitchen was a heavy tank up on a sturdy platform. Daily, an employee brought in big blocks of ice to melt in the tank. We drew off pots of water to heat and a kettle of water was kept on the stove so that we could have some boiled water to cool for drinking, as well as warm water for washing.

Daily Charlie Gordon and Tom Arey deliver ice. Tommy and Mora Kerr watch.

Mary and Tommy. X indicates the back of our house.

Tommy helps Joe prepare a garden site village in background.

I actually found the organizing and adjusting very exciting and wished I didn't find it so tiring. I thought the rough plane ride in had made me feel quite ill but the feeling prevailed for several weeks. 1955 had been an exciting year but 1956 would be moreso with another baby on the way.

Winter was fast approaching. Joe had to plan and begin his outdoor research. One midday while Tom played on the walk we hurriedly cleared the dead plants from the surface of a ten-feet square at the front of the house. We thought if it were black in the spring it would thaw earlier. We had plans for a garden.

Day by day we met the people around us. "Moose" and Ellie Kerr were generous with help and their daughters found a brother in Tommy, often taking him with them to the store or on errands. Mora, the youngest of their four, made a good playmate for him.

There had been a great change in the administrative staff – it was much larger with many new faces. I knew only three or four of the Anglican Mission staff. Except for "Moose" Kerr, Principal of the Day School, I never did get to know any teachers, either in the Residential School or the Day School.

I had a new rôle – a wife, a mother, a soon-to-be-mother again and a neighbour.

Things changed quickly when Joe had to undergo emergency surgery for acute appendicitis. We got to know the Anglican Hospital medical staff and they became very good friends. Frequently nurses coming off night duty would drop in, have breakfast and a visit. On their days off they were often our supper guests. Pru Hockin, Biddy Worsely, Merlyn Randall, Thelma Benham, Helena Sowden were frequent visitors with whom we maintained contact for many subsequent decades.

Tommy could play by himself but he enjoyed having playmates, too. Tim Timmins, the Game Warden had a boy, Bobby, a little older than Tom but, like Mora Kerr, a good playmate.

<u>Excerpt from a Christmas letter to friends, December 1955.</u>

On August 17th we left The Pas to begin another adventure. Joe had accepted an appointment with the Canadian Wildlife Service as Mammalogist at Aklavik, N.W.T. While he went to Ottawa to sign on, Mary and Tom spent two weeks on the farm with her parents.

September 5th saw us transferred from Edmonton to Norman Wells on a DC3 and on to Aklavik in an Otter.

Since then the days have flown until now we have no sun and scarcely any daylight except at noon. A while ago Joe remarked, "You know, it takes me from dawn to dusk just to eat lunch!" One doesn't notice the darkness a great deal though, for the Arctic winter sky with its brilliant moon and stars, the amazing Aurora Borealis, the reflections from the snow, and the bright lights scattered throughout the town are an unusual change.

A comfortable 4-room house became 'home' until the late fall boat brought our possessions and a year's supply of groceries. Ever since we have been undecided which should have the limited space, us or our belongings.

Joe has made a few trips by plane — to Norman Wells on a beaver survey, to Old Crow, Y.T. on a caribou survey (no caribou seen) and to the Reindeer Station, 40 miles N.E. of Aklavik to attend the annual reindeer slaughter. Rudolph still has his red nose. Joe also spent a couple of weeks in hospital getting his appendix chopped out (and preserved for posterity).

Mary has met many old acquaintances and expects to enjoy living in Aklavik even more than on her previous sojourn.

Snow to jump in, playmates close by, and the days as they come keep Thomas happy.

With all good wishes for 1956.

The Bryants.

"An igloo for Tommy"

Mary's Lino-cut

1956

As spring 1956 approached I was desperate to ready a layette. There was nothing in our own supplies anticipating a new baby. Mrs. Holman at All Saints School came to my rescue. The Anglican Church women of southern Canada had sent diapers and clothing to promote outreach to needy northern mothers and so I became a recipient. When a little red-headed girl arrived, she was showered with little dresses, blankets and then some. Joe prepared the fish box we had used as a crib for Tom and which came to Aklavik full of books. It just fit on top of the trunk in our bedroom. The loving care in the hospital extended to our home with our baby.

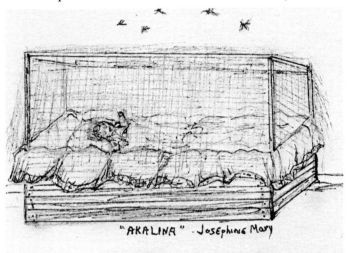

"AKALINA" - Josephine Mary

We appreciated the support as we had sad news: Joe received word through the Signal Corps that his father had suddenly passed away just a few weeks after our little girl had arrived. Not being able to be with his mother and family to lend and share support and without telephone contact, we were very appreciative of support from our new friends in Aklavik.

I became a thoroughly employed domestic person. The days were full and happy. Daily diaper washings, taking daily outings with Tom and baby Josephine and just coping with the domestic chores, sandwiched with tea parties and visits, filled the days. Joe put some hooks high on opposite walls of the living room. In the evenings when we no longer expected drop-in visitors, he strung cords on them from side to side. Up went the laundry to dry over night. It was the only way we could manage. As well it added moisture to the dry air.

It also, however, added thick frost to the windows. When the house
warmed up the windows dripped and required vigilance with a mop.
Tom enjoyed climbing up on a chair and scratching holes in the inch-
thick frost. He liked to see "the brown-cheeks boys and girls going to
school." I painted the noon-day sky as seen through that same peep
hole.

I was more aware of the weather than I had been ten years previously.
With Joe away in the frozen Delta with no communication, with a
little boy who liked nothing more than digging in the snow (as he told
Mr. Kerr: "Looking for Jack Frost") and a thermometer on the back
door that read minus 30°F day after day, I programmed the days to
match.
Spring gave way to summer and Joe took us in the canoe for a picnic.
We slung the baby in a blanket between two willows, Joe and Tom
made a fire, I unpacked canned wieners, canned corn on the cob and
we even toasted marshmallows. Mosquitoes were a bane as they
were in swarms. We could put netting over the baby until she either
pulled or kicked it off. Tom could tolerate "612" (mosquito repellant)
and seemed to have no effect from the stings. Cool winds from the
northern ice always turned warm days cold but they temporarily

banished the insects.

During the following winter I had been attempting some night school classes in Mr. Kerr's Day School. They were open to any Aklavik persons who wished help in elementary reading and writing English and in fundamental arithmetic. I was able to re-connect with some students I had had ten years before and for most of them it was rewarding – access to books and help to recall some reading and number work. For a few it was a pleasant place to talk and socialize. I had one student who had never mastered writing; and to him arithmetic was incomprehensible. But he was a pleasant happy fellow who cheered us all. One evening I took some peppermints to class. When I passed them around Ivan said, "No," and I recalled an earlier event.

When ships pulled in to the riverside dock at Aklavik workers would construct a gangplank from the barge to the dock. Depending on the water depth, it could vary in slope and length, Not infrequently a box would fall from a wheelbarrow as cargo was being pushed ashore. Often it would seem to sink into the muddy river, irretrievable – or so it seemed. Nevertheless, after the ships departed thirsty youth would reclaim boxes in anticipation that they might contain "treasures." Ivan was apparently good at that. Upon one occasion after such a retrieval he was rushed to hospital. I arrived shortly after to visit friends and was puzzled by the strong mint smell throughout the halls. Ivan had, indeed, found a "treasure" – a whole case of 12 bottles of peppermint extract, which he consumed! The nurses felt nearly as badly as he did after they had pumped his stomach.

It was several nights before Ivan reappeared at school. The story had made the rounds so no one was surprised when he refused the proffered peppermints.

1. *Tommy moves water from potholes to the ditch.*

2. *He helps the "ice man."*

3. *Knut Lang gave us this grandfather whitefish.*

4. *Tom moves building blocks for a "new" house.*

1. A favourite pet from Game Officer Jim Angus.

2. Jim helped Joe make a deck where Josephine often plays.

3. The R.C. Brothers built an Igloo. Tommy & Mary look it over.

4. Joe takes Tommy and Josephine to see the river in flood.

1957
A Spring Migration South

In late June Joe had some business in Ottawa so the children and I met Joe's mother in Edmonton and went with her to stay with my parents on the farm. Joe's mother was a great help as Josephine could now run about and needed to be watched. Later Joe joined us and the two grandmas managed while I was in the University of Saskatchewan Hospital for ten days. Before we left there was a big family reunion at Pike Lake. We returned Mrs. Bryant Sr. to her home near Creston, B.C., visited for a few days and returned by train to Edmonton where we met Joe's sister, Bea, who had dropped in from Jasper for a visit.

In Edmonton we had some anxious hours until we found our return tickets to Aklavik in a book that had been packed inadvertently in surplus luggage which we finally located in the C.P.R. shipping shed.

On August 19 we were up before 5 a.m. and arrived at 8 p.m. in Aklavik after two months away. I came back resolved to be more loyal in writing my diary daily. People had been so interested and anxious to learn about our lives, "away up North."

On Tom's 4th birthday his sister, Josephine, Bobby Timmins and Mora Kerr came for supper. Besides the horse-drawn cookie wagon they also ate three ice cream cones each.

From my diary: *Tom's first idea was – "Now we must see Miss Keyho and see about Sunday School." [Age 4 was the starting age for Sunday School.]*

Joe out for the evening with government visitors, Ward Stevens, Alex Reeve and Rory Flanagan.

Sunday, August 25. The three visitors came for dinner. Joe had helped me clear the groceries out of the living room and tidy up. He vacuumed, I dusted. Weather clearing, roads muddy.

Mixing bread dough. The living room is full of boxes.

Sunday, September 1. A beautiful day . . . In a.m. Joe and Tom went to the "woods" and brought 2 small spruce trees home to plant in the garden. They also brought berries, mushrooms, moss and leaves for the table decoration. We all walked with Tom for his first Sunday School. I went in with him but followed him out before the last part of the lesson! Sadie Hunter and the Gorlicks came for dinner.

The days passed pleasantly. We'd had some greens, beet leaves and radishes from our garden. On the Second of September I picked all the remaining garden produce – a large bowl of small lettuce leaves – as we expected frost any day. On the Eighth I picked another big radish and brought in the seed pods to pickle in vinegar. Ellie Kerr helped me cut the material for Delta-type parkas for the children so they'll be ready for winter. By the first heavy snowfall on the Fourteenth I had the parkas ready.

Fresh snow on our garden!
Sept. 10, 1957

Our little houses were connected by pipes to the river pumps but as soon as the above ground pipes started to freeze, the pumps were shut off. We had some days without water before Dave Jones' tank truck came and pumped some muddy water into two barrels that Joe had ready in the porch. For drinking, we used only ice blocks that I melted and boiled the water. Despite our precautions all of us were very ill with stomach flu. The whole village seemed to have this discomfort at least twice a year.

Joe and Tom set mouse traps in the vicinity of our house, a trapline with runways in the deep snow. The National Museum wanted a collection of small rodent skins from the Delta. Joe and I had learned the techniques at U.B.C. but as the rodents were small it was easier for me to do the skins. Many evenings were spent preparing the shrews, red-backed voles and meadow mice.

The entire village seemed sick with the 'flu so we were fortunate to be the first to be almost recovered and able to help. Usually Hallowe'en was a busy time but in '57 only three children came to the door, the schools were closed and there were no parties.

By mid-November a post-Hallowe'en masquerade was scheduled. Joe and I went to our first public party in nearly three years. We were masked and dressed as "Before" (Joe, very well stuffed and minus his mustache for the first time in many years) and "After" (I with an

18" waist). We got home at 2 a.m. and paid our baby sitter, Karen Kerr the then handsome sum of three dollars.

Joe had been working in the Day School workshop building experimental covers to put over muskrat pushups. They were 4 feet X 2.5 feet X 1.5 feet and very well insulated. They were part of his research studying the movements of muskrats under the ice through the winter.

We had our radio hooked up and got some news from Grande Prairie, Edmonton, Fairbanks, etc. We heard this week (November 10) "The Russians launched a satellite with a dog in it." It was a broadcast review of the November 3 event but "new" to us.

As it got near Christmas Joe took Tom out with the toboggan to get a little Christmas tree. It was a bitterly cold day (-40°C). He carefully scooped the snow from around a small spruce tree but as he tried to saw the trunk of the tree, the branches shattered like glass. After two more tries he ended up putting Tom on the toboggan and piling the stem and branches on top for the short trip home. After slowly warming the pieces he and Tom put them together again by drilling a hole in the stem for each branch. After our 4-year and one-year olds added some coloured trinkets it was a work of art!. We remember this little Delta spruce as our most precious Christmas tree.

December "AKLAVIK, NWT.

Joe's notes

I had met Mary in the fall of 1949 at UBC and in the following six years had heard quite a bit about her years at Aklavik. When the opportunity came to apply for a position there with the Canadian Wildlife Service, I jumped at it. I placed second in the competition but, as luck would have it, the person who placed first had to forego accepting because his wife refused to move to such a remote location. Fortunately, for my wife going to Aklavik was almost like going home and we were delighted at the prospect. After several happy years of working among the Cree, Métis and white hunters and trappers of northern Manitoba, with the support of many dedicated Game Officers and other members of the Manitoba Game Branch, I would have an opportunity to work with the Loucheux and Eskimo of the Canadian northwest. It would also mean working within a very much larger professional organization – an important consideration for a young biologist.

In Ottawa I was briefed on a variety of administrative details and the Chief Mammalogist, Dr. Frank Banfield, provided some background on what my two predecessors in the position had been doing. I would be expected to design my own program, subject to budget approval from Ottawa.

Very shortly after arriving in Aklavik I was requested to meet another CWS colleague, Bill Fuller, who was stationed at Fort Smith, to participate in an aerial beaver survey out of Norman Wells. Getting there from Aklavik was easy but Bill ran into delays caused by weather. To fill in the time, I ran a small-mammal trapline to collect specimens for the National Museum. After several days Bill arrived and we were able to carry out the survey in beautiful autumn weather. It provided my first chance to get a feel for part of the landscape of my new territory and to learn from my much more experienced colleague.

Not long after returning to Aklavik from that trip I underwent emergency surgery for acute appendicitis. Two Scottish surgeons Drs. Black and Hagen, did a fine job on what turned out to be a very difficult procedure but as they were salaried federal employees they were not allowed to charge for their services. A gift of a bottle of overproof rum each, however, helped to indicate my appreciation. The Anglican hospital charged just $5.00 per day for its top notch service. That was fortunate because the CWS office in Ottawa hadn't got around to completing the paper work for my government health insurance.

While convalescing I had time to review all the wildlife files left by my predecessors. Based on that review I decided to follow up on some of the work on muskrats that Ward Stevens had started. Muskrats were the primary source of income for trappers in the Delta and to a somewhat lesser extent for those at Old Crow, Yukon. Better understanding muskrat ecology might enable me to help put more jingle in the pockets of those trappers. Knut Lang, a Danish trapper and trader and a long-time resident of the delta, had provided a knowledgeable field base for Ward and very kindly did the same for me. He became a good friend and a never-ending source of helpful advice and fascinating stories. When Ward's research had demonstrated that muskrats were "old" at three years of age and "ancient" at four, most trappers wouldn't believe it: they were convinced that the rats lived at least ten years. Knut's standing in the trapper community was such that when he accepted Ward's results, others gradually followed. From a resource management standpoint, it makes a great deal of difference whether individual animals live for two years or for ten.

"Man does not live by bread alone." And the residents of the Delta could not live by muskrats alone, either. They needed big game for food and other furbearers for cash income. In the early years of Mary's time at Aklavik, very few people lived at Aklavik. They came to trade, to enjoy "community" get togethers, etc. but quickly moved back to their hunting and trapping areas. By the time I arrived on the scene a few years later things were changing very rapidly. Family allowances had come in and government Day Schools had blossomed. In order to collect Family Allowance, parents had to see that their children were attending school. To do that either the children had to be placed in residential schools or mothers had to stay in the villages to enable them to attend Day Schools. The male hunters and trappers were unhappy to be out on the land without their wives and children and so the villages grew quickly. Where hunters had traditionally stayed out on the land for months at a time and collectively covered vast areas of huntable terrain, now they stayed out for a few days at best and concentrated their hunting near the villages. Wildlife populations near the villages declined, forcing families to depend increasingly on welfare in order to survive. I wanted to document this 'common knowledge' and undertook a brief study along the Arctic Red River.

In late September, 1956, I travelled by canoe to establish a cache of food and equipment near the abandoned "Bernard House," about 80 miles above the settlement of Arctic Red River (now Tsiigèhtchic). Then in late November, with the very able assistance of Antoine André, a local trapper, I returned to the cache by dog team and proceeded to scout the area for game. I was assured that no one had ventured that far up the river since 1946. In the lower 60 miles of the river we saw tracks of only four moose: in the next twenty miles we saw tracks of another 18. The habitat in both areas was roughly comparable. Presence of other wildlife followed a similar pattern. Antoine was enthusiastic to return later to hunt and trap in the vicinity of Bernard House but realized it would be extremely difficult without money for a grubstake or means of transporting it so far under severe winter conditions. [1]

A subsequent aerial survey of moose in the northern Mackenzie District resulted in a similar tale of increasing abundance with increasing distance from the settlements.

Travelling in extremely cold weather necessitated high calorie foods – for man and dogs. In my few trips by dog team the dogs were fed on frozen fish often supplemented by cooked cereals with lots of lard. We also munched on frozen dried fish at tea breaks, occasionally supplemented by Pilot Biscuits slathered with lard. That may not sound very appetizing to southerners but it was and provided needed calories. Mary devised an even more appetizing "break" snack. She made patties about four inches in diameter of a mixture of peanut butter and honey with chopped dried fruit and nuts mixed in. When frozen they were easily carried in a pocket and no matter how cold, could always be chewed. Mary often also sent me off with a supply of frozen bannocks made with extra lard and filled with calorie-rich

[1] *A few years later, as Superintendent of Game for the Mackenzie District I was able to build on my experience at Aklavik and in northern Manitoba to help trappers. Some of the changes included exchanging the Game Officers' dog teams for twin-tracked Bombardier Snowmobiles so they could assist trappers who wanted to move into the back country with their families and to check on them occasionally to ensure their well being. I was also able to persuade the territorial government to institute a trappers' grub stake program, managed by the local trappers' councils, to enable capable trappers to obtain sufficient goods to be able to spend extended periods of time in the back country. Legislation was also passed to establish a system of Fur Traders' Record Books whereby all traders had to provide written records of all transactions involving furs. That didn't sit very well with some of the traders but it ensured that each trapper was given a written account of all sales and purchases. It tied in well with the increasing literacy of the northern population and provided a more accurate record of the economics of the fur industry.*

additions of raisins, other dried fruits such as apples and apricots. Sometimes chopped nuts were also added. My native travelling companions loved them as much as I did.

Trappers in the Old Crow Flats (about 2000 square miles of lakes, ponds and streams north of the settlement of Old Crow and a prime source of income from muskrat pelts) were finding that the muskrats one spring had many white spots in their livers. They asked the

R.C.M.P. stationed in the village to request that a biologist be sent over from Aklavik to see what the problem was and (a) whether the muskrats were likely to die off and (b) whether it was safe to eat them. The R.C.M.P. relayed the message to me and sent a map of the "Flats" with an "X" marked on one of the myriad lakes as the spot where I should meet my guide. Towards the end of March I flew over with a

Joe and supplies on "Lake X." Old Crow Flats, March 1957

Charlie Peter Charlie's camp in the Old Crow Flats, March 1957.

"Main Street," Old Crow, Yukon, March 1957. Note the absence of sled dogs. As a prophylactical measure against hydatid disease instituted by Chief Charlie Peter Charlie, the dogs were kept in a community compound.

two-weeks supply of food for two men and a team of dogs, landed on what appeared to be the lake marked "X" and unloaded my gear. The plane took off and I waited. Not too long later I heard the bells of a dog team approaching. It turned out to be the young Chief, Charlie Peter Charlie, who was to be my guide and interpreter. We moved my supplies off the lake into the shelter of some little trees and made camp.

After supper, as we lay on our bedrolls having a smoke, Charlie asked if I knew anything about hydatid disease.[2]   I was surprised that he knew the term but, as I had studied the subject and had given many public talks about it in villages along the Mackenzie River, I quickly told him what I knew. He listened patiently. When I was finished he pulled out of his packsack a typescript copy of a report on hydatid disease that my old professor at the University of British Columbia, Dr. Ian Cowan, had prepared a few years previously for a meeting of Conservation Officers, guides and outfitters in northern British Columbia. Somehow that report had come into Charlie's hands and he had typed out a copy for every head of household in Old Crow. He knew the stuff frontwards and backwards.   I was very grateful that I had known it, too. For two weeks we travelled from camp to camp, talking with trappers such as Peter Lord, Ben Thomas, Donald Frost and Philip Joe (whose artificial leg did not seem to impede his trapping success) and examining the muskrats they had caught.   The liver spots turned out to be relatively innocuous from the standpoint of survival of the muskrats, but I suggested it would be as well for people not to eat the livers.

Chief Charlie epitomized for me the great intellectual and moral strength of the Old Crow people. It was a community at that time of just 186 people, largely cut off from southern Yukon and from the N.W.T.   I was told that until I invited the Indian Agent from Whitehorse to come to Old Crow for a trappers' meeting, none had ever been there. The R.C.M.P. were responsible for issuing welfare when needed but were very rarely called upon: the people looked after their own. Charlie had been born "in the bush," had never had an opportunity to go to school, yet had taught himself to read English and, as mentioned above, had learned to operate a typewriter and

[2] *Hydatid disease is caused by a parasite that, in northern Canada, normally infects wolves, caribou and moose. It is transmittable from caribou & moose to dogs and from dogs to humans. Precautionary steps include keeping dogs isolated from homes and taking sanitary precautions when handling dogs and dog harnesses. Chief Charlie brought the subject clearly to all the people at Old Crow, resulting in much reduced infection rates, compared to villages in the Mackenzie Valley.*

carried on official correspondence on behalf of the Band (now "First Nation"). In 1988 he was invested in the Order of Canada. His citation reads:

Charlie Peter. Charlie shortly after being invested in the Order of Canada, 1988.

As Chief and Band Councillor, he led the Old Crow People with intelligence, dedication and confidence during a period when they were confronted with a number of major social and political issues. He is an astute and learned man whose eloquence, experience and commitment are invaluable to the linguists, anthropologists and others whom he has assisted for over forty years in documenting the language, human and geologic history and biology of the northern Yukon.

It is worth noting that Chief Peter Moses, one of Charlie's predecessors, was awarded the OBE in recognition of his leadership in raising enough money during World War II to purchase a field ambulance for the Allied cause. The community's sole income from which to make that great donation was derived from the fur harvest.

In May 2007 Bertha (Moses) Allen, a granddaughter of Chief Peter

Moses, was invested in the Order of Canada. Her citation reads:

Bertha Allen is a champion of social, political and economic equality for Aboriginal and Northern women. An elder whose counsel is continually sought, she is a former president of the Native Women's Association of Canada and helped found the NWT Training Centres in Yellowknife

and Inuvik. Grounded in her traditions and community, she was appointed to the Council of Grandmothers, which advises the territorial government on health, wellness and social development issues. After serving as president of the Status of Women Council of the Northwest Territories, she is now a member of the steering committee of its Women's Voices in Leadership initiative to increase the participation of women at all levels of government.

Three such awards in three consecutive generations to members of a population as tiny as that of Old Crow must surely be a record!

Back at Aklavik I learned that as one progressed farther north in the delta, the lakes gradually became shallower. They still functioned well as breeding and nurturing areas for muskrats in the summer and fall but many froze to the bottom in winter, killing all the muskrats. At first I tried to convince some of the trappers to trap out such lakes early in the winter, before the ice got too thick but they considered that time of year as their mink season and weren't interested in going after the much less valuable muskrats. So I experimented with artificially creating snowdrifts over pushup areas to see if the added insulation would effectively reduce ice thickness. It worked but was far too labour intensive to be a useful management practice.

Joe at work on one of his snow depth studies on a lake near Aklavik.

Summer muskrat studies included live-trapping, tagging and releasing animals in the expectation that some of the tags would be returned by trappers in the next year or two. The return rate was disappointingly low but did add to the store of information on distribution and longevity. One summer I was assigned a Quebec biology student as a field assistant and together we undertook a survey of many dozens of delta lakes, analysing habitat quality for muskrats. The information added to our understanding of the variable rates of productivity reported by trappers in different areas.

During the spring ratting season I examined the carcasses of a few hundred muskrats each year to observe general condition, parasites and reproductive organs to assess condition and reproductive history. One of my favourite places to work at that time was at Tom Arey's camp – the same one that Mary had visited in the '40s when it belonged to Bert and Marjorie Boxer. Unfortunately, Tom's wife had to be under permanent medical care in the south, leaving Tom with three children, the eldest a girl of 8 when I first met them. That little girl was a marvel. Besides looking after her younger siblings, she looked after the household, cleaning, washing, getting meals, baking bread, etc. She also helped with skinning muskrats and preparing the skins. One spring a teen-aged female relative of Tom's joined the ratting team. She was a very quick, bright young lady who became interested in what I was doing and soon joined in to help. It was a real eye-opener for me to see her using an ulu to nip out the reproductive tracts at least as quickly and neatly as I could with a scalpel. In the hands of such women the ulu was an almost magical instrument with a broad array of uses.

Odd jobs sometimes landed at the Mammalogist's door. One was autopsying sled dogs that had been shot or died of unknown causes. In one case the dog – a particularly good one – had become so ill that the owner shot it to put it out of its misery. He and I were both surprised to find that the poor animal had somehow ingested a piece of heavy canoe canvas about 18 inches square that had completely plugged the digestive tract. Other instances concerned animals suspected of having rabies. To obtain a positive diagnosis, the head of the animal had to be shipped out to a laboratory in southern Canada where tests of brain tissue could be carried out. Because of the danger to humans such shipments had to be made in thoroughly sealed metal containers and packed to ensure that they arrived in a refrigerated state. Although no human cases of rabies appeared during my time at Aklavik, we always tried to ensure that everyone knew enough about the danger to take reasonable precautions.

Throughout the north ravens were present at all seasons and how they managed to find enough to eat in the depth of winter was the subject of much local lore. In the village of Aklavik their "songs," their play and feeding habits provided unending fascination. It may sound odd to refer to ravens' "songs" but, although I do not have a particularly good ear, I recognized at least two dozen voices ranging from their typical raucous croak to an imitation of a gull, a dove and a tinkling silver bell. The latter was <u>really</u> unexpected. In winter we often watched from our house as a flock of perhaps 30 or 40 ravens played in the updraft caused when strong north winds hit the two-story R.C. Mission buildings. The birds would swoop low into the updraft, be carried forcefully upward then roll out and tumble down to near the ground only to swoop back into the updraft and play it over and over again. It was also amusing to see the clever ravens steal food from sled dogs chained near the houses. They usually worked in pairs, one approaching the dog from the front but remaining just out of reach. While the dog tugged at its chain and barked at the bird, the second raven would approach from the rear and pull the dog's tail. The dog would invariably spin around to catch that bird while bird number one jumped in, snatched the dog's food and quickly retreated.

One of the little mysteries about the ravens, however, was where and when they nested. Very few trappers ever reported having found an active raven nest but local lore was that they nested in spruce trees in February. I wanted to find out more and had made arrangements to start a study in late winter 1958. Unfortunately we were gone before then and none of my successors were interested in taking it on. I still regret that lapse.

In the autumn of 1957, although I had several interesting projects underway and others planned, and although I had expected to be at Aklavik for 5 to 10 years, I was persuaded by colleagues in Ottawa and Fort Smith to let my name stand for the position of Superintendent of Game for the Mackenzie District. It's incumbent, Ward Stevens, was moving to a senior position with the Canadian Wildlife Service. Later, having won the competition, the crunch came: should I take it? It would mean leaving behind interesting biological work, many friends among the trappers and villagers and another disruption for the family but it also offered possibilities of changing some management practices to the benefit of both the hunters and trappers and of the resource itself. Mary and I discussed it at length and finally decided to move. The Territorial government wanted me to move as quickly as possible.

1958
We move again

We worked rapidly over the last days of the old year. It was no easy task to find suitable materials for packing cases. We had to decide what to crate to go by boat in the summer, seven months away and what could be shipped by air as soon as possible. For the two children there were things very necessary each day that had to go as hand luggage. We packed some other things to go on the first plane with space and the rest we gave away. Our provisions, having been ordered for a year, were no problem to give away (except for our cash flow in the coming months).

Soon the cosy little home was a pile of boxes and crates. Tommy at four was delighted with the whole packing process. To our little one-year-old, however, it was disturbing and tiresome. She couldn't understand what was happening to her peaceful world.

Not knowing for sure when a plane would be able to take us was difficult but friends kept asking us out for supper which proved a welcome respite, except perhaps for the children.

Finally, early on January 5, 1958 departure time arrived, cold, dark and windy with a storm threatening from the north. The Pacific Western Airlines pilot, "Pappy" Hill, was very anxious to get away before that storm caught us. We woke Tommy who, eager and excited, was soon dressed and clutching the toy polar bear. Josephine was sound asleep so Joe picked her up, pillow, blankets and all. Mary carried as many of the bags as she could and we left our little house in the Arctic darkness. Our friend, Game Officer Jim Angus, must have heard us pass his house and soon caught up. He relieved Joe of the crib and also took some of Mary's load. It was -30°F. The wind was fierce, blowing snow into our faces. We finally reached the plane, already warming up on the river ice. The pilot helped us in, slammed the passenger door, ran around to the other side, jumped in and we were off. Mary called above the roar of the plane, "Where's the crib?" Joe shook his head, "No room. Pappy wouldn't take it." In no time we were airborne – no time to say farewell and no light for even a last glance at our Aklavik home. We were off on a new venture.

1. *Joe & Mary sorting plants before placing them in a plant press for drying.*
At home in Aklavik, July 1956.

2. *And then some more Bryants: Tommy and Josie in Fort Smith, 1958*

APPENDICES

1. Arctic Mission Uniforms for Women Workers
2. Menu, S.S. Distributor, September 5, 1944
3. Hudson's Bay Company advertisement for travel,
   Waterways to Aklavik, 1933
4. Artwork by Children at the
   Anglican Mission School, Aklavik, 1944-48

DIOCESE OF THE ARCTIC

Outfits for Women Workers

ARCTIC MISSION UNIFORMS

Arctic missionaries are required to wear the navy blue Arctic
Mission uniforms, especially when travelling to and from the field.
Wives of missionaries may wear the uniform if they care to do so.
(1) Black or brown shoes.
(2) Hat, navy blue felt hat with red feather for nurses, and blue for
other workers. Can be obtained at Eaton's Down-Town Store,
Toronto, Ont. Miss Lancaster, $4.29.

(3) Coat, made of good quality serge, navy blue and lined with
Grenfell cloth which is wind and water proof. Nurses have a red
lining and other workers blue. Made by T. Eaton Company,
Toronto. Ladies' Tailoring Dept., Second Floor, Ask for Mrs. Carr.
$33.50.

(4) Dress, navy blue rayon for travelling. Can be made by the T.
Eaton Company, Toronto, Ladies Tailoring Dept., (Mrs. Carr.) for
$16.70. Extra collars and cuffs (white pique) $2.00

(5) Similar dresses to the above in any navy blue wash material are
needed for work dresses. The pattern is the Girl Scout (America)
Uniform pattern carried by the Butterick Pattern Service, #8606.
No zipper is used at the neck but two buttons on a shank
connecting two buttonholes, and white cotton pique collars and
cuffs are added. It is well to be supplied with three such work
uniforms with which to begin.
Nurses require at least two such for night duty, etc.

NURSES Nurses will need a supply of white uniforms, white
shoes and stockings, besides the above. Especially at Aklavik, the
nurses wear their white uniforms probably three-quarters of the
time.

OFF DUTY CLOTHES A moderate supply of ordinary silk
afternoon dresses and one or two summer dresses. One would use
the dresses one happened to have at the time of going out. Knitted
suits, woollen dresses, and especially heavy cloth skirts with

pullover sweaters are good for the long winter months.

SPORTS CLOTHES For outdoor wear leather coats or windbreakers and ski pants are good for hiking.

WINTER OUTER GARMENTS An old fur coat is found very useful, especially at Aklavik. Workers usually purchase fur parkas of native manufacture. Occasionally a duffle (blanket cloth) parka is made by a native of materials supplied by the missionary, over which is worn a larger one made of duck. However, few of the Aklavik workers have cared for this outfit in the past years and it is not advisable to purchase the necessary material ahead of time.

UNDERWEAR A moderate supply of ordinary silk or rayon for summer wear; medium weight woollens for winter; at least one suit of heavy wool with long sleeves for out-door wear; extra wool bloomers or knitted pants to pull on.

OTHER WOOLLENS Mitts, scarf, cap. Berets are more useful than hats. Warm sweater coat.

NIGHT WEAR Mostly flannelette pyjamas or nighties, with limited supply of summer weight.

FOOTWEAR (A) Stockings For one year a half dozen pairs of wool cashmere and probably one or two pairs of heavier home knit stockings. 1 dozen lisle or cotton hose for summer wear. Limited number of silk hose (or substitute) for "dress up" occasions.

(B) Shoes At Aklavik a good fitting Oxford for every-day wear. Sport shoes with crepe soles useful for out of doors. If not possible to take in sufficient shoes to last a term, obtain maker's name, size, width, where obtainable, etc. for mail orders for work shoes.

Rubbers and galoshes to fit shoes and a pair of women's knee rubber boots two sizes larger than regular size. At other points workers usually wear native footwear both indoors and out of doors after the first few months. In the summer time crepe soled sport shoes would be useful, and one would have their travelling shoes with the. Rubbers to fit shoes would be necessary also knee rubber boots.

MISCELLANEOUS NECESSITIES:
1 FLASHLIGHT, 1/2 dozen batteries, 2 extra bulbs
1 pair good dark colored glasses
Toilet articles, dental floss,
Sewing notions, especially ample supply of mending wools for stockings
Stationery and writing materials (include ink)
Hot water bottle
2 pairs canvas work gloves
Warm dressing gown and house slippers
MISCELLANEOUS OPTIONAL ARTICLES
Things to make one's own room homelike: chintz, cushions, candles, artificial flowers, etc.
Gifts (value about 75¢) for birthdays and Christmas for other staff members.
Paper, ribbon, seals, etc. for wrapping gifts.
a few Christmas and Birthday cards.
Table decorations for occasions, Diary,
Milk chocolate, Kodak and films, Books, Binoculars, Personal Radio
Portable typewriter, Materials for teaching Sunday School such as leaflets, quarterlies, etc.
TRADE ARTICLES AKLAVIK – (For payment to natives for sewing, etc)
Lengths of print in different designs (6 yards each)
Braids such as LLama or rick-rack
Balls of colored wool, remnants of bright colored prints, or gingham
Needles: round, Glover's or knitting.
EXTRA NOTES Skates & skiis are usable at most missions, snow shoes are unnecessary. Advise taking extra eye glasses or false teeth if they are used.

MENU September 5. 1944

S.S. D I S T R I B U T O R

L U N C H

S O U P

Puree of White Beans   x

F I S H

Keta Salmon Sliced Lemon

E N T R E E S

Denver Omlette
Baked Beef Short Ribs Country Gravy
Roast Leg of Lamb Mint Sauce   x
Cold Pork with Mixed Pickles

V E G E T A B L E S

Boiled Potatoes
Buttered Carrotes

D E S S E R T

Rice and Raisin Pudding
Peach Pie
Lemon Pie   x

Cheese

Tea   Coffee

George Gordon

MARGARET STEWART

I have ten dogs and sled and ten harnesses.